The Widening Road:
from Bethlehem to Emmaus

Exploring the Gospel of Luke
Leith Fisher
with foreword by Professor John Barclay
Lightfoot Professor of Divinity,
University of Durham

Scottish
Christian PRESS

First published in Great Britain
In 2003 by Scottish Christian Press
21 Young Street
Edinburgh EH2 4HU

ISBN 1904325114

Cover image by Iain Campbell

Cover layout and page layout by Heather Macpherson
Printed and bound in the UK by Bookchase

To Iona, for years of care and inspiration.

Contents

foreword:

Widening the Road...

The Gospel of Luke is one of the treasures of the Christian church. Artful and engaging in his narrative style, Luke has the wonderful capacity to surprise his readers, to tell stories with a devastating twist in the tale, or to show a sudden new vista on reality. The style matches the content. Luke is absorbed by the grace of God in the healing, teaching, death and resurrection of Jesus; and grace, he sees, has the habit of catching us unawares and turning us inside out.

New Testament scholars are convinced that Luke used the Gospel of Mark as the basis for some of his Gospel, but drew on several other sources to fill out Mark's picture. The result is a narrative less tightly structured than Mark, but full of arresting stories, including Luke's famous parables. On a careful reading, a number of common themes emerge: notably power, family, wealth, generosity and the breaking of boundaries. In all of these Luke is recognised by many scholars to be a radical; sometimes overtly so, sometimes more subtly. He may not always fit our definitions of what a radical should care about or say, but his work stands at that cutting edge where the gospel of grace disturbed the value-systems which Luke's well-heeled Christian readers absorbed from the urban society of the Roman empire.

Leith Fisher here guides us with immense skill around Luke's marvellous 'picture-gallery' and back out into our own world of 21st century society. By dwelling longest on the key texts, but commenting on all, he gives us a well-balanced reading of the Gospel and identifies very clearly its most challenging themes. As he rightly notes, this is a gospel which turns many things upside-down and outside-in, and he repeatedly shows how the question of boundaries, barriers, limits and horizons could serve to challenge and inspire the church today. As in his earlier book on Mark, Leith's remarkable range of knowledge offers something for everyone: he makes judicious use of biblical scholarship and contemporary theology, but draws also on poetry, art, contemporary stories and a range of reflection on contemporary church and society. This expert and provocative guide should be welcome to everyone - ministers and priests, lay readers, Bible-study leaders, and all who simply want to study the Gospel of Luke for their own spiritual growth or to aid that of others. The study is well worth the effort, and Leith Fisher is to be thanked for helping release the extraordinary resources which this treasure still has to offer the church today.

Professor John Barclay,
Lightfoot Professor of Divinity,
University of Durham

Introduction

The gospel of Luke has exerted a massive influence on the way we see our world. Phrases and images from Luke have been part and parcel of our culture for centuries, and some of Luke's basic themes have shaped both faith and culture enormously. To read Luke's gospel is to accept an invitation to browse in a wonderful and varied gallery; the word-pictures Luke paints of incidents from the life of Jesus and of the stories he told are unforgettable. Many of the pictures are profoundly familiar; this exploration invites us to look at these once more with fresh eyes. Other parts of Luke's gospel are roads less trodden; here is an opportunity to linger on the less familiar way. Before engaging with the gospel itself, here is a word of very brief background to Luke and his story.

Who Luke was, and when his gospel was written, continue to be the subjects of endless debate. There is strong evidence that he is the only Gentile of the four gospel writers, was possibly from Syria, and that he had close links with St Paul and the Pauline mission to the wider Gentile world. One of the most persistent themes of the gospel is the way in which Luke sees Jesus as for ever pushing beyond the boundaries and expanding horizons on the widening road of faith and grace. Although he was in a sense an 'outsider', Luke shows such a degree of knowledge of the Greek version of the Hebrew scriptures, the Septuagint, that he may well have been a 'God-fearer', before he became a follower of Jesus. 'God-fearers' were Gentiles who came as inquirers and seekers after the God of Israel. As to the date of writing, the original form of transmission of the story of Jesus was by word of mouth in what was a largely oral culture. The gospels were written down around the time when the first generation of eye-witnesses to Jesus' life and death were dying out. We can reckon the date of the writing of this gospel between 60 and 80 CE, probably after the year 70 when Jerusalem suffered the cataclysmic events of recapture by the Roman army and saw the Jerusalem Temple, the heart of the people's life and faith, reduced to rubble.

If we think of the books of Luke and Acts as, at the very least, two closely related works, long regarded as the work of the one author (coming from Acts 1:1 itself), then Luke is telling a story which begins in Jerusalem, the heartland of the people of promise, and ends in Rome, the pivotal centre of the known world. At the gospel's end, the risen Jesus commissions his disciples to preach to all nations 'the message about repentance and forgiveness of sins, beginning in Jerusalem' (24:47). The focus of this gospel is Jerusalem, although Luke does tell of Jesus' ministry in Galilee. We are both receivers and inheritors of that commission. Read on to learn more of the road which beckons in this most universal of the gospels.

How to use this book - some suggestions.

Any book has a life of its own once it finds itself in the hands of a reader or a group of readers. This book is offered both for personal and group reading. It can be read either at a sitting, or in smaller doses over a period of a month or a year. It could form the basis for a year's preaching through Luke or for a series of group studies. Its forty sections also make it suitable for the days of Lent.

After each section in the book, some stimulus for personal reflection is suggested. Keeping your own journal of your thoughts as you journey through the gospel will deepen your study. The material from your journal can also provide excellent material for group discussion. Another aid to reflection is to read over the text for each section and mark it thus:

?   With a question mark against anything which puzzles you.

x   With a cross against anything you find difficult or don't agree with.

!   With an exclamation mark against anything you find surprising or see in a new light.

✓   With a tick against anything that makes you want to cry out 'Yes!'

Material for group work is also offered for around half of the sections. These can be picked and mixed: do them all or simply pick out a few. Some require more 'homework' than others; it will be a good idea to look at what 'homework' is needed in advance. In particular, the best results will be achieved if the group leader has done her/his homework well in advance, rather than picking up the book the night before the meeting. The burden of leadership/enabling can be shared out among members of the group. You may find the following 'Icebreaker' book helpful in getting your group started and its members at ease with one another: *75 Icebreakers for great gatherings: Everything you need to bring people together* by Nan Booth, published by Brighton Books.

Luke's telling of the good news of Jesus Christ is something of a patchwork, with the threads of strong common themes binding the separate pieces together. Before you begin reading you might jot down your answers to this question: What do I know about Jesus which excites, scares, perplexes, challenges, reassures me? Ask yourself the same question when you come to the gospel's end.

Acknowledgements

The writing of this book was made possible thanks to a period of study leave granted under the Church of Scotland's Department of Ministry study scheme. I am once more hugely indebted to Professor John Barclay for acting as my supervisor throughout the writing. His wisdom, friendship and encouragement have been constant, not just in this project, but over many years, and his departure (or elevation!) to Durham is a great loss.

Muriel Pearson has brought her considerable theological and educational skills to bear in helping form the prayer and study material at the end of each section. Nonie, my wife, has again endured life with (or without) a frequently absent or preoccupied husband. Over many years she has constantly taught me about the widening road of the gospel. After my book on Mark, the Scottish Christian Press have been bold enough to invite me to write another gospel study and for the skill and encouragement of Gill Cloke, Janet de Vigne and Kate Blackadder I am indeed grateful.

chapter 1

Birth announcements———

LUKE 1:1-25

Dear Theophilus:

Many people have done their best to write a report of the things that have taken place among us. They wrote what we have been told by those who saw these things from the beginning and who proclaimed the message. And so, your Excellency, because I have carefully studied all these matters from their beginning, I thought it would be good to write an orderly account for you. I do this so that you will know the full truth about everything which you have been taught.

The Birth of John the Baptist is Announced.

During the time when Herod was king of Judea, there was a priest named Zechariah, who belonged to the priestly order of Abijah. His wife's name was Elizabeth; she also belonged to a priestly family. They both lived good lives in God's sight and obeyed fully all the Lord's laws and commands. They had no children because Elizabeth could not have any, and she and Zechariah were both very old.

One day Zechariah was doing his work as a priest in the Temple, taking his turn in the daily service. According to the custom followed by the priests, he was chosen by lot to burn incense on the altar. So he went into the Temple of the Lord, while the crowd of people outside prayed during the hour when the incense was burnt.

An angel of the Lord appeared to him, standing on the right of the altar where the incense was burnt. When Zechariah saw him, he was alarmed and felt afraid. But the angel said to him, "Don't be afraid, Zechariah! God has heard your prayer, and your wife Elizabeth will bear you a son. You are to name him John. How glad and happy you will be, and how happy many others will be when he is born! He will be a great man in the Lord's sight. He must not drink any wine or strong drink. From his very birth he will be filled with the Holy Spirit, and he will bring back many of the people of Israel to the Lord their God. He will go ahead of the Lord, strong and mighty like the prophet Elijah. He will bring fathers and children together again; he will turn disobedient people back to the way of thinking of the righteous; he will get the Lord's people ready for him."

Zechariah said to the angel, "How shall I know if this is so? I am an old man, and my wife is old also."

"I am Gabriel," the angel answered. "I stand in the presence of God, who sent me to speak to you and tell you this good news. But you have not believed my message, which will come true at the right time. Because you have not believed, you will be unable to speak; you will remain silent until the day my promise to you comes true."

In the meantime the people were waiting for Zechariah and wondering why he was spending such a long time in the Temple. When he came out, he could not speak to them, and so they knew that he had seen a vision in the Temple. Unable to say a word, he made signs to them with his hands.

When his period of service in the Temple was over, Zechariah went back home. Some time later his wife Elizabeth became pregnant and did not leave the house for five months. "Now at last the Lord has helped me," she said. "He has taken away my public disgrace!"

DEDICATION

'One of the main troubles the church has today is that it's an institution publicly perceived as cocooned in formality, in an increasingly informal world.' I've never forgotten that comment from a perceptive and sympathetic young journalist some years ago. Luke's gospel begins with a highly formal dedication in the best of classical Greek. In it, he gives his reasons for writing down his account of the life of Jesus Christ. In beginning his gospel in this way, Luke is echoing the practice of classical Greek historians. He is using the dedication to say to the reader that this is a serious, solid piece of work. The work is dedicated to 'most excellent Theophilus' or 'Your Excellency, Theophilus', who may be a real person, an official of some standing, or may simply be a literary device, inviting all to read on. 'Theophilus' is the Greek for 'a lover of God'; the invitation is to all who would love God to learn more through Jesus Christ. If you're an informal 'modern', don't let the formal introduction put you off; Luke has a story to tell which is the polar opposite of 'stuffy.' 'Subversive' might be a better word for it.

REALISING THE PROMISE

Immediately after the formal opening to Luke's gospel, we plunge into a series of dramatic stories and exuberant songs in the first two chapters of Luke. This material, much of which is very familiar and precious to us, is found only in Luke. Chapter 1 of the gospel centres round the promise of the births of John the Baptist and his second cousin, Jesus. The form of Luke's writing here strongly echoes the Septuagint. From the gospel's start, Luke wants to show on the one hand that the event of Jesus of Nazareth is firmly rooted in the promises of God to Israel, his people; yet also, on the other, that the realising of these promises in Jesus will burst the old bounds in a fresh blooming of the wonder of God's grace.

AN OLD MAN'S BIG DAY

It's in Jerusalem the story begins. Zechariah and Elizabeth were an elderly couple, both well-connected in the religious life of their people. Zechariah was a priest of the Jerusalem Temple and both came from priestly families. They lived good lives, and scrupulously kept the law of God, yet their lives were blighted: they had no children.

We know today how much pain can be felt by couples who wish for children but are unable to have them. In biblical times the pain was compounded because children were seen as one of the greatest signs of God's blessing, and the absence of children was often interpreted as a sign of God's disapproval through some hidden fault in the would-be parents' lives. Underneath the physical barrenness of Zechariah and Elizabeth, a symbolic meaning lurks. This was a time of barrenness not just for this particular couple but for the whole people of Israel. In religious terms prophetic voices had ceased, and in political terms they were caught between a rock and a hard place, between the cruel and arbitrary rule of Herod's dynasty and the overarching power of the Roman Empire. Signs of the Lord's disfavour rested not just on this couple but on the whole life of the nation.

Even though times were hard, personally and nationally, the story begins with Zechariah preparing for his big day. It has been reckoned that there were around 20,000 priests serving the Jerusalem Temple in a multitude of different ways. To be the one chosen to burn incense at the holy place would be a once-in-a-lifetime experience. Luke tells of how, as the old man went into the holy place, the crowd gathered outside (1:10). As he came to burn the incense, Zechariah was about to lead the prayers of all his people. We can well imagine the pride and passion which Zechariah would bring to his prayers. In the prayers, priest and people would be praying fervently that God would keep his promises to Israel. Would they be praying with expectation, that God would act, that something new would come to birth; or would their prayers however fervent, be without hope?

Zechariah's big day suddenly got a lot bigger. Before the altar of God, he discovered that he was not alone, but stood in the presence of the angel Gabriel; who announced to him that he and Elizabeth, notwithstanding their age, were to be the parents of a son called John, who would be filled with the Holy Spirit (1:15), and make the people ready for the Lord's coming (1:17). In shock and disbelief, the old priest was struck dumb; he could only communicate his experience by way of signs, though everyone was aware that he had seen a vision. Back home with Elizabeth, the miracle happens, and she becomes pregnant. 'Now at last the Lord has helped me. He has taken away my public disgrace!' (1:25)

The crowd gathered for prayer outside the holy place would have expected the priest returning from the altar to bless them. This, of course, the dumb Zechariah is unable to do. Raymond Brown makes a fascinating suggestion. 'The priestly blessing that could not be given at the beginning of the Gospel by Zechariah will be given at the end of the Gospel by Jesus. In 24:50-53 we are told that Jesus led his disciples out to Bethany, lifted his hands over them, and blessed them; then they worshipped him, and returning to Jerusalem with great joy, they were continually in the Temple praising God. ...It is not far-fetched to think that Luke has attached to the risen Jesus the fulfilment or replacement of the Temple ritual' (Brown 1993, p. 280-1).

GABRIEL'S ANNOUNCEMENT

Before we leave the scene of Zechariah in the Temple, it is worth looking more closely at Gabriel and his announcement, as a number of significant themes first crop up here. The opening chapters of Luke are punctuated by angelic appearances (1:11, 1:26, 2:9). At the time of Luke's writing, belief in angelic intermediaries between God and human beings had developed widely in Hebrew culture. Angels were accepted as the normal bearers of the extraordinary. The root meaning of the Greek word *'angelos'* is 'messenger,' 'envoy', 'one who announces, proclaims'. The name 'Gabriel' means 'man of God' or 'God has shown himself strong', and he has previously appeared in the book of Daniel (8:15-16, 9:21), though there he is not described as an angel.

Reference to Daniel reminds us of the key role of that book in the gospels, for interpreting the significance of Jesus in terms of the Son of Man and the Kingdom of God and, in particular, Daniel 7:13-14. Watch for it later. This whole passage is full of Old Testament references. The coming of fertility to the old couple Zechariah and Elizabeth recalls us to the foundational story of the promise of God to Abraham and Sarah out of which the people Israel came to be born. The reference to John being in the Nazirite tradition of abstaining from wine and strong drink recalls Samuel, the Nazirite prophet, born to the barren woman Hannah in answer to her prayers (1 Samuel 1). The great prophet Elijah appears in verse 17 where, in describing his role of turning the children back to their fathers and getting the Lord's people ready, Luke quotes from Malachi 3:1 and 4:5-6. Malachi was the last of the Old Testament prophets. From Abraham and Sarah to Malachi, the whole span of biblical history has been encompassed. More specifically, at the time of Jesus many believed that after the time of Malachi the voice of God had grown silent. The Malachi reference prepares us for God's speaking again to his people.

The plethora of scripture references make clear that this speaking will be in continuity with the old. It will also announce the new. Four times in this first chapter,

Luke makes reference to the Holy Spirit (1:15, 35, 41, 67). At the beginning of his own ministry, Jesus will announce his vocation in terms of the coming of the Holy Spirit, 'The Spirit of the Lord is upon me' (4:18). The theme of God's Holy Spirit, coming to dwell in his people in power and joy and bring the new to birth, is one which develops through Luke and Acts from the very beginning.

LUKE 1:26-38
The Birth of Jesus is announced

In the sixth month of Elizabeth's pregnancy God sent the angel Gabriel to a town in Galilee named Nazareth. He had a message for a young woman promised in marriage to a man named Joseph, who was a descendant of King David. Her name was Mary. The angel came to her and said, "Peace be with you! The Lord is with you and has greatly blessed you!"

Mary was deeply troubled by the angel's message, and she wondered what his words meant. The angel said to her, "Don't be afraid, Mary; God has been gracious to you. You will become pregnant and give birth to a son, and you will name him Jesus. He will be great and will be called the Son of the Most High God. The Lord God will make him a king, as his ancestor David was, and he will be the king of the descendants of Jacob for ever; his kingdom will never end!"

Mary said to the angel, "I am a virgin. How, then, can this be?"

The angel answered, "The Holy Spirit will come on you, and God's power will rest upon you. For this reason the holy child will be called the Son of God. Remember your relative Elizabeth. It is said that she cannot have children, but she herself is now six months pregnant, even though she is very old. For there is nothing that God cannot do."

"I am the Lord's servant," said Mary; "may it happen to me as you have said." And the angel left her.

A YOUNG WOMAN'S SURPRISE

We come to the second of Luke's vivid pictures. The scene changes to a hill-town some 70 miles north of Jerusalem. In the place of the old man stands a young girl. Gabriel is the constant. The angel has more announcing to do. This moment of the meeting of Mary and Gabriel is so full of intensity, beauty and mystery that it has fascinated poets and artists down through history. It is well caught by the Orcadian poet Edwin Muir when he writes:

'The angel and the girl are met. ...

See, they have come together, see,
While the destroying minutes flow,
Each reflects the other's face
Till heaven in hers and earth in his
Shine steady there. ...

Outside the window footsteps fall
Into the ordinary day
And with the sun along the wall
Pursue their unreturning way. ...

But through the endless afternoon
These neither speak nor movement make,
But stare into their deepening trance
As if their gaze would never break.
(Edwin Muir 1963, p 223-4)

It is a moment when the extraordinary breaks in upon the ordinary, a theme repeated in these early chapters of Luke. Mary's surprise, her initial reactions on hearing the angel's message are more than understandable, as is her second question, 'I am a virgin. How, then, can this be?' (1:34) This first chapter of Luke is all about God's initiative, God's new actions on the scene of human history. The last words of Gabriel to Mary say it all. 'For there is nothing that God cannot do' (1:37).

MARY'S 'YES'

The initiative may well be God's, but for the promise to find fulfilment needs human agency. God's new initiative is dependent on Mary's saying 'Yes.' Beyond the sterile battles about the possibility or impossibility of virgin birth, this story encompasses two realities - God's initiative and Mary's 'Yes.' Mary occupies a very important place in the life of faith as the mother of Jesus, the bearer of the Lord. She is also a significant model for us of what it means to be a disciple. In terms of Luke's gospel, we could well call her the first disciple. She is the first to say 'Yes.' That's how following Jesus always begins, and continues, through learning to say 'Yes'.

LUKE 1:39-45
Mary Visits Elizabeth

Soon afterwards Mary got ready and hurried off to a town in the hill country of Judea. She went into Zechariah's house and greeted Elizabeth. When Elizabeth heard Mary's greeting, the baby moved within her. Elizabeth was filled with the Holy Spirit and said in a loud voice, "You are the most blessed among women, and blessed is the child you will bear! Why should this great thing happen to me, that my Lord's mother comes to visit me? For as soon as I heard your greeting, the baby within me jumped with gladness. How happy you are to believe that the Lord's message to you will come true!"

THE COUSINS' MEETING

Mary goes to visit her cousin Elizabeth. The third scene is of the meeting of the cousins. We can well imagine the young girl and the older woman coming together to share their extraordinary stories, to encourage and reassure each other. Elizabeth tells of the mighty kick she had received from the unborn John in her womb. 'The baby within me jumped with gladness' (1:44). Here is another theme which appears frequently in these early chapters, the theme of joy, gladness. It continues in Mary's song which immediately follows and swells to a climax in the song of the angels over Bethlehem, 'good news.... which will bring great joy to all the people' (2:10).

LUKE 1:46-56

Mary's Song of Praise

Mary said,

> "My heart praises the Lord;
> my soul is glad because of God my Saviour,
> for he has remembered me, his lowly servant!
> From now on all people will call me happy,
> because of the great things
> the Mighty God has done for me.
> His name is holy;
> from one generation to another
> he shows mercy to those who honour him.
> He has stretched out his mighty arm
> and scattered the proud with all their plans.
> He has brought down mighty kings
> from their thrones,
> and lifted up the lowly.
> He has filled the hungry with good things,
> and sent the rich away with empty hands.
> He has kept the promise he made
> to our ancestors,
> and has come to the help of his
> servant Israel.

He has remembered to show mercy
to Abraham,
and to all his descendants for ever!"
Mary stayed about three months with Elizabeth and then went back home.

MAGNIFICAT

We turn to Mary's great swelling song of joy, echoing the song of Hannah in 1 Samuel 2:1-10. Mary's song has become part and parcel of the song of the church, one of the great shouts of affirmation and praise appropriate for every season. This heart-warming, soul-soaring song, rooted in Mary's personal experience, rightly belongs within the church's communal praisegiving; expressing, as it so powerfully does, the hope of all God's people. Its great themes are the faithfulness of the holy and merciful God from generation to generation; the God who keeps faith by a kind of continual revolution in which He humbles the proud and lifts up the lowly, fills the hungry and sends the rich away empty. Mary's song is prompted by the kingly presence in her womb. It fulfils these instructions from the short book of the prophet Zephaniah:

Sing aloud, O daughter Zion;
shout, O Israel!
Rejoice, and exult with all your heart,
O daughter Jerusalem!
...The king of Israel, the Lord, is in your midst;
you shall fear disaster no more.
(Zephaniah 3:14,15 NRSV)

'In your midst' can be rendered, 'in your womb.' Some verses from the prophet immediately preceding these ones also find echo in Mary's song. They are worth close attention.

...I will remove from your midst your proudly exultant ones,
and you shall no longer be haughty in my holy mountain.
For I will leave in the midst of you a people humble (*ani*) and lowly (*dal*).
They shall seek refuge in the name of the Lord - the remnant of Israel.
(Zephaniah 3:11b,12 NRSV)

In the Bible, the theme of liberation from oppression as the work of God is as old as Moses and the Exodus. The Old Testament has much to say about both God's initiative and our human duty of care for the poor and oppressed. *Ani* and *dal* are the classic Old Testament words for describing the poor. However, it is the little-known prophet Zephaniah who makes a new connection between liberation, justice and humility. Zephaniah speaks of the *anawim*, translated into English as either 'the righteous remnant', 'the humble poor,' 'the little poor ones'. The word that came to Zephaniah was that the people of Israel would be redeemed, after the downfall of their proud, haughty ones, by having in their midst this remnant of those who, in the eyes of the world, had nothing, who felt themselves as barren and empty, but whom God would fill in a visitation of renewing power and hope. The translators are indeed right to render *ani* and *dal* here as 'humble' and 'lowly'. They speak of both the social and economic reality of poverty and powerlessness and an attitude towards God of humble expectation (see Weber 1989, p 117-120).

Mary is a classic example of one of the *anawim*. Here she is, young, poor, not yet a child-bearer, not specially gifted, insignificant really, and yet... One commentator says: 'Mary is the summation of Israel. She is Israel prepared for two thousand years - one woman, one person who sums up Jewish spirituality. She is the virgin/mother, physical impossibility but spiritual pattern. It is henceforth clear that we bring to God our *emptiness* (virginity) as opposed to our fullness and fertility. It is the barren and the virgins (the *anawim*) who become mothers, not the perfect and the self-made. It is a 'spirituality of imperfection' as opposed to our modern philosophy of progress... The little one is the fruitful one' (Rohr 1997, p 64,5).

WHO SINGS THE SONG TODAY?

Mary's song encompasses both physical poverty and humility of spirit. The themes of wealth and poverty loom large in Luke's gospel. One commentator reckons that every fourth verse in the gospel relates to these subjects, while another reckons that one-seventh of Jesus' teaching in Luke is a condemnation of riches. Many scholars think that Luke was the most comfortable of the gospel writers, yet he finds it inconceivable that Christians could live side by side with poverty and feel and do little about it. So, how does a comfortable church sing Mary's song?

From the mid 1960s to the end of the 1970s I lived and worked in the East End of Glasgow, in one of its poorest parishes, while the area was slowly demolished around its residents. Ironically the district, which had about the lowest car ownership in the city, was afflicted by planning blight, while the city authorities decided on where to route the flank of a motorway, fortunately still unbuilt. For me these were years of profound education, when I began to glimpse what it is to see and hear the gospel from the perspective of the poor.

I vividly remember an experience in the late 70s. Kay Carmichael, a respected teacher of social work at Glasgow University, lived for three months in a small local authority East End housing scheme, almost under the lights of Celtic Park, the home of the East End's most illustrious football team. Out of her experiences, the BBC made a series of three television programmes which were introduced by an English cathedral choir's sublime singing of the Christmas carol, 'Once in royal David's city'. The contrast between the polished privilege of the choir and the poverty which the programmes revealed was gut-wrenching. It's a contrast caught in the following quotation from Christopher Rowland's *Radical Christianity*:

> When one attends Anglican evensong... it is difficult to hear the words of
> Mary's song, the Magnificat, in the midst of the surroundings and the close

identification of that institution with the dominant cultural ethos of the powerful. What do the worshippers make of the claim that the God they have come to worship is about to put down the mighty from their seat and exalt the humble and meek? ...What incongruence that the song of a young woman celebrating the poor and the outcast will be sung, often with macho zeal, by a choir of men when women are frequently excluded from participating in the music and leadership of the worship in that beautiful building.
(Rowland 1988 p. 14)

Mary's song is certainly a challenge to Christian action in the face of poverty. It is also a challenge to Christian vision. The vision and the action belong together and inform one another. Luke will develop the theme of the blindness of riches. In that context, let's not think of money alone, but of all the wealth that surrounds us, of knowledge, power, comfort, security. The truth is, while we are surrounded by so much wealth, we're about the most driven generations who have ever lived on this earth. For there's so much to do, we've no time to be. There's no time for us to stop and look and listen to the heavens, to wait for *our* angel, to announce what God would say to us. Eugen Drewermann is a priest and a psychotherapist. He says this about us modern people:

We always think that the important and essential things must be done by our own hands, that when something decisive is to occur in our lives, we are the ones who must *do* it. But what if the old images are true? The issue is not what *we* want and what we decide to do, but what grows inside us under the grace-giving eye and the sheltering wing of God; *that is* our truth, and our beauty lies therein...

We take ourselves too seriously, convinced that everything depends on us. So the day goes by, the weeks pass, and the years come and go. But who are we really?.... What we really are grows in the depths. We can't plan it or decide it; it is suddenly simply there. ... But where do we find the still places, the places like Nazareth, where we can simply be?
(Eugen Drewermann 1991, p. 88)

LUKE 1:57-66
The Birth of John the Baptist

The time came for Elizabeth to have her baby, and she gave birth to a son. Her neighbours and relatives heard how wonderfully good the Lord had been to her, and they all rejoiced with her.

When the baby was a week old, they came to circumcise him, and they were going to name him Zechariah, after his father. But his mother said, "No! His name is to be John."

They said to her, "But you have no relatives with that name!" Then they made signs to his father, asking him what name he would like the boy to have.

Zechariah asked for a writing tablet and wrote, "His name is John." How surprised they all were! At that moment Zechariah was able to speak again, and he started praising God. The neighbours were all filled with fear, and the news about these things spread through all the hill country of Judea. Everyone who heard of it thought about it and asked, "What is this child going to be?" For it was plain that the Lord's power was upon him.

WHAT'S IN A NAME?

Scene four tells of the birth of John the Baptist. Once again there is a note of joy, as family and neighbours meet together around the safe arrival of the baby and give their thanks to God. At the circumcision ceremony, parallel to infant baptism in many ways, the baby is about to be named Zechariah after his father, when mother Elizabeth interrupts the expected flow of the proceedings. 'No! His name is to be John.' Consternation reigns. 'There are no Johns in our family. Where did you get a name like that?' Babies' names can be a touchy business in family circles today; in the time of John's birth there were clear traditional guidelines which laid down that the first-born male should inherit the name of his father. Father Zechariah gets a writing tablet and makes it clear: 'His name is John.' The tradition is broken, all are surprised and at once father can speak again, with the praise of God on his lips.

What's in a name? The name 'John' means, 'the Lord has given.' The implication is that God has acted with grace. Grace is a persistent theme in Luke's gospel; it unfolds the story of an abundant and surprising grace. As we leave the naming celebrations we too can wonder with the neighbours and the people of the Judean hill country, 'What will these two children, John and Jesus, be?'

LUKE 1:67-80

Zechariah's Prophecy

John's father Zechariah was filled with the Holy Spirit, and he spoke God's message:

> "Let us praise the Lord, the God of Israel!
> He has come to the help of his people, and has set them free.
> He has promised for us a mighty Saviour,
> a descendant of his servant David.
> He promised through his holy prophets long ago
> that he would save us from our enemies,
> from the power of all those who hate us.
> He said he would show mercy to our ancestors

and remember his sacred covenant.

With a solemn oath to our ancestor Abraham

he promised to rescue us from our enemies

and allow us to serve him without fear,

so that we might be holy and righteous before him

all the days of our life.

You, my child, will be called a prophet of the most High God.

You will go ahead of the Lord to prepare his road for him,

to tell his people that they will be saved

by having their sins forgiven.

Our God is merciful and tender.

He will cause the bright dawn of salvation to rise on us

and to shine from heaven on all those who live in the dark shadow of death,

to guide our steps into the path of peace."

The child grew and developed in body and spirit. He lived in the desert until the day when he appeared publicly to the people of Israel.

ZECHARIAH'S SONG

The long first chapter of Luke ends with Zechariah's song of praise, named and treasured in the church's liturgy as the Benedictus, after the Latin of the hymn/prayer's first words, 'Blessed be God.' As Zechariah begins his song, Luke tells us he was 'filled with the Holy Spirit' (1:67). At least 20 times in the gospel this phrase will reappear.

Zechariah's song is a shout of thanksgiving and hope, thanksgiving for God's past faithfulness and hope for what he will accomplish through the child John. It ends with the wonderful words:

'Our God is merciful and tender.

He will cause the bright dawn of salvation to rise on us

and to shine from heaven on all those who live in the dark shadow of

death,

to guide our steps into the path of peace.' (1:78,9)

These grace-filled words would have special significance for Zechariah and his people, living in dark times. The picture of the dawning of the new day is striking. We watch more sunsets than sunrises. How powerfully the sunrise can speak to us of God's unfailing purposes, and the inexhaustible hope God offers.

After the end of the song we are given a brief glimpse of the growing up of John. He grew in body and spirit. Early on he went into the desert, where he would be both physically and spiritually prepared for his task. In a gospel which has a special place for outsiders, it's as an outsider, from outside society and the system, that John will reappear.

STUDY

BY YOURSELF

'Dear Luke....' As you engage with Luke's letter to 'Theophilus', keep a notebook in which you write back: your thoughts, observations, feelings and questions as a 21st century 'Theophilus', or lover of God. (See 'How to use this book', in *Introduction*.)

Find either a prose or metrical version (there are plenty!) of Mary's song from Luke 1:46-55. Learn it and make it part of your life of prayer on a daily or a weekly basis. Let it sing in your life! ('Tell out my soul the greatness of the Lord', is probably the best-known hymn version today.)

chapter 2

Bethlehem

LUKE 2:1-20

The Birth of Jesus
(Mt. 1:18-25)

At that time the Emperor Augustus ordered a census to be taken throughout the Roman Empire. When this first census took place, Quirinius was the governor of Syria. Everyone, then, went to register himself, each to his own town.

Joseph went from the town of Nazareth in Galilee to the town of Bethlehem in Judea, the birthplace of King David. Joseph went there because he was a descendant of David. He went to register with Mary, who was promised in marriage to him. She was pregnant, and while they were at Bethlehem, the time came for her to have her baby. She gave birth to her first son, wrapped him in strips of cloth, and laid him in a manger - there was no room for them to stay in the inn.

The Shepherds and the Angels

There were some shepherds in that part of the country who were spending the night in the fields, taking care of their flocks. An angel of the Lord appeared to them, and the glory of the Lord shone over them. They were terribly afraid, but the angel said to them, "Don't be afraid! I am here with good news for you, which will bring great joy to all the people. This very day in David's town your Saviour was born - Christ the Lord! And this is what will prove it to you: you will find a baby wrapped in strips of cloth and lying in a manger."

Suddenly a great army of heaven's angels appeared with the angel, singing praises to God:

"Glory to God in the highest heaven,
and peace on earth to those with whom he is pleased!"

When the angels went away from them back into heaven, the shepherds said to one another, "Let's go to Bethlehem and see this thing that has happened, which the Lord has told us."

So they hurried off and found Mary and Joseph and saw the baby lying in the manger. When the shepherds saw him, they told them what the angel had said about the child. All who heard it were amazed at what the shepherds said. Mary remembered all these things and thought deeply about them. The shepherds went back, singing praises to God for all they had heard and seen; it had been just as the angel had told them.

INTRODUCING CAESAR

He is only once mentioned by name in the gospel, yet the reality he represents provides a pervasive background in Luke. His name is Gaius Julius Caesar Octavianus, titled Augustus. Augustus - a word that translates as 'majestic', 'venerable', or 'consecrated', but used as a proper name for this individual and his successors - had stamped his authority on the Roman world from 30 BCE, when he had emerged the victor from a bloody and unsettling civil war which had consumed the last days of Republican Rome. The ensuing peace which Augustus enforced was generally welcomed and he was then to rule as the first Roman Emperor until his death in 14 CE. The imperial propaganda machine did its best to have the rule of Augustus not merely welcomed, but seen as a golden age. His *Pax Romana* was proclaimed throughout the extensive empire.

Writing in the immediate aftermath of the Iraq war of spring 2003, it is not hard to see parallels between Augustus and George W. Bush, and between the so-called Pax Romana and the would-be Pax Americana. Both men could lay claim to being the most powerful in their world. Both 'empires' are undergirt and enforced by efficient organisation, superior technology, economic strength and military might. Both would insist that their intentions and effects were benign, a view far from universally shared.

Luke is interested in the relationship between Augustus, Son of the Divine, as he got himself called, and Jesus of Nazareth, the Son of God. Augustus never heard of this lowly provincial from the eastern reaches of his empire, but his successors certainly would learn all about him and his followers. There are arguments, which we will pick up as we go through the gospel, that Luke is a bit soft on Roman power, as he is anxious to portray both Jesus and the young church in the Gentile world as law-abiding and unthreatening. On the other side, there are arguments that Luke's witness to Jesus of Nazareth is frequently subversive of the power of Rome, and indeed of the power of any big battalions, past or present. The gospel does not present any direct threat to the political or military power of the Empire; its challenge is to the Empire's ideological roots, through its witness to a very different set of powers and values. We will come upon one of these moments of subversion as early as the song of the angels over Bethlehem (2:10-14).

If there is any validity in the accusation that Luke is soft on Caesar, he is only one example of a long list of Christians and churches guilty of cultural and political subservience. The accusation of toadying to Caesar can frequently be substantiated. Yet one of the great strengths of gospel and church is that embedded in our foundations and tradition are the seeds of divine unrest. Christopher Rowland expresses the tension: 'One of the most interesting characteristics of the Christian tradition is that it has not only worked for accommodation with established powers but also has never rested content with that settlement. A compromised church contained within its life traditions which undermined any cosy settlement' (Rowland 1988, p. 14-5).

QUIRINIUS WAS GOVERNOR OF SYRIA?

Luke has a concern to locate the events of his gospel within the framework of secular history. In Chapter 1 we are told that the events of the birth announcements took place 'during the time when Herod was king of Judea' (1:5). By beginning the story of the birth of Jesus with a reference to Caesar Augustus, Luke seeks to put the birth onto the world stage, to signal that the significance of the one born at Bethlehem is universal, for all the world. To get Mary and Joseph to Bethlehem, where the child should be born as a descendant of David, he tells of a census which required males to return to their town of origin. 'This took place,' he says, 'when Quirinius was the governor of Syria' (2:2).

Unfortunately, the weight of evidence suggests he wasn't. There are a number of problems with this census. The dates of Herod and Quirinius don't tally. Quirinius did hold a census but Herod was dead several years before Quirinius became governor. There is also no evidence that the Emperor ever ordered a universal census of his realms 'that all the world should be taxed' (2:1 *AV*). It would have been an act of provocation to do so. There is also little evidence of people being required to return to the place of their origin for census purposes. We will come across a number of instances in this gospel where Luke does not get the detail right. Two things should be remembered here. First, while the story of Jesus is told forwards, from birth to death to resurrection, it was out of the events at the end of the life of Jesus that the young church was born. It is from his ministry and out of the crucible of his passion that the story of Jesus is told. About the first thirty years of his life, before he goes public, we know virtually nothing. Second, the gospel writer is concerned principally with meaning. Luke may be considered more of a historian than the other gospel writers, but he is a late-coming outsider who is not totally familiar with the history, geography and practice of the Jewish people and sometimes he does get things wrong. Historians in the ancient world are not academic historians in the sense we would use that term. In general they have a point of view, and the gospel writers in particular have a message to proclaim. For them, the meaning of the message is paramount. Our purpose is to listen to Luke, and hear what he has to say, to let the light of his gospel illuminate our lives, and act on our conclusions. So, whether Quirinius was governor of Syria, or there ever was a census, or the child was born in Bethlehem, or Nazareth, is not the bottom line. The bottom line is that a child is born, and the world has never been the same since.

'IN A MANGER FOR HIS BED'

How often has the story of the journey of Mary and Joseph from Nazareth to Bethlehem and the birth of the child outside the inn been told and retold? Down the years accretions multiply. The birthplace becomes filled with animals, with the ox and the ass (possibly through reference to Isaiah 1:3) and sometimes mice (the product of pious imaginations). The weather becomes that of northern Europe, 'In the bleak midwinter', and there is much concentration on the hardship of the journey and the exclusion of the family from a place of warmth, shelter and security. Searching for fodder for innumerable nativity plays and watchnight homilies, ministers and teachers walk the tightrope between honest respect for Luke's text and the demands for a dramatic and imaginative presentation.

Luke's text tells the story of the birth of Jesus with bare simplicity. Our attention is focused on two places; Bethlehem itself - 'the house of bread,' 'royal David's city,' where the Messiah, the new David, was expected to be born - and the manger bed. The prophetic significance of Bethlehem as the place of royal birth contrasts sharply with the mean manger. The new-born child is wrapped in strips of cloth, 'swaddling clothes' (AV), the recognised babywear of the time, and laid down in the animals' feeding trough, the manger. The baby in strips of cloth, to be found lying in a manger, outside the house, is an important sign for what immediately follows in the angel's announcement (2:12).

Luke tells of the circumstances of Jesus' birth being dictated by the decree of the dominant imperial political power of the day. We do no justice to Luke's witness if we are not sharply aware of the reality of life in present day Bethlehem, a Palestinian town like the rest of the West Bank, under siege from the Israeli army in recent times. Raja Shehadeh, a Palestinian lawyer, activist and writer, has written a diary of his life in the West Bank town of Ramallah during the events of the year 2002. He writes:

> The invading army carried out its wild acts of wanton destruction and murder and withdrew to the peripheries retaining their siege on our town and our life. Those harrowing times were followed by months of a twenty-four hour curfew that the army lifted only for a few hours every two or three days. For months Ramallah, along with most of the towns and villages of the West Bank, remained in a state of involuntary dormancy, its workers not allowed to work, its students struggling to get to their schools and universities, its economic life brought to a halt. The West Bank had been turned into the biggest detention camp in the world...

> Curfew is an extraordinary measure. It is usually imposed during a state of emergency, for a short period of time, when the authority in power is unable to restore public order. When it is inflicted on a civilian population for a prolonged, open-ended period, it is meant to serve a wholly different, more pernicious purpose: the slow strangulation of the community...

I don't know why it was yesterday that I felt the full horror of our situation. Perhaps because I realized that this would be the third Christmas that we will spend in these terrible conditions...
(Shehadeh 2003, p. 148-50)

'WHILE SHEPHERDS WATCHED THEIR FLOCKS BY NIGHT'

We move to the outskirts of the town and the encounter of the shepherds with the angels. This scene marks the third and final angelic appearance in Chapters 1 and 2, and is the occasion of the third of the four songs in these chapters, songs which are deeply embedded in Christian hymnody. Commentators view the shepherds from two different angles. Some regard them as outsiders, pointing out that Palestinian shepherds lived on the margins of local communities with which they often had strained relationships. In that view, it's to the suspect outsider that the news of the birth of the saviour is first announced. They can also be seen as insiders, the lineal descendants of David, Bethlehem's shepherd king, the inheritors of the traditions of Israel and the people's present longings for a saviour.

Out on the hillside, in the darkness of the night, literal and symbolic, their watch is interrupted by the breaking in of the light from heaven. Their reaction to the appearance of the holy in their midst is typical of the Bible: these tough men were frightened. The messenger from heaven reassures them, 'I am here with good news for you, which will bring great joy to all the people' (2:10). The coming of a saviour, deliverer, liberator, is announced and the unlikely, surprising directions as to where this saviour is to be found are given, '...you will find a baby wrapped in strips of cloth and lying in a manger' (2:12). In an instant the heavens are filled with a host of angels singing their great song of glory...

'ALL GLORY BE TO GOD ON HIGH'

Think back to the mention of Caesar Augustus in the context of the angel's announcement and the angels' song. The announcement is of 'good news, gospel'. The Greek word here is the word which was used to announce news of victory of a Roman army. Augustus also claimed the titles of 'saviour,' 'lord'... of the whole known world. Here is the claim that the child laid in the manger will grow to challenge in his own way the rule, claims and values of the emperor and his empire, the ways of the world.

The saviour is called, 'Christ, the Lord.' 'Christ' is of course the Greek translation of Messiah, the one on whom Jesus' people placed their hopes of deliverance. 'Lord' is a title which belongs much more to the Graeco-Roman world. Once again, while Luke places the new-born child firmly within the traditions and hopes of Israel, he also shows him as the one who bursts the bounds to have a universal saving significance. The angels' song is correctly translated, 'Glory to God in highest heaven, and peace on earth to those with whom he is pleased' (2:14). 'Those with whom he is pleased', 'those whom he favours' is often mistranslated to have a universal application, 'peace to all on earth.' It is a mistranslation which captures well the spirit of Luke's gospel. 'Those whom he favours' we will meet again in Jesus' sermon at Nazareth when he begins his ministry by announcing the year of Jubilee, 'the year of the Lord's favour' (4:19 *RSV*).

We follow the shepherds as they make their way to see the child in the manger. As we watch with them, we can brood over the strange conjunctions of this night of light and darkness, power and vulnerability, the particular and the universal, the light of heaven on the hillside and the smelly earthiness of the stable. We can share the joy of shepherds and angels, of mother and father, before the new life and reality which has come to birth:

> 'Great Little One, whose all-embracing birth,
> lifts earth to heaven, stoops heaven to earth.'
> (Richard Crawshaw 1613-1650, 'At Bethlehem')

'O MAY WE KEEP AND PONDER IN OUR MIND'

What happened next, after the amazing event of this night? The shepherds told their story, those who heard it were amazed, and Mary remembered all these things and thought deeply about them. Luke gives us a picture of Mary as not only the mother of Jesus, but his companion, and disciple. She is shown as someone who is deeply reflective. Events don't simply happen to her, she is aware and alive to their meaning. Even without having the stories of the first two chapters of Luke to reflect upon, when we think of the life of Jesus it is clear that his mother must have been a remarkable woman. As Jesus' mother, accompanying him on life's way, she certainly had the deepest experience of life, of light and darkness, joy and sorrow. Think of her pondering, reflecting on the meaning of her life and the life of her son as a model for our prayer lives. Think of her tasting life's heights and depths; life with Jesus is not an anaesthetising, sectarian, out-of-this world experience. To live with Jesus is to be plunged into this world's heart, agonisingly and joyfully present to whatever comes.

STUDY

FOR YOURSELF

Take this very familiar story and try to be present at the scene. Use your imagination to enter into it.

- What can you see, hear, smell, taste, feel as you imagine being present at the scene?

- What is the atmosphere like? Inviting, threatening, lively, solemn?

- How are you feeling? Curious? Attracted? Disturbed? Afraid? Excited?

- Do you want to speak to anyone? To Mary? To Joseph? To the child? To the innkeeper? To the announcing angel? To the shepherds? What do you want to say? What do you hear being said to you?

- If any of the scenes particularly attracted you, go back to it. Without forcing anything, see if you can identify what is attracting you.

Learn what you can about the plight of the people of Bethlehem today. Make the plight of Palestinians and Israelis, and their common need for peace with justice, a focus for informed and continuing prayer and action.

FOR GROUP WORK

We celebrate Christmas by having meals together. No need for the turkey and all the trimmings; share a simple meal together. Suggestions for a meal and an accompanying liturgy can be got from Alternativity, 759a Argyle Street, Glasgow G3 8DS, telephone: 0141 221 4242; email: mlunan@christian-aid.org; web: www.alternativity.org.uk.

The events of the nativity have provided endless material for artists down through the centuries. At the beginning of the year 2000, an exhibition called, 'Seeing Salvation: Images of Christ in Art' was mounted at the National Gallery in London. Neil MacGregor, the gallery's director wrote a book about the exhibition. In it he tells of how powerfully the image of Christ, God in our humanity, captured western imagination. In particular, so much art has concentrated on the beginning and end of the life of Christ, as they are concerned with the great human universals, birth and death.

Track down some different images of Christ's birth, from different ages and perhaps cultures, and discuss them together, beginning by asking what people see in the pictures and going on to uncover what they feel and what meaning they have for us in our situation. (Try Neil MacGregor's book referred to above (with Erika Langmuir), *Seeing Salvation: Images of Christ in Art*; or alternatively, Hans-Reudi Weber's *Immanuel: The Coming of Jesus in Art and the Bible*, 1984. This book contains also contains modern art from the younger churches of Africa, Asia and the Americas. There are also extensive art resources available through the Net, accessible through using a search engine such as Google.)

chapter 3

Jerusalem

LUKE 2: 21-52

Jesus is Named

A week later, when the time came for the baby to be circumcised, he was named Jesus, the name which the angel had given him before he was conceived.

Jesus is Presented in the Temple

The time came for Joseph and Mary to perform the ceremony of purification, as the Law of Moses commanded. So they took the child to Jerusalem to present him to the Lord, as it is written in the law of the Lord: "Every firstborn male is to be dedicated to the Lord." They also went to offer a sacrifice of a pair of doves or two young pigeons, as required by the law of the Lord.

At that time there was a man named Simeon living in Jerusalem. He was a good, God-fearing man and was waiting for Israel to be saved. The Holy Spirit was with him and had assured him that he would not die before he had seen the Lord's promised Messiah. Led by the Spirit, Simeon went into the Temple. When the parents brought the child Jesus into the Temple to do for him what the Law required, Simeon took the child in his arms and gave thanks to God:

"Now, Lord, you have kept your promise,
and you may let your servant go in peace.
With my own eyes I have seen your salvation,
which you have prepared in the presence of all peoples:
A light to reveal your will to the Gentiles
and bring glory to your people Israel."

The child's father and mother were amazed at the things Simeon said about him. Simeon blessed them and said to Mary, his mother. "This child is chosen by God for the destruction and the salvation of many in Israel. He will be a sign from God which many people will speak against and so reveal their secret thoughts. And sorrow, like a sharp sword, will break your own heart."

There was a very old prophet, a widow named Anna, daughter of Phanuel of the tribe of Asher. She had been married for only seven years and was now 84 years old. She never left the Temple; day and night she worshipped God, fasting and praying. That very same hour she arrived and gave thanks to God and spoke about the child to all who were waiting for God to set Jerusalem free.

The Return to Nazareth

When Joseph and Mary had finished doing all that was required by the law of the Lord, they returned to their home town of Nazareth in Galilee. The child grew and became strong; he was full of wisdom and God's blessings were upon him.

The Boy Jesus in the Temple

Every year the parents of Jesus went to Jerusalem for the Passover Festival. When Jesus was twelve years old, they went to the festival as usual. When the festival was over, they started back home, but the boy Jesus stayed in Jerusalem. His parents did not know this; they thought that he was with the group, so they travelled a whole day and then started looking for him among their relatives and friends. They did not find him, so they went back to Jerusalem looking for him. On the third day they found him in the Temple, sitting with the Jewish teachers, listening to them and asking questions. All who heard him were amazed at his intelligent answers. His parents were astonished when they saw him, and his mother said to him, "My son, why have you done this to us? Your father and I have been terribly worried trying to find you."

He answered them, "Why did you have to look for me? Didn't you know that I had to be in my Father's house?" But they did not understand his answer.

So Jesus went back with them to Nazareth, where he was obedient to them. His mother treasured all these things in her heart. Jesus grew both in body and in wisdom, gaining favour with God and people.

RITES OF PASSAGE OBSERVED.

The birth of a child remains in our society an occasion for celebration, and within the church a time for a ceremony of baptism or dedication. After the birth of Jesus, Luke tells of three accepted rites undertaken by Joseph and Mary. Eight days after his birth, Jesus was circumcised. The circumcision of a male child on the eighth day was considered so important that it was allowed even if the eighth day fell on the Sabbath. At the circumcision rite the boy received his name, in this case Jesus, as Gabriel had instructed Mary. Jesus, the Greek transliteration of Joshua, Yeshua, means 'the one who saves,' 'the liberator', 'the one who leads into freedom'.

The family now move to Jerusalem to observe the two further rites, of presentation and purification. In this story there is a strong echo of Hannah's presentation of her son Samuel, in 1 Samuel 1. The background to the act of presentation was that every firstborn male was regarded as sacred, devoted to God. It can be seen as an act of thanksgiving, a sacrificial returning to God, who is the giver of all life. Obviously society would be severely disrupted if every firstborn male entered the priesthood. There was therefore a ceremony of the redemption of the firstborn (Numbers 18:15), at which the child could be bought back on payment of a small sum to the sanctuary. It is not clear in Luke's account whether this money was paid, perhaps deliberately so, for while Jesus never enters the official priesthood, his whole life is an act of dedication to God.

The lack of clarity perhaps arises because Luke with his Gentile background is confused about the difference between presentation and purification. It was the child's mother who underwent the rite of purification, for a male child about forty days after the birth. Until purification she could not share in any communal religious practices (Leviticus 12). She then had to go to the priest and make two offerings, a lamb for a burnt offering and a pigeon for a sin offering. If the family were poor, a pigeon could be substituted for the lamb. The offering of two pigeons was known as 'the offering of the poor.' It is this offering which Mary makes at the Temple. Again we are recalled to the humble human origins of Jesus.

SIMEON AND ANNA

At the Temple the family meet with an old man and an old woman. The part played by older people in these early chapters is notable. In a sense Zechariah and Elizabeth at the start and Simeon and Anna at the close form the book-ends for the birth stories. It's also worth noting that in them we meet two couples. With the prominence given to Mary, we can already see the significant place Luke will give to women in this gospel. The two couples highlight another of the gospel's features, namely that men and women are often paired together. For example, the story of the healing of the centurion's servant in Chapter 7 is immediately followed by the raising of the son of the widow of Nain, and the Sabbath healing of the man with the paralysed hand (6:6-11) is paralleled by the Sabbath healing of the crippled woman (13:10-17).

Simeon and Anna are pictured as two devoted older people whose lives revolved around the Temple where they hoped and prayed, and prayed and hoped, for a new dawn for their people. Simeon has the larger part. Once again the agency and activity of the Holy Spirit is involved. The Spirit leads Simeon to be in the Temple precincts at the right time to meet the family and to recognise and discern who this child will be. With the most human of touches, Luke tells how the old man took the child into his arms and breaks out into thanksgiving for what he has seen and touched.

'MY EYES HAVE SEEN YOUR SALVATION'

Simeon's song is the fourth and last of the great songs of the birth narratives, the Nunc Dimittis. It makes quite explicit the universal theme of the gospel. Simeon says he has seen the salvation, the deliverance God has prepared not for some, but for all people. The child will become a light for the Gentiles and Israel's glory. The picture of the light of God's glory shining from Israel to illuminate the nations echoes Isaiah 42:6,16 and 60:1-3.

Simeon sees something else also, a shadow which will fall across the path of Mary in the sufferings of her son. Luke and Matthew are the only two gospels to tell the story of Jesus' birth, before and after; the stories they tell are quite different. However, it is interesting to see how many parallel themes they share. Both tell of the work of angels, of the virgin mother, of light to the Gentiles, and both link the birth of this child to suffering. Matthew tells the story of the slaughter of the innocents at Bethlehem (Matt 2:16-18); Luke tells of Simeon's far-seeing prediction to Mary, that her child will be both a liberating and disruptive force in the house of Israel, and that he will bring sorrow to her heart. Here the shadow of the cross falls across our gospel journey for the first time. No doubt Mary kept these words in her heart also, and pondered them deeply. The invitation to reflect on all we hear and see is extended to us, the readers. We remember that Mary is the only adult from the birth stories who survives to see Jesus' ministry, death and resurrection, and indeed into the first days of the young church in Acts (1:14).

BACK HOME

In two short verses Luke tells of Jesus growing to the age of twelve. In these verses he tells us more than the other three evangelists put together, as there is total silence about Jesus before the start of his public ministry. Luke tells us that the boy grew strong and wise, and that God's blessings were upon him. We can also infer from the following story that he grew up within the framework of a strong and lively extended family and we have already seen that his mother was a remarkable woman. And he grew up in Nazareth in Galilee.

Nazareth was not Jerusalem, indeed Galilee was suspectly distant from the Judean heartland. Galileans were characterised by sufficient distinctiveness of speech to have them stand out in the metropolitan centre, as Peter learnt to his cost (22:59). Galilee was not only far from cosmopolitan, it was suspected of being bandit territory - to the inhabitants of Jerusalem anyway, it wasn't just full of country bumpkins, but was seen as actually quite wild and frightening. But Nazareth of Galilee was no tiny backwater. It may well have had around 20,000 inhabitants in and around it. And the world came and went very close to its front door. It was significantly close to the sites of a number of the events told of in the Old Testament, and much of the considerable traffic both through and in and out of Israel passed close by. As William Barclay comments; 'Jesus was brought up in a town in sight of history and with the traffic of the world almost at its doors' (Barclay 1953, p. 43-4).

Changing times

The story of Jesus lost and found in the Temple at Jerusalem is the only other story we have of his early years. We find the growing Jesus travelling with his parents to keep the great feast of Passover at Jerusalem as he approaches adulthood. Thirteen was the age at which he assumed responsibility for keeping the holy law. Maybe this first visit was preparatory so that the boy would know what to expect when he came to assume full participation as a young man. Then the parents start on their journey home, and after they have travelled for a day they discover that Jesus is not with them. 'How careless,' we may be tempted to say - and we would be wrong. The parents would have travelled separately, with the slower-moving group of women with young children setting off earlier in the day, and meeting up with their menfolk in the evening. They would be travelling in extended family groups and it would be quite likely the boy would be with relatives or friends rather than father or mother.

Children are particularly protected in our society today, even more than since my childhood. I remember my mother taking me to school on the 1st of February 1946 and I never remember her taking me to school again. I walked, alone or with friends, and never thought a thing about it. Today in the neighbourhood where I live, most children are driven to school, often in mobile fortresses called 4x4s. While it may make 'my' child safer, it does tend to make 'our' children less so.

When Joseph and Mary discover that Jesus is not with the party going home, they hurry back into the city and search for him, no doubt increasingly frantically. It's not till the third day (is that symbolic?) that they find him again, sitting among the teachers in the Temple, listening and asking questions, and impressing everyone with the intelligence of his answers. Again we should be aware of a cultural difference. To sit and debate with the rabbis around the Temple precincts was the accepted way of learning. There is no suggestion here of an unhealthy or arrogant precocity.

It is mother Mary, always the dominant parent in Luke's narration, who gives voice to their anxieties. 'Why have you done this to us? Your father and I have been terribly worried' (2:48). Jesus' answer, 'Why did you have to look for me? Didn't you know that I had to be in my Father's house?' distances himself from his parents. 'You don't have to look after me any longer, I can look after myself.' That's a typical response of the adolescent growing into maturity. 'My Father's house,' must have been even sorer for his parents to bear as in these words Jesus displaces the human father, Joseph, who has provided for him and nurtured him. Parents everywhere will identify with this moment of growing up and growing away which is part of our relationship with our children. We leave the family returning home, where Jesus continues to grow within the respectful care of his family circle. As we come to the end of these opening chapters of Luke, we have already met a wide variety of human experience, spanning birth to old age. Luke's rich humanity is one of his greatest treasures.

Two final words about this incident are appropriate. Here we see the first break in Jesus' relationship with the family circle. Jesus lived in a society where ties of blood and kin were immensely strong, yet one of the characteristics of his teaching and his actions is to loosen these ties. Jesus never idolises the family; on the contrary he questions it as being constrictingly exclusive. Luke's gospel is particularly ambivalent (see eg 8:19-21, 9:57-62, 12:49-53).

This incident is once again located in the Jerusalem Temple which has already loomed large in Luke's narrative. Here Jesus speaks of it fondly as 'my Father's house'. The Temple occupies centre stage in the gospel. In these opening chapters, in Jesus' teaching in the Temple courts during his final days (from Chapter 19), and in the book of Acts, it is symbolic of the heart of Judaism. It will also be shown as flawed, by the way its power is abused by those leaders entrusted with its stewardship. About the Temple there is also ambivalence.

STUDY

BY YOURSELF

Where are you in these stories?... Growing up like the young boy Jesus, on the threshold of an adult life?... Watching your children grow like Mary and Joseph, and aware that growing older means growing away?...Growing old yourself like Simeon and Anna, but still with hopes and dreams?... Reflect on your life and remember the one who comes to bring it peace.

FOR GROUP WORK

This passage raises issues about how our churches provide ministry to older people and children. Reflect on your own experiences and find out what your church practises.

In our society there are many older people with considerable resources of time, energy and skill who have massive amounts to contribute to the life of church and society. There are also older people who have come to the stage in life where they need extra care and attention as their physical and mental powers fail. How do you relate caringly with those in each group?

What is the place of children in your church community? What is the ministry to and with children? How does the church provide a ministry to children in which they are kept safe, nurtured in faith and also allowed to grow to be their own person?

Do the results of this discussion need to be shared with a wider group?

PAUSE

A word about sources

As we move to Chapter 3 of Luke's gospel, we may well be struck by the appearance of familiar material on Jesus' life, if we already know something of the gospels of Matthew and Mark. We have already seen that the material in Luke's first two chapters appears nowhere else in the gospel records. We pause to address the question, 'Where did Luke get the material for his gospel? What are his sources?' It is generally, though not universally, accepted that both Luke and Matthew knew Mark's gospel when they came to setting down their own account. Large chunks of Mark's gospel crop up throughout Luke - about half of Mark appears in Luke - though not without, on numerous occasions, significant amendment at the hands of Luke the editor. The motives of the editor are threefold: literary, stylistic and theological. The literary and stylistic questions are quite technical. A more detailed discussion of the questions of sources and editing is to be found in the Introduction of C F Evans' commentary, *St Luke* (1990) and particularly from p 13-43. We need to be aware that each of the gospel writers brings their own theological view to their work of editing. Luke's view will become apparent as we go through the text itself.

In the second place, there are around 200 verses in Luke which also occur in Matthew's gospel. On occasions these verses are sufficiently different to suggest that Luke and Matthew used different sources originating from the same material, (e.g. in their versions of the Beatitudes and the Lord's Prayer) but it has long been held that Luke and Matthew had access to a common source, mainly of the sayings of Jesus, called Q.

There remains a significant amount of material peculiar to Luke. This includes some of the best-known of Jesus' parables, e.g. the Good Samaritan and the Prodigal Son, and the extremely familiar beginnings and ends of the gospel, the birth narratives at the start and the story of the walk to Emmaus at the end. There are also a number of occasions when the material peculiar to Luke finds an echo in John's gospel, suggesting a source known to both writers.

We can think of Luke's gospel as a patchwork; skilfully, conscientiously and imaginatively woven together by the author, the raw material of which was supplied by Mark, Q and significant other sources, both written and oral, whose precise origins are now beyond recall.

chapter 4

Things new and old

LUKE 3

The Preaching of John the Baptist.
(Mt 3:1-12; Mk 1:1-8; Jn 1.19-28)

It was in the fifteenth year of the rule of the Emperor Tiberius; Pontius Pilate was governor of Judea, Herod was ruler of Galilee, and his brother Philip was ruler of the territory of Iturea and Trachonitis; Lysanias was the ruler of Abilene, and Annas and Caiaphas were high priests. At that time the word of God came to John son of Zechariah in the desert. So John went throughout the whole territory of the River Jordan, preaching, "Turn away from your sins and be baptized, and God will forgive your sins." As it is written in the book of the prophet Isaiah:

'Someone is shouting in the desert;
Get the road ready for the Lord;
make a straight path for him to travel!
Every valley must be filled up,
Every hill and mountain levelled off.
The winding roads must be made straight,
And the rough paths made smooth.
The whole human race will see
God's salvation!"

Crowds of people came out to John to be baptized by him. "You snakes!" he said to them. "Who told you that you could escape from the punishment God is about to send? Do those things that will show that you have turned from your sins. And don't start saying among yourselves that Abraham is your ancestor. I tell you that God can take these stones and make descendants for Abraham! The axe is ready to cut down the trees at the roots; every tree that does not bear good fruit will be cut down and thrown in the fire."

The people asked him, "What are we to do, then?"

He answered, "Whoever has two shirts must give one to the man who has none, and whoever has food must share it."

Some tax collectors came to be baptized, and they asked him, "Teacher, what are we to do?"

"Don't collect more than is legal," he told them.

Some soldiers also asked him, "What about us? What are we to do?"

He said to them, "Don't take money from anyone by force or accuse anyone falsely. Be content with your pay."

People's hopes began to rise, and they began to wonder whether John perhaps might be the Messiah. So John said to all of them, "I baptize you with water, but someone is coming who is much greater than I am. I am not good enough even to untie his sandals. He will baptize you with the Holy Spirit and fire. He has his winnowing shovel with him, to thresh out all the grain and gather the wheat into his barn; but he will burn the chaff in a fire that never goes out."

In many different ways John preached the Good News to the people and urged them to change their ways. But John reprimanded Herod, the governor, because he had married Herodias, his brother's wife, and had done many other evil things. Then Herod did an even worse thing by putting John in prison.

The Baptism of Jesus
(Mt 3:13-17; Mk 1:9-11)

After all the people had been baptized, Jesus also was baptized. While he was praying, heaven was opened, and the Holy Spirit came down upon him in bodily form like a dove. And a voice came from heaven, "You are my own dear Son. I am pleased with you."

The Ancestors of Jesus.
(Mt 1:1-17)

When Jesus began his work, he was about 30 years old. He was the son, so people thought, of Joseph, who was

> the son of Heli, the son of Matthat,
> the son of Levi, the son of Melchi,
> the son of Janni, the son of Joseph,
> the son of Mattathias, the son of Amos,
> the son of Nahum, the son of Esli,

the son of Naggai, the son of Maath,
the son of Mattathias, the son of Semein,
the son of Josech, the son of Joda,
the son of Joanan, the son of Rhesa,
the son of Zerubbabel, the son of Shealtiel,
the son of Neri, the son of Melchi,
the son of Addi, the son of Cosam,
the son of Elmadam, the son of Er,
the son of Joshua, the son of Eliezer,
the son of Jorim, the son of Matthat,
the son of Levi, the son of Simeon,
the son of Judah, the son of Joseph,
the son of Jonam, the son of Eliakim,
the son of Melea, the son of Menna,
the son of Mattatha, the son of Nathan,
the son of David, the son of Jesse,
the son of Obed, the son of Boaz,
the son of Salmon, the son of Nahshon,
the son of Amminadab, the son of Admin, the son of Arni,
the son of Hezron, the son of Perez,
the son of Judah, the son of Jacob,
the son of Isaac, the son of Abraham,
the son of Terah, the son of Nahor,
the son of Serug, the son of Reu,
the son of Peleg, the son of Eber,
the son of Shelah, the son of Cainan,
the son of Arphaxad, the son of Shem,
the son of Noah, the son of Lamech,
the son of Methuselah, the son of Enoch,
the son of Jared, the son of Mahalaleel,
the son of Kenan, the son of Enosh,
the son of Seth, the son of Adam,
the son of God.

'THE WORD OF GOD CAME TO JOHN'

We fast forward about fifteen years to the start of the work of John the Baptist. Luke assembles such a cast of the great and not-so-good to introduce John, that it has been suggested Chapter 3 was the original beginning of this gospel and that the birth narratives were added at a later editing. Tiberius was the Roman Emperor who succeeded on the death of Augustus in 14CE, the powerful ruler of the known world. Herod and Philip were the sons of Herod the Great, the Herod of 1:5 who died in 4 BCE.

On his death his will divided his kingdom among his sons, who ruled somewhat shakily under the eagle eye of Rome and the largely hostile eye of their Jewish subjects. Another son, Archelaus, had inherited Judea, but he had been deposed in 6 CE and since then the province had been under the direct rule of a Roman procurator, at this time Pilate. Of Lysanias we know little: Abilene to the north of Iturea contained part of modern Lebanon. Strictly speaking, Caiaphas was the high priest in Jerusalem, Annas was his father-in-law and a real power behind the throne.

In introducing this list, Luke does two things. He locates the ministry of John and the coming ministry of Jesus firmly on the stage of human history, both on the broad canvas of the known world and within the narrow confines of Palestine. Once more the evangelist stresses that the events to be unfolded are not the story of some hole-in-the-corner pious cult, but are of significance for the whole human story.

But Luke does something else. The key words are 'the word of God came to John in the desert' (3:2). Within the kingdoms of this world there is a new arrival on the scene. Prepare for an explosion as God's word comes to John the Baptist. From the wilderness, the desert, the periphery, comes a force to challenge the central powers. Writing during the times of the struggle against apartheid in South Africa, Alan Boesak quotes from two of the foremost church leaders engaged in that struggle, one white and one black.

> When Beyers Naude opted for justice in South Africa, he was hated by his own people, dishonoured by his church, called a traitor by his colleagues and banned by the government. He could only say, 'If the Word of God is not the fire that renews us, other fires shall devour us; if the Word of God is not the hammer that crushes rocks, other hammers will destroy us. Listen, O people of God!'
>
> And Desmond Tutu says to the Minister of Law and Order: 'Mr Minister, we must remind you that you are not God. You are just a man. And one day your name shall be merely a faint scribble on the pages of history, while the name of Jesus Christ, the Lord of the Church, shall live forever...'
>
> (Boesak 1984, p 9,10)

'The word of God came to John'. The word comes first. Before we speak, we listen, see, hear. That's always the way with any prophet or preacher worth listening to. They must first of all have listened to discern what God is saying and doing in their lives, the lives of others and the life of their society. The real message, though it is filtered through our experience and limitations, is never our own message. It's the word that comes to those who listen and wait.

CHANGE!

John bursts upon the scene after the years of his formation in the Judean desert, a barren, inhospitable scrubland. The desert wilderness had a special place in the consciousness of the Hebrew people as a place of promise, testing and transformation from the time of Moses. Soon we shall see Jesus himself go off for his desert experience (4:1-13). Desert is both place and symbol, location and experience. Even if we've never been to the desert, we've known the experience of confrontation with the elemental forces of life, of struggling with dry, tough times, of deprivation and desolation. Daniel Berrigan, modern prophet and critic of contemporary America, writes in commenting on Isaiah 40, the passage Luke quotes here:

> Ancient understanding looked on the desert as a place of combat and rebirth. There the demonic spirits lurked, there in solitude, prayer and fasting, one's vocation was wrested from a hidden God. Thus went the story of the people of Israel and of their greatest sons, John the Baptist and Jesus Christ. The geographical details are symbols, clues to meaning. We have, today and then, entire cultures that are spiritual deserts; the mountains to be levelled are the arrogant pride of nations.
> (Berrigan 1996, p. 103)

At the start of this new section, Luke directly quotes scripture in the words of Isaiah 40:3-5 to give weight to the message of John. Once again we cannot miss the universal reference in the last line of the quotation. 'The whole human race will see God's salvation.' What was John's message? 'Repent, be baptised, and be forgiven.' 'Repent' belongs largely these days to the vocabulary of street corner preachers. Its basic meaning is, 'Change, turn your life round'. My life experience in church and society would be that if you want an easy life, don't ask people to change. But the call to change, to be converted, lies at the heart of the teaching not just of John, but of Jesus.

John can hardly be called a popular preacher with his austere and demanding message, but the crowds flocked to hear him. It wasn't like going to the football or the theatre, this was no mere entertainment. The prophet's words struck a chord with his people that chimed with both their moral and political longings. Because this was more than entertainment, the crowds around John represented a threat to Herod, as would soon become evident. Yet the language John uses to awaken the people is robust to say the least. 'Brood of vipers fleeing from the wrath to come', he calls them. William Barclay suggests the vivid image comes from the frequent bush-fires which broke out in the desert scrub, sending the snakes among the other wild animals scurrying for cover. John goes on to tell the people that it's neither belonging to a religious tradition or a religious fellowship which will save them. It will not be enough to say, 'I am a child of Abraham,' - a central Jewish identity symbol - nor 'I am a member of the most prestigious, or most orthodox, or most zealous congregation in the neighbourhood'. What matters is how you behave in your relations with other people. The demand of God is for an egalitarian, outgoing and compassionate sharing.

Two specific and unlikely groups are singled out for special mention, tax collectors and soldiers. Both come to ask John what they should do. Both would be connected in the popular mind with unpopular authority. The collection of taxes at this time was operated on something like a contemporary franchise system. The senior collectors operating under authority would tender out tax-raising powers to others, who would then collect the due payment and a bit extra for their own living. It is clear that the 'bit extra' could be a very flexible amount and the whole system was open to obvious abuse. To the tax collectors John says, 'don't extort in your dealings'. Soldiers, by dint of their authority and their arms, were also particularly open to the temptation to oppress. To the soldiers John's word is, 'don't abuse your power, and be content with your pay'. It has been suggested that the inclusion of these two specific groups here by Luke is indicative of his desire to show authority in a favourable light. It is equally possible to read the example of the tax collectors and the soldiers as further evidence of inclusion. The message their presence gives is, 'anyone can repent'. This theme also will develop in the ministry of Jesus.

THE COMING ONE

Herod was right to be worried. John created such a stir that people began to wonder if he himself was the Messiah, the deliverer (3:15). John is quick to disabuse them. There is a greater one coming who 'will baptize with the Holy Spirit and with fire' (3:16). Fire could be taken as a sign of the coming judgement, the whole phrase 'the Holy Spirit and with fire' can also be taken as a reference forward to the day of Pentecost in the companion volume of Acts (2:1-4), when the Spirit descends with empowering tongues of fire on the waiting disciples.

Luke rounds off the story of John the Baptist by describing the circumstances of the end of his mission. His outspoken criticism of Herod's illegal marriage to Herodias, his brother's wife, proves too much for the ruler, and he is incarcerated in the fortress of Machaerus to the east of the Dead Sea. The awakening voice will not be silenced however.

JESUS IS BAPTISED

The story continues with Jesus' baptism. Luke's description of the baptism is much terser than that of Matthew and Mark. Specifically, he does not link the descent of the Spirit like a dove to the moment when Jesus comes out of the waters of Jordan. He simply says the Spirit came as Jesus was praying. He may well be wishing to downplay the significance of Jesus' baptism, lest it be thought that this was the moment when the Spirit came upon Jesus for the first time. For Luke, Jesus is God's son from the time of his conception. The baptism is but a moment of confirmation of his mission. Luke does quote the voice from heaven which in turn is a conflation of two Old Testament texts: 'You are my own dear Son' from the royal coronation Psalm 2, and 'I am pleased with you' from Isaiah 42:1, the first of the four songs of the servant of God who will carry God's truth to the Gentiles and fulfil the mission through rejection, suffering and death. Once more the crucified Messiah is foretold.

BACK TO ADAM

Jesus' ministry begins after his baptism. Uniquely, Luke gives us the information that his work began when he was about 30 years old (3:23). He then gives us the genealogy of

Jesus, through Joseph, his nurturing but not his natural father, back to Adam. Tracing family trees has become a widespread hobby of our times; in the world of New Testament times ancestry held much more significance. Both Luke and Matthew give a genealogy of Jesus early in their gospel. There is an interesting and a significant divergence; the line of names from David to Jesus' father Joseph is different, and scholars argue inconclusively about why this should be so. The names from that period are largely unheard of, people of obscurity as compared to the earlier, much better-known names. The more significant difference is that Matthew traces the line of Jesus back to Abraham while Luke goes all the way back to Adam, the first human being. Luke gives us a picture of Jesus, rooted in our humanity right back to the beginnings of the world's creation, linked not only to the father of a tribe, Abraham - though Abraham has been given a universal significance by John (8:39) - but to our first human father, Adam. We can be left to wonder at the puzzle as to why Luke both acknowledges that Joseph was only thought to be Jesus' father, and then gives a genealogy which is surely redundant if Joseph is not the father of Jesus!

STUDY

BY YOURSELF
The summons of John is perennial: 'Turn your life round!'
Take time to reflect on your life. Where does it need to change in attitude and action?
Ask for the aid of God's spirit to move in new ways; and pray this prayer in hope:
>Turn again, good God, and give us life
>that your people may rejoice in you.
>Make me a clean heart, good God,
>and renew a right spirit within me.
>Give me again the joy of your help,
>with your Spirit of freedom sustain me. *Amen.*
>(*Iona Community Worship Book* 1988, p. 26)

chapter 5

A testing time

LUKE 4:1-15

The Temptation of Jesus
(Mt 4:1-11; Mk 1:12-13)

Jesus returned from the Jordan full of the Holy Spirit and was led by the Spirit into the desert, where he was tempted by the Devil for 40 days. In all that time he ate nothing, so that he was hungry when it was over.

The Devil said to him, "If you are God's Son, order this stone to turn into bread."

But Jesus answered, "The scripture says, 'Human beings cannot live on bread alone.'"

Then the Devil took him up and showed him in a second all the kingdoms of the world. "I will give you all this power and all this wealth," the Devil told him. "It has all been handed over to me, and I can give it to anyone I choose. All this will be yours, then, if you worship me."

Jesus answered, "The scripture says, 'Worship the Lord your God and serve only him!' "

Then the Devil took him to Jerusalem and set him on the higher point of the Temple, and said to him, "If you are God's Son, throw yourself down from here. For the scripture says, 'God will order his angels to take good care of you.' It also says, 'They will hold you up with their hands so that not even your feet will be hurt on the stones.'"

But Jesus answered, "The scripture says, 'Do not put the Lord your God to the test.'"

When the Devil finished tempting Jesus in every way, he left him for a while.

Jesus begins his Work in Galilee
(Mt 4:12-17, Mk 1:14-15)

Then Jesus returned to Galilee, and the power of the Holy Spirit was with him. The news about him spread throughout all that territory. He taught in the synagogues and was praised by everyone.

INTO THE DESERT

Between Jesus' baptism and the beginning of his ministry comes his temptation in the wilderness. Jesus, the new Adam, knows the reality of human life from the inside. Again the Spirit is involved, that voice of the inner ear, of discerning prompting. We are told that Jesus came from the Jordan 'full of the Holy Spirit' and that the Spirit led him into the wilderness (4:1). Jesus endures his wilderness testing for forty days, echoing the forty years of the wilderness testing of the children of Israel on their journey into freedom. This testing of Jesus is part of his freedom journey and a clear preparation for the work he will undertake very shortly. He is tested by the Devil, the personification of the forces of evil in the world. Luke portrays the temptations as a conversation between Jesus and the Devil; the reality his testings point to is the inner struggle we all know. Jesus is about to go public, to live a life and die a death before the eyes of the world. The same Jesus continues to speak to innumerable people around the world now, 2000 years after his life and death, to guide, influence, challenge and cheer them. It's through his inner struggles and battles that *all* becomes possible. This is a crucial moment.

In the lonely place, by himself, deprived of all external stimuli, fasting throughout, Jesus struggles... about who he is and the nature of his mission. The temptations are subtle and relate to what he will go on and do. It's significant that it's right at the end of the forty days' experience the Devil moves in. Is this because Jesus relaxes his guard... because he thinks he has endured the period successfully? We're not told, but this psychologically acute observation rings true.

Luke gives us three specific instances of Jesus' testing. Each is prefaced by a little word, 'If?' Remember, Jesus has just come from hearing the heavenly voice confirming that he is God's son. Within each temptation the Devil says 'If...' Twice he says, 'If you really are God's son...' One commentator writes, 'This is what we all doubt. We doubt we are really God's son, God's daughter... Basic conversion is a reconstituted sense of one's own identity, a different sense of the 'I' that I am - not me apart and alone, but me-in, me-with, and me-and Another' (Rohr 1997 p. 99-100). It's when we doubt our identity as God's children, chosen and precious, that our world closes in around us and life becomes dominated by 'I' and 'me', and my needs and desires become the things which drive us. Remember Luther's graphic picture of sin, 'Man turned in on himself.' Jesus refuses to get turned in. He has another resource in God's word.

'MAKE THESE STONES BREAD'

The first temptation is to turn stones into bread. Maybe after his period of deprivation Jesus is beginning to hallucinate. 'How great if these stones were bread'. Maybe his mind goes back to the experience of his people in the wilderness when God fed them with the manna bread night and morning (Exodus 16). From what we know of Jesus it is much more likely that he is thinking not of bread for himself but bread for the world. He could be the deliverer who could feed the people, lead them into plenty. It is no bad thing for people to have enough to eat. The temptations are subtle. But simply to feed people without teaching them about the sharing of bread, which is also the sharing of life, is not what Jesus is about. To turn the stones into bread, which can be called *the economic temptation*, is a distraction. Jesus answers it from scripture, from the time of the Exodus, in the words of Deuternomy 8:3: 'Human beings must not depend on bread alone to sustain them, but on everything that the Lord says.'

'JUST WORSHIP ME'

In the second temptation Jesus is given a vision of the world and its peoples stretched out before him. 'You can have all this,' says the Devil, 'if you only worship me.' Jesus would look and see his own people sweating under oppressive and alien rule. Jesus had in his own band of disciples members of the Zealot group who were committed to armed struggle against the Roman authorities. The temptation to take up the sword would be very real. Underneath the temptation to take power the world's way is a deeper temptation - to deny that the Kingdom of God is a present reality, to see the world's ways of power as the only way that works. To see the world in that way is to deny the hidden presence of God in His world, to find nowhere the presence, promptings and activity of the Holy Spirit. It's easy, too easy, to submit to what is a deep kind of doubting despair. Jesus doesn't. He has come not to conquer, but to serve. He knows the world belongs to God already (Psalm 24:1) and that his own way is the other way, the servant way. He quotes Deuteronomy again, 'Worship the Lord your God and serve only him!' (Deut 6:13) We could call this *the political temptation*, or the military option. It's a temptation which has not lost its potency today.

'GO ON, JUMP!'

The third temptation, which offers no attractions to someone like me with no head for heights, is for Jesus to throw himself down from one of the Temple's pinnacles - and here the Devil quotes scripture to him - God will rescue him and the wonder of it all will claim everyone's attention. This is *the spiritual temptation*. It's the temptation to be the wonder-worker, to offer a ministry of signs and wonders, instant success religion. Throughout the gospels there's no one more suspicious of such a ministry than Jesus himself; yet for many people today faith seems to be based more on Jesus the doer of miracles than on the saviour of the world who redeems us through his cross and passion. Jesus is clear: he is not here to do tricks, however wonderful. It will only be when he is lifted high on a cross that he will make known who he is. The third

Deuteronomic quotation is from 6:16: 'Do not put the Lord your God to the test'. All the quotations Jesus uses to counter the lures of the Devil come from the Old Testament stories of Israel's testing in the desert.

For a time
The time of testing is over - or is it? Certainly Jesus is now ready to begin his work. But the temptation story is left unfinished, in a sense. Luke reports 'The devil left him, for a while' (*GNB*), 'until an opportune time' (*NRSV*). The clear implication is that the time of testing for Jesus is not over, and that it would continue throughout his life, as it continues in our own. Luke reports a final decisive moment of testing at the Mount of Olives (22:39-44), where Jesus again wrestles to do his Father's will before the cross. The journey continues and the battle goes on.

Into Galilee
Traditionally the story of the temptation of Jesus is read on the first Sunday of Lent, the period when we are all asked to look at our lives again in the light of Jesus' cross and passion. Lent is an old English word for springtime, the season of preparation and promise when life returns to a cold earth, 'bursting out all over'. It's been suggested that Luke 4:14-15, two short verses which tell of the beginnings of Jesus' ministry in Galilee, are like the voice of springtime when he bursts forth in new life, all the time of preparation over. In the gospels there are often these short summary verses where a few words signify a great deal of activity. We leave Jesus, having come out of the narrow way of his testing, taking Galilee by storm, to the joy of all.

STUDY

Savour this prayer:

> And now we are come into Lent
> to the time of tears and terrors,
> the season of sorrows and sins.
> It is a time to look *down*
> and say to our souls.
> 'Here we are come to the worst,
> to the chasm where all has fallen.'
> But it is also a time to look *up*
> and hear another voice which says,
> 'Before you ever were, I spanned the abyss.
> You are free, and freedom is unbounded.'
> And so Lent can be a time
> when the soul is afoot and light-hearted,
> when it is done with indoor complaints and querulous criticisms,
> when it is strong and content to travel the open road
> and look around and see the timeless mystery of Love.
> (Charles Robertson)

In his temptations Jesus relies on the presence and reality of God's kingdom, on signs of 'the timeless mystery of love.' Think where you see these signs in your own life and in the life of world and other people around you. It is these moments of grace, when we know and feel God's love, which are our bulwark in times of testing.

chapter 6

Nazareth and Capernaum

LUKE 4:16-44

Jesus is Rejected at Nazareth
(Mt 13:53-58, Mk 6:1-6)

Then Jesus went to Nazareth, where he had been brought up, and on the Sabbath he went as usual to the synagogue. He stood up to read the Scriptures and was handed the book of the prophet Isaiah. He unrolled the scroll and found the place where it is written:

> "The Spirit of the Lord is upon me,
> because he has chosen me to bring good news to the poor.
> He has sent me to proclaim liberty to the captives
> and recovery of sight to the blind;
> to set free the oppressed
> and announce that the time has come when the Lord will
> save his people."

Jesus rolled up the scroll, gave it back to the attendant, and sat down. All the people in the synagogue had their eyes fixed on him, as he said to them, "This passage of scripture has come true today, as you heard it being read."

They were all well impressed with him and marvelled at the eloquent words that he spoke. They said, "Isn't he the son of Joseph?"

He said to them, "I am sure that you will quote this proverb to me, 'Doctor, heal yourself.' You will also tell me to do here in my home town the same things you heard were done in Capernaum. I tell you this," Jesus added, "prophets are never welcomed in their home town.

"Listen to me: it is true that there were many widows in Israel during the time of Elijah, when there was no rain for three and a half years and a severe famine spread throughout the whole land. Yet Elijah was not sent to anyone in Israel, but only to a widow living in Zarephath in the territory of Sidon. And there were many people suffering from a dreaded skin disease who lived in Israel during the time of the prophet Elisha; yet not one of them was healed, but only Naaman the Syrian."

When the people in the synagogue heard this, they were filled with anger. They rose up, dragged Jesus out of the town, and took him to the top of the hill on which their town was built. They meant to throw him over the cliff, but he walked through the middle of the crowd and went his way.

A Man with an Evil Spirit
(Mk 1:21-28)

Then Jesus went to Capernaum, a town in Galilee, where he taught the people on the Sabbath. They were all amazed at the way he taught, because he spoke with authority. In the synagogue was a man who had the spirit of an evil demon in him; he screamed out in a loud voice, "Ah! What do you want with us, Jesus of Nazareth? Are you here to destroy us? I know who you are: you are God's holy messenger!"

Jesus ordered the spirit, "Be quiet and come out of the man!" The demon threw the man down in front of them and went out of him without doing him any harm.

The people were all amazed and said to one another, "What kind of words are these? With authority and power this man gives orders to the evil spirits, and they come out!" And the report about Jesus spread everywhere in that region.

Jesus Heals Many People
(Mt 8:14-17, Mk 1:29-34)

Jesus left the synagogue and went to Simon's house. Simon's mother-in-law was sick with a high fever, and they spoke to Jesus about her. He went and stood at her bedside and ordered the fever to leave her. The fever left her, and she got up at once and began to wait on them.

After sunset all who had friends who were sick with various diseases brought them to Jesus; he placed his hands on every one of them and healed them all. Demons also went out from many people, screaming, "You are the Son of God!"

Jesus gave the demons an order and would not let them speak, because they knew that he was the Messiah.

Jesus Preaches in the Synagogues
(Mk 1:35-39)

At daybreak Jesus left the town and went off to a lonely place. The people started looking for him, and when they found him, they tried to keep him from leaving. But he said to them, "I must preach the Good News about the Kingdom of God in other towns also, because that is what God sent me to do."

So he preached in the synagogues throughout the country.

SOME SERMON!

Reading through the early chapters of Luke is to be struck by the cumulative force of a series of beginnings. There's Chapter 1, with the birth announcements, chapter two with the story of Jesus' birth, Chapter 3 telling of the impact of the ministry of John the Baptist and the baptism of Jesus, and the start of Chapter 4 with the time of testing and the brief announcement of the beginnings of his teaching in Galilee. It is striking how little Jesus speaks in these opening chapters. Apart from replying to his mother at the Jerusalem Temple and countering the Devil in the desert, as yet he has not spoken directly. This is about to change, dramatically.

Luke locates the first recorded incident in the ministry of Jesus in his own home town of Nazareth. The scene is the local synagogue, the time the Sabbath day, and the report is that Jesus was found in the synagogue on the Sabbath, as usual. The attendant gives him the scriptures to read, on this occasion the scroll of the words of the prophet Isaiah. Jesus stands to read; he unrolls the scroll, finds the place at the beginning of Isaiah 61. He reads (I quote from the *NRSV* translation which is closer to the original than the *GNB*):

> The Spirit of the Lord is upon me,
> because he has anointed me
> to bring good news to the poor.
> He has sent me to proclaim release to the captives
> and recovery of sight to the blind,
> to let the oppressed go free,
> to proclaim the year of the Lord's favour.
> (Luke 4:18,19 *NRSV*)

The drama continues. Jesus rolls up the scroll, hands it back to the attendant, and sits down - the sitting position is the accustomed posture for teaching. All eyes are on him. He says, quite simply. 'Today this scripture is fulfilled, come alive, in your very hearing' (4:21).

What does this mean? Think of Magna Carta, the Gettysburg Address, the Declaration of Arbroath - many nations have their founding and foundational documents. In contemporary society all manner of human groupings from public bodies to business enterprises spend time and effort in constructing 'mission statements' which seek to summarise and encapsulate what they are about. The words Jesus takes from Isaiah 61 and makes his own can be seen as Jesus' foundational mission statement according to Luke. They have been called, 'The Nazareth Manifesto,' in which Jesus announces who he is and what he is about. They are therefore worth looking at with some care.

THE SERMON'S THEMES

Jesus quotes from Isaiah. From the prophet Isaiah the gospel writers derive a mass of material on Hebrew hopes for the Messiah which they will link with the person and purpose of Jesus. Isaiah links his words about the coming Messiah to his picture of the Servant of the Lord. Key passages are the prophecies of Isaiah 2, 9 and 11 (which are embedded for us in Advent liturgies) and the four servant songs of Isaiah 42:1-13, 49:1-6, 50:3-9, and above all 52:13 - 53:12, which underpins the whole narrative of Jesus' passion. Jesus' words here from Isaiah 61 are also the words of the Servant Lord.

Once again they contain a reference to the Spirit. It is the descending, indwelling Spirit of God which fills the servant with power to undertake his commission. The Spirit blows with a mighty wind of freedom. It is an overflowing, gracious, liberating sense of freedom which comes from the words of Jesus. For the poor, joy in freedom from want; for prisoners, liberty from captivity; for the blind, liberation from their blindness; and for the oppressed, the lifting of their burden. In the offering of release from captivity and the freeing of the oppressed there is also an undertone of another of the gospel's main themes, the offer of forgiveness and specifically the removal of the burden of debt. That theme intensifies in the final phrase of Jesus' quotation, 'to proclaim the year of the Lord's favour' (*NRSV* 4:19).

The 'year of the Lord's favour' was the year of Jubilee, the fiftieth year. Its far-reaching regulations are found in Leviticus 25. It was a year when the land lay fallow, when slaves were released from their burden, and debts incurred were remitted. Jubilee therefore offered a new beginning for land and people alike. It was expected that the coming Messiah would proclaim and enforce Jubilee. There are considerable doubts as to how far the regulations of Jubilee with their serious demands for wealth redistribution were observed in Israelite society. What is true is that the Jubilee regulations gave a key reference point for prophets in their insistence that the people return to ways of justice. John Howard Yoder, in his book *The Politics of Jesus,* makes out a case that the redistributive demands of the Jubilee were taken with sufficient seriousness around Jesus' time for the great rabbi Hillel to produce a device to get round the regulations for debt repayment (Yoder 1972, pp. 69-70). Was 'Jubilee dodging' the earlier equivalent of today's tax avoidance? Do both carry an unwarranted veneer of respectability among the better-off?

Taken as a whole, the Nazareth Manifesto represents a great announcement of the coming of one who will open up ways of freedom and justice. The 'year of the Lord's favour' suggests an overflowing abundance of God's grace, lifting people out of their own preoccupations and wounds to see and become part of the Kingdom of the gracious God at work in the world. Jubilee has become a contemporary theme among the churches and others in the campaign for the relief of debt for the world's poorest countries, a campaign for both justice and freedom. The promise and the struggle goes on. Listen to the words of Nelson Mandela, who in recent years has come to embody so much of the spirit of Jesus in his Nazareth sermon. At the end of the autobiography of his life up to the 1994 election he writes:

> It was during those long and lonely years [in prison] that my hunger for the freedom of my own people became a hunger for the freedom of all people, white and black. I knew as well as I knew anything that the oppressor must

be liberated just as surely as the oppressed. A man who takes away another man's freedom is a prisoner of hatred, he is locked behind the bars of prejudice and narrow-mindedness. I am not truly free if I am taking away someone else's freedom, just as surely as I am not free when my freedom is taken away from me. The oppressed and the oppressor alike are robbed of their humanity.

When I walked out of prison, that was my mission, to liberate the oppressed and oppressor both. Some say that has now been achieved. But I know that is not the case. The truth is that we are not yet free; we have merely achieved the freedom to be free, the right not to be oppressed. We have not taken the final step of our journey, but the first step on a longer and even more difficult road. For to be free is not merely to cast off one's chains, but to live in a way that respects and enhances the freedom of others. The true test of our devotion to freedom is just beginning.

I have walked the long road to freedom. I have tried not to falter; I have made missteps along the way. But I have discovered the secret that after climbing a great hill, one only finds that there are more hills to climb. I have taken a moment here to rest, to steal a view of the glorious vista that surrounds me, to look back on the distance I have come. But I can rest only for a moment, for with freedom come responsibilities, and I dare not linger, for my long walk is not yet ended.
(Mandela 1994, p. 751)

Yes, but.....

In his reflections on Luke, *The Good News According to Luke*, Richard Rohr comments wryly that when he speaks on this passage, when he stresses the themes of hope and freedom, he receives the warm applause of his audience, but when he speaks about the social and redistributive aspects of Jesus' message he is greeted with at best polite, tepid and sporadic handclaps (Rohr 1997 p. 103). Something akin happens to Jesus at his home synagogue in Nazareth. The mood of the crowd changes from admiration to anger, very quickly. Luke is not very clear in relating the moment of transition but the movement itself is obvious.

The people of Nazareth are delighted at the accomplishments of one of their own, the carpenter's son. They have no doubt heard of his healings elsewhere in Galilee, and they would like to claim him for themselves. 'He's our boy, after all.' Jesus is more than doubtful. 'Prophets are never welcomed in their home town' (4:24).

What rouses the crowd to fury is his telling of two stories, one about Elijah and one about Elisha; the point of both is that it is to an outsider the prophet becomes an instrument of God's grace. It is the widow of Zarephath in Lebanon and Naaman the Syrian who receive blessing. What Jesus has come to proclaim and inaugurate cannot be limited to the home town, the home family, the homeland.

As we struggle to be a 'Church without Walls', we are aware that parochialism still exercises its divisive undertow. I remember speaking with people in a small Scottish rural parish who were telling me they were simple people, unused to change. From their front doors they could see an international airport, two inter-city motorways, an inter-city rail link and a modern petro-chemical complex (where many of them worked). Change was all around them. However, we remained good friends which is more than could be said for the people of Nazareth. They lay hands on Jesus, the home boy who has grown too big for them. They would silence this now uncomfortable voice in their midst. He evades them, and goes his way, he 'dare not linger, for his long walk is not ended.' It has scarcely begun.

ANOTHER TOWN, ANOTHER SYNAGOGUE

The scene changes to the lakeside town of Capernaum. Jesus is again found in the synagogue on the Sabbath. In telling the story of Jesus' encounter with the man with an evil spirit (4:31-36), Luke extracts one particular incident out of a more general pattern. Luke says, 'Jesus is to be found teaching in the synagogue every Sabbath, here's one example of what happened.' From the general pattern Luke shows Jesus teaching with such authority that people were amazed. They were caught up in the directness and power of his teaching. His power, however, produced a reaction, and in the synagogue on one Sabbath day a voice rang out to challenge him. 'What do you want with us, Jesus of Nazareth? Are you here to destroy us? I know who you are: God's holy messenger!' (4:34) Luke says that the voice came from a man with an evil demon in him. (There is a note on Luke's world of angels and demons at the end of this chapter.) Jesus' authority extends to demanding that people be released from evil demons or spirits. The demon comes harmlessly out of the man and the people are further amazed at this display of authority. News of Jesus spreads far and wide in the region. His name has power (4:37). In the casting out of the evil spirit, as in his teaching, his directness causes people wonder. In his healings, there is a complete lack of elaborate ritual or esoteric rites. We begin to see the outworking of the Spirit's power in the anointed, chosen one (4:18-19).

This story and the following one of the healing of Simon's mother-in-law belong at the start of a section in the gospel (up to 6:16) which Luke has sourced from Mark. In Mark this story occurs very early (Mark 1:21-28). There, it is suggested that the evil spirit which perceives Jesus as a threat is symbolic of a collective voice from the synagogue authorities who see Jesus as a dangerous challenge to the old ways. The same case can be made here in Luke, that this is another instance of the opposition Jesus will encounter.

From the synagogue we move to the private place of Simon's house. Simon's mother-in-law is sick with a fever. Jesus orders the fever to leave her, with the same authority he has shown in dealing with the evil spirit. She makes their dinner.

There follows another of these short verses covering a great deal of activity (40-41). When the sun had set, i.e. when the Sabbath was over, many were brought to Jesus for healing. The sick were healed as he laid hands on them and the demons were peremptorily driven out. First thing the following morning, Jesus leaves the town to go to a lonely place where he is pursued by the crowd from the town who want him back. He explains to them that he must keep moving. No more than the people of his home town, Nazareth, can these townsfolk claim him. He has other towns to visit and other places to preach; that is what God has sent him to do (4:43). Here for the first time he makes mention of the Kingdom of God: the present reality of God, which becomes real to people through his preaching and healing; the two activities which always belong together through his ministry in Galilee, and major themes in this gospel. Jesus goes on his way, preaching through the synagogues of the region.

STUDY

BY YOURSELF
Make the words Jesus quotes from Isaiah at Nazareth the focus of your prayer life for the coming week:

> The Spirit of the Lord is upon me,
> because he has anointed me
> to bring good news to the poor.
> He has sent me to proclaim release to the captives
> and recovery of sight to the blind,
> to let the oppressed go free,
> to proclaim the year of the Lord's favour.
> (4:18,19 *NRSV*)

Learn these words. Recall them in the morning, in the middle of the day and in the evening. Reflect on what they are saying to your life in the midst of your daily activity.

FOR GROUP WORK
These words of Jesus at Nazareth have been called his 'mission statement'. Draw up a mission statement for your church group, a short and punchy summary of what your purpose is. (Jesus found his 'mission statement' in the words of the Bible; you could try to do the same.)

Luke's world of angels and demons

Luke's view of angels/demons reminds us of the distance between his world and ours; though the same unseen forces are encountered in both, albeit with different names. The world of Luke, which would be as familiar to his first readers as the world of the daily diet of media is to us, was one where belief in spirits and their influence was an accepted reality. These unseen forces were divided into the good and the bad.

The good are represented by the angels. In Luke these appear at the beginning and end of the gospel; in the birth narratives (1:11 & 26, 2:9), and at the empty tomb (24:4 & 23). In these appearances Luke uses the familiar tradition of the Old Testament usage of angels as a way of describing how the unseen God appeared to human beings. With the specific reference to Gabriel (1:19, 26), Luke uses a development from late in the Old Testament which came to see angels as personal intermediaries between God and his people. In the gospel the angels are uniformly messengers, heralds of good tidings of birth and new birth.

Demons are more numerous and more complex. They occur frequently throughout Jesus' ministry. In the time of Jesus, through the influence of apocalyptic writing, they were believed to have their origin in the fall of the angels and to further the work of Satan in this present age, working all manner of seduction, evil and corruption until meeting their end in the age to come. In the common mind, demons or evil spirits were also connected with popular animistic belief in unseen spirits who invaded people's lives and afflicted them with a variety of illnesses and madness (see Evans 1990, p. 278-9). Illnesses producing symptoms of loss of control, such as epilepsy, convulsions, tremors or other clear signs of derangement, were characterised as the work of evil spirits. However, Luke, more than the other evangelists, sees the work of malign spirits even in more clearly physical illness. Note in the immediately preceding story of the healing of Simon's mother-in-law, where Mark says Jesus took her by the hand and lifted her up (Mk 1:31) - a very human touch - Luke says Jesus commanded the fever to leave her, as if the fever were personified (4:39).

In all cases, the presence of evil spirits or demons was seen as the work of the Devil, Beelzebul, Satan. Jesus made war on them and cast them out (9:1f, 10:19f, 11:20). Their expulsion was both a sign of Jesus' victory in his warfare against Satan and all evil powers, and a mark of deliverance and release in the person afflicted. It was therefore in part fulfilment of the promise of the Nazareth Manifesto of 4:18 - freedom to the captives. Jesus' power over demons and the healing he brings to those afflicted are signs of the new age he inaugurates.

chapter 7

Genessaret

LUKE 5

Jesus Calls the First Disciples
(Mt 4:18-22, Mk 1:16-20)

One day Jesus was standing on the shore of Lake Gennesaret while the people pushed their way up to him to listen to the word of God. He saw two boats pulled up on the beach; the fishermen had left them and were washing the nets. Jesus got into one of the boats - it belonged to Simon - and asked him to push off a little from the shore. Jesus sat in the boat and taught the crowd.

When he finished speaking, he said to Simon, "Push the boat out further to the deep water, and you and your partners let down your nets for a catch."

"Master," Simon answered, "we worked hard all night long and caught nothing. But if you say so, I will let down the nets." They let them down and caught such a large number of fish that the nets were about to break. So they motioned to their partners in the other boat to come and help them. They came and filled both boats so full of fish that the boats were about to sink. When Simon Peter saw what had happened, he fell on his knees before Jesus and said, "Go away from me, Lord! I am a sinful man!"

He and the others with him were all amazed at the large number of fish they had caught. The same was true of Simon's partners, James and John, the sons of Zebedee. Jesus said to Simon, "Don't be afraid; from now on you will be catching people."

They pulled the boats up on the beach, left everything, and followed Jesus.

Jesus Heals a Man
(Mt 8:1-4, Mk 1:40-45)

Once Jesus was in a town where there was a man who was suffering from a dreaded skin disease. When he saw Jesus, he threw himself down and begged him, "Sir, if you want to, you can make me clean!"

Jesus stretched out his hand and touched him. "I do want to," he answered. "Be clean!" At once the disease left the man. Jesus ordered him, "Don't tell anyone, but go straight to the priest and let him examine you; then to prove to everyone that you are cured, offer the sacrifice as Moses ordered."

But the news about Jesus spread all the more widely, and crowds of people came to hear him and be healed from their diseases. But he would go away to lonely places, where he prayed.

Jesus Heals a Paralysed Man
(Mt 9:1-8, Mk 2:1-12)

One day when Jesus was teaching, some Pharisees and teachers of the Law were sitting there who had come from every town in Galilee and Judea and from Jerusalem. The power of the Lord was present for Jesus to heal the sick. Some men came carrying a paralysed man on a bed, and they tried to take him into the house and put him in front of Jesus. Because of the crowd, however, they could find no way to take him in. So they carried him up on the roof, made an opening in the tiles, and let him down on his bed into the middle of the group in front of Jesus. When Jesus saw how much faith they had, he said to the man, "Your sins are forgiven, my friend."

The teachers of the Law and the Pharisees began to say to themselves, "Who is this man who speaks such blasphemy! God is the only one who can forgive sins!"

Jesus knew their thoughts and said to them, "Why do you think such things? Is it easier to say, 'Your sins are forgiven you,' or to say, ' Get up and walk'? I will prove to you, then, that the Son of Man has authority on earth to forgive sins." So he said to the paralysed man, "I tell you, get up, pick up your bed, and go home!"

At once the man got up in front of them all, took the bed he had been lying on, and went home, praising God. They were all completely amazed! Full of fear, they praised God, saying, "What marvellous things we have seen today!"

Jesus Calls Levi
(Mt 9:9-13, Mk 2:13-17)

After this, Jesus went out and saw a tax collector named Levi, sitting in his office. Jesus said to him, "Follow me." Levi got up, left everything, and followed him.

Then Levi had a big feast in his house for Jesus, and among the guests was a large number of tax collectors and other people. Some Pharisees and some teachers of the Law who belonged to their group complained to Jesus' disciples. "Why do you eat and drink with tax collectors and other outcasts?" they asked.

Jesus answered them, "People who are well do not need a doctor, but only those who are sick. I have not come to call respectable people to repent, but outcasts."

The Question about Fasting
(Mt 9:14-17, Mk 2:18-22)

Some people said to Jesus, "The disciples of John fast frequently and offer prayers, and the disciples of the Pharisees do the same; but your disciples eat and drink."

Jesus answered, "Do you think you can make the guests at a wedding party go without food as long as the bridegroom is with them? Of course not! But the day will come when the bridegroom will be taken away from them, and then they will fast."

Jesus also told them this parable: "No one tears a piece off a new coat to patch up an old coat. If he does, he will have torn the new coat and the piece of new cloth will not match the old. Nor does anyone pour new wine into used wineskins, because the new wine will burst the skins, the wine will pour out, and the skins will be ruined. Instead, new wine must be poured into fresh wineskins! And no one wants new wine after drinking old wine. 'The old is better,' he says."

OF FISH AND FISHERMEN

The crowds do indeed flock round Jesus. By the lake of Genessaret, Luke's unique naming of the sea of Galilee, the numbers are so thick that Jesus presses into service one of the fishing boats by the shore where the fishermen were busy with their nets after a fruitless night's work. The boat he uses belongs to Simon, and from the boat pushed off a little from the shore, Jesus sits and teaches the people.

When the teaching is over, Jesus turns to Simon. Luke highlights this first conversation with the one who is to be his chief apostle, in the light of the key role he will play in the book of Acts. Jesus and Simon get to talking about fishing, Simon's daily work. It is out of a conversation about work that Jesus 'catches' Simon. Work continues to be the place which devours a major amount of people's commitment and energy. The workplace is a realm of all manner of challenges, achievements, relationships, disappointments and ambiguities. We live a long way from the medieval monastic ideal of life as a balanced and intermingled order of work and prayer, prayer and work. Today our experience of life is so often fragmented and compartmentalised. Yet, in the vows of membership in the Church of Scotland there is a promise to 'serve Christ in our daily work' (*Common Order* 1994, p. 118). As a minister, I wonder whether I listen enough in an informed way to people's stories about their daily work; as congregations, do we spend enough time exploring the world of work in our changing society; as church members, do we see the world of work as a vital place for the fulfilling of our Christian vocation?

The conversation between Jesus and Simon, about fish and fishing, has an extraordinary twist to it. The story itself has strong echoes of the post-Resurrection story of Jesus and Peter in John 21:1-14. Jesus tells Simon to put back out into the lake, and when he and his partners with their boat do so, they are rewarded with a catch fit to break their nets (and nearly sink their boats). Simon, now called Peter for the first time in the gospel, is so overcome by the wonder of it all that he sinks to his knees before Jesus and says, 'Go away from me, Lord! I am a sinful man!' (5:8) There's a certain irony in these words since what immediately follows is that Simon together with his partners, James and John, who will form the inner core of the disciples, all go away with Jesus. The discipleship journey has begun. Once again Jesus has displayed an awesome power; it is a power which does not repel, it attracts.

'BE CLEAN!'

Encounters multiply thick and fast. Jesus is next met by a man with a skin disease (possibly leprosy, in which Luke has a particular interest - see 7:22, 17:11-19). The leper not only suffered from the physical effects of the illness, but also carried the burden of a rigid social exclusion which could only be lifted by priestly decree. Lepers were 'untouchables' because of the contagious nature of their illness, yet in face of the man's desperate request, Jesus reaches out to touch him and declare him 'clean'. Jesus tells the man to go to the priest and perform the duly appointed sacrifices (5:14). We are shown Jesus' respect for the Jewish law and its ways as they assist in the healing process. He also bids the man tell no one what has happened, but news about Jesus' teaching and healing cannot be contained and spreads like wildfire.

The crowds press round, but Luke relates that there was another rhythm to Jesus' life. While he was incessantly in demand and giving of himself without stint, he would also go away, 'far from the madding crowd', to be alone to pray. That rhythm of engagement and withdrawal, activity and reflection, work and prayer is central to a fruitful life in the spirit. It's an important word for a generation of driven activists, just so long as the withdrawal, reflection and prayer don't become part of our drivenness also.

'PICK UP YOUR BED AND GO HOME!'

By now the activity of Jesus has come to the attention of more than the ordinary people, 'the people of the land'. In the next encounter we are introduced for the first time to those who will form the personal opposition to Jesus, the Pharisees and the teachers of the Law, some of whom have come from the heartland, Jerusalem. The Pharisees represented a lay group within Israel who sought reform and hope for the people through the rigorous practice of the Law and the pursuit of personal holiness. In many ways they are close to Jesus and the disciples; with the key difference that while their practice is exclusive (the name 'Pharisee' means 'separated one'), that of Jesus and the disciples is inclusive. Luke is more gentle in his characterisation of the Pharisees than the other gospel writers, probably because converted Pharisees played an important role in the church of the book of Acts - Paul was one. Here we are introduced to 'some' Pharisees. The teachers of the Law, Luke's name for the scribes, were, as the name suggests, the interpreters of the Mosaic law and the traditions which had grown up around it. They were both religious teachers and lawyers, as the distinction between sacred and secular is anachronistic in terms of Hebrew faith and practice.

The main character in this story is a paralysed man brought by his friends to Jesus. It's one of the gospels' most dramatic stories; as the man is brought by his friends to Jesus and they can't get near because of the crowd, until they resort to the ingenious method of removing some roof tiles and lowering the man on his bed down in front of Jesus (5:17-26). The message of the story is of a two-fold deliverance. The man gets up and walks, freed from his paralysis and released from his sin.

It is the second which causes controversy and confrontation: the release from sin. Jesus is not saying that all illness is caused by sin, though this was a commonly-held view of the time (see John 9). He does discern that some physical illnesses have psychic roots and that is why his word of forgiveness here is liberating. The argument with the authorities is over power. Who has power to forgive sins? Strictly speaking, scripture said that only God had power to forgive sins. The scribes, teachers of the Law, however, had drawn up an elaborate system by which people could make atonement for their sins through the sacrificial system and find release. The ones who complain here about Jesus were the operators of the official system for releasing people of their burden of indebtedness, usually for a price. They are not quite disinterested. But God can delegate his authority to another, and it's that authority Jesus claims here. Forgiveness is a major theme of the gospel and Jesus will go on to teach more not only of the wonder of God's forgiving grace but also of the way that grace is given to us to enable us freely and heartily to forgive one another.

'THE SON OF MAN IS ABLE......'

For the first time in the gospel Jesus refers to himself with the title of 'Son of Man', 'Human One'. This is a key title in the gospels, one with a long Old Testament background; and Jesus' choice of it and its importance and significance is well brought out in the following quotation from G B Caird's commentary on Saint Luke:

> There is adequate evidence that it was Jesus' own choice of title, perhaps a deliberately mysterious and ambiguous one. It enabled him, without actually claiming to be the Messiah, to indicate his essential unity with mankind, and above all with the weak and the humble, and also his special function as predestined representative of the new Israel and bearer of God's judgement and kingdom. Even when he used it as a title, its strongly corporate overtones made it not merely title, but an invitation to others to join him in the destiny he had accepted. And when he spoke of the glory

of the Son of Man he was predicting not so much his own personal glory as the triumph of the cause he served.
(Caird 1963, p. 94-5)

'NOT THE RESPECTABLE, BUT OUTCASTS'

The final dramatic encounter of this chapter is of Jesus with Levi, the tax collector (5:27-32). In looking at the message of John the Baptist (3:12-13), we have already seen the dubious position of tax collectors in the society of Jesus' time. They were doubly despised, as agents of an alien authority and as entrepreneurs more than liable to make an extortionate profit at the expense of ordinary people. They were nobody's friends. But Jesus calls Levi, the tax collector, to follow him. Levi immediately leaves his work, and we next find Jesus as the guest at a party in his house where most of the other guests are - tax collectors. Once again the guardians of the straight and narrow are scandalised. 'Why do you eat with tax collectors and other outcasts?' Jesus answer is to point once again to the boundary-bursting grace he has come to show. 'I have come not to call the righteous, but sinners to turn their lives round' (5:32). These words will echo through the gospel and break out very soon in the longer story of Jesus' anointing in the house of Simon the Pharisee (7:36-50).

OF OLD AND NEW WINE

The chapter ends with Jesus being questioned about why his disciples do not fast as the disciples of the ascetic John do. Jesus points forward to the time when he will no longer be with them; that will be an appropriate time for fasting, but not now in this time of joy when the good news is being spread. It's like being at a wedding feast! (5:33-35)

Jesus then adds two sayings about the problems of grafting the new on to the old. Too often all that is heard is the sound of tearing, of new cloth from old; or the noise of explosion, of the new wine bursting the old wineskins. As confrontation looms in this chapter, in these final sayings about the departure of the bridegroom and the explosive nature of the meeting of old and new, Jesus shows he is well aware of the costly nature of his ministry. The final verse, 'No one wants new wine after drinking old wine. "The old is better", he says' (5:39); this can only be an ironic warning of the difficulties in getting the human species (and maybe in particular homo religiosus) to change. At a recent conference, a speaker offered the following seven last words for the Scottish church. 'We never did it that way before!'

STUDY

BY YOURSELF
Reflect on the question:
What does it mean to me to serve Jesus in my daily work - whether that work is paid, voluntary, or in the home?

FOR GROUP WORK
Share the reflections on what following Jesus means in the workplace today.
Think together about the changing place of work in our changing society.
Do we see the world of work as a vital place for the fulfilling of our Christian vocation? Which of these frequently-heard sentences do you hear yourself saying?
• It's just a job.
• It pays the rent.
• It's what God wants me to do.
• I really enjoy my work.
• My work's hard, but someone needs to do it.
How do we work out that vocation in practice?

chapter 8

Challenging custom and choosing apostles

LUKE 6:1-16

The Question about the Sabbath
(Mt 12:1-8, Mk 2:23-28)

Jesus was walking through some cornfields on the Sabbath. His disciples began to pick the ears of corn, rub them in their hands, and eat the grain. Some Pharisees asked, "Why are you doing what our Law says you cannot do on the Sabbath?"

Jesus answered them, " Haven't you read what David did when he and his men were hungry? He went into the house of God, took the bread offered to God, ate it, and gave it also to his men. Yet it is against our Law for anyone except the priests to eat that bread."

And Jesus concluded, "The Son of Man is Lord of the Sabbath."

The Man with a Paralysed Hand
(Mt 12:9-14, Mk 3:1-6)

On another Sabbath Jesus went into a synagogue and taught. A man was there whose right hand was paralysed. Some teachers of the Law and some Pharisees wanted a reason to accuse Jesus of doing wrong, so they watched him closely to see if he would heal on the Sabbath. But Jesus knew their thoughts and said to the man, "Stand up and come here to the front." The man got up and stood there. Then Jesus said to them, "I ask you: what does our Law allow us to do on the Sabbath? To help or to harm? To save someone's life or destroy it?" He looked around at them all; then he said to the man, "Stretch out your hand." He did so, and his hand became well again.

They were filled with rage and began to discuss among themselves what they could do to Jesus.

Jesus Chooses the Twelve Apostles
(Mt 10:1-4, Mk 3:13-19)

At that time Jesus went up a hill to pray and spent the whole night there praying to God. When day came, he called his disciples to him and chose twelve of them, whom he named apostles: Simon (whom he named Peter) and his brother Andrew; James and John, Philip and Bartholomew, Matthew and Thomas, James son of Alphaeus, and Simon (who was called the Patriot), Judas son of James, and Judas Iscariot, who became the traitor.

THE CONFRONTATION OVER THE SABBATH

The argument and the action continue directly from the previous chapter. Luke places two controversial incidents side by side; both involving the Sabbath Law. In the first, Jesus is taken to task, once again by 'some Pharisees', for allowing his disciples to pick, rub and eat some wayside ears of corn. The argument is not about the theft of another's corn: the picking of corn nearest the path was allowed for the poor and the traveller. The problem is the Sabbath Day. Picking the corn was technically reaping, and rubbing the ears was technically milling. Both activities were classified as work, and work on the Sabbath was forbidden. By Jesus' time the initial commandment had become weighed down by myriad regulations.

It is difficult for a Scot to deal dispassionately with the Sabbath. In my lifetime the long-established practice of a Sabbatarianism with many negative and legalistic characteristics has now been replaced by a day seemingly designed mainly for compulsive shopaholics. Two comments, however, are in order. First, keeping the Sabbath was a vital part of Jewish identity, particularly when that identity was continually coming under attack from outside and from alien forces. Second, the intention of the original commandment was to give a day of rest to people whose daily lives involved sweat, sweat and more sweat, and for whom leisure was an unknown concept and reality. Both the Sabbath year - every seventh year when the land lay fallow (i.e. rested) - and the Jubilee year of restitution and debt cancellation, were developments from the original weekly Sabbath day. Jesus is certainly not hostile to the basic humanising and liberating purposes of Sabbath regulation. What he has problems with is nit-pickingly legalistic attitudes over its application.

In the story of the cornfields, he invokes the example of King David, who fed his men when they were hungry from the bread in the sanctuary which was dedicated to God. If David out of necessity could eat the dedicated bread, then the disciples out of necessity could break the regulations surrounding the dedicated day. Jesus ends, 'The Son of Man is Lord of the Sabbath' (6:5). The conjunction of that statement and the invocation of David's example raise the question. Is Jesus here making claims for himself as a Messianic figure?

MORE CONTROVERSY OVER THE SABBATH

Another dramatic incident immediately follows, though on a different Sabbath. We are back in a synagogue. This time there are some scribes and Pharisees waiting and watching to see if Jesus will put a foot wrong. Sure enough, knowing well what they are thinking, he deliberately puts his foot over the mark. He calls a man with a paralysed hand out to the front. Then he speaks, 'I ask you: what does our Law allow us to do on the Sabbath? To help or to harm? To save someone's life or destroy it?' (6:9) He casts his eye round the congregation. No answer. Then he says to the man, 'Stretch out your hand,' and it was restored to health. The authorities are furious, they begin to discuss what they could do to Jesus.

The man's hand wasn't in urgent need of mending. It could have waited to the next day. This is a deliberate confrontation on the part of Jesus. Luke does not include Mark's quotation of Jesus' words, 'The Sabbath was made for the good of human beings; they were not made for the Sabbath' (Mark 2:27). The sense of these words is clearly implied, since for Jesus the whole thrust of Sabbath is towards human liberation. If Jesus is making claims for himself as a Messianic figure, it is the figure of one who brings release to those bearing burdens. The Nazareth Manifesto is being acted out in its fullness. And the cost of the action begins to loom clearer.

In a very short space of time Jesus has been shown in confrontation with scribe and Pharisee about the purity code, over the touching of the leper and the question of the company he keeps; the debt code, in the incident of the paralysed man and the forgiveness of sins; and the Sabbath law. The Pharisees and scribes recognise a threat to all that is most precious to them. The people get a sense of the coming of the abundant Kingdom of liberating joy.

PRAYING AND CHOOSING

We have seen the tension beginning to mount in Jesus' ministry. He goes apart to pray (6:12). He prays throughout the night. He has important decisions to make. He will wrestle hard with the decision and seek discernment and ponder with God on the way ahead. He is about to choose twelve men to be his closest disciples. The naming of twelve echoes the twelve tribes of old Israel, men are chosen as 'fathers of the tribe'. These men, together with an important group of women (8:2-3), will form the nucleus of the new community around Jesus, the community of the new Israel. Once again we see the promise of the new arising out of the old. It has to be said that we don't know very much about them, as individuals. Luke's list doesn't correspond exactly with those of Matthew and Mark. Luke lists Judas the son of James, where the other two evangelists have Thaddeus. In Luke's account only Peter receives a new name. And, of course, within the twelve is the one who will betray him, Judas Iscariot. It is the ordinariness of the disciples which is striking. And the number twelve, sign of the new community.

STUDY

BY YOURSELF

In the previous section we saw the rhythm of engagement and withdrawal, prayer and action, which was the pattern of Jesus' life. Here we have been reminded that the Sabbath has been given us for rest and liberation.

Reflect on this:

• What is the rhythm and pattern of my life of work, engagement, withdrawal, prayer and reflection?

• Is prayer something I need to explore further? (There are a huge number of books and other resources on prayer and how to pray. Most churches publish a prayer diary of some kind, such as the Church of Scotland's *Pray Now,* a yearly guide to devotions published by St Andrew Press.)

• How do I make time for rest and renewal in my life?

chapter 9

'But I tell you'

LUKE 6:17-49

Jesus Teaches and Heals
(Mt 4:23-25)

When Jesus had come down from the hill with the apostles, he stood on a level place with a large number of his disciples. A large crowd of people was there from all over Judea and from Jerusalem and from the coastal cities of Tyre and Sidon; they had come to hear him and to be healed of their diseases. Those who were troubled by evil spirits also came and were healed. All the people tried to touch him, for power was going out from him and healing them all.

Happiness and Sorrow
(Mt 5:1-12)

Jesus looked at his disciples and said,

"Happy are you poor;
the Kingdom of God is yours!
Happy are you who are hungry now;
you will be filled!
Happy are you who weep now;
you will laugh!

"Happy are you when people hate you, reject you, insult you, and say that you are evil, all because of the Son of Man! Be glad when that happens, and dance for joy, because a great reward is kept for you in heaven. For their ancestors did the very same things to the prophets.

"But how terrible for you who are rich now;
you have had your easy life!

How terrible for you who are full now;
you will go hungry!
How terrible for you who laugh now;
you will mourn and weep!

"How terrible when all people speak well of you; their ancestors said the very same things about the false prophets.

Love for Enemies
(Mt 5:38-48, 7:12a)

"But I tell you who hear me; love your enemies, do good to those who hate you, bless those who curse you, and pray for those who ill-treat you. If anyone hits you on one cheek, let him hit the other one too; if someone takes your coat, let him have your shirt as well. Give to everyone who asks you for something, and when someone takes what is yours, do not ask for it back. Do for others just what you want them to do for you.

"If you love only the people who love you, why should you receive a blessing? Even sinners love those who love them! And if you do good only to those who do good to you, why should you receive a blessing? Even sinners do that! And if you lend only to those from whom you hope to get it back, why should you receive a blessing? Even sinners lend to sinners, to get back the same amount! No! Love your enemies, and do good to them; lend and expect nothing back. You will then have a great reward, and you will be children of the Most High God. For he is good to the ungrateful and the wicked. Be merciful just as your Father is merciful.

Judging Others
(Mt 7:1-5)

"Do not judge others, and God will not judge you; do not condemn others, and God will not condemn you; forgive others, and God will forgive you. Give to others, and God will give to you. Indeed, you will receive a full measure, a generous helping, poured into your hands - all that you can hold. The measure you use for others is the one that God will use for you."

And Jesus told them this parable: "One blind man cannot lead another one; if he does, both will fall into a ditch. No pupil is greater than his teacher; but every pupil, when he has completed his training, will be like his teacher.

"Why do you look at the speck in your brother's eye, but pay no attention to the log in your own eye? How can you say to your brother, 'Please, brother, let me take that speck out of your eye,' yet cannot even see the log in your own eye? You hypocrite! First take the log out of your own eye, and then you will be able to see clearly to take the speck out of your brother's eye.

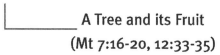

A Tree and its Fruit
(Mt 7:16-20, 12:33-35)

"A healthy tree does not bear bad fruit, nor does a poor tree bear good fruit. Every tree is known by the fruit it bears; you do not pick figs from thorn bushes or gather grapes from bramble bushes. A good person brings good out of the treasure of good things in his heart; a bad person brings bad things out of his treasure of bad things. For the mouth speaks what the heart is full of.

The Two House Builders
(Mt 7:24-27)

"Why do you call me, 'Lord, Lord,' and yet don't do what I tell you? Anyone who comes to me and listens to my words and obeys them - I will show you what he is like. He is like a man who, in building his house, dug deep and laid the foundation on rock. The river overflowed and hit that house but could not shake it, because it was well built. But anyone who hears my words and does not obey them is like a man who built his house without laying a foundation; when the flood hit that house it fell at once - and what a terrible crash that was!"

DOWN TO WORK

Jesus and the newly appointed disciples come down from the hill. Picture Jesus standing in the midst of a larger crowd of disciples, a reminder that the recently appointed twelve are but the symbolic inner core of a much greater number of followers. There is also a crowd, waiting for teaching and healing, come from all over the surrounding region. They were not disappointed. After a time of healing Jesus begins to teach, and this section of teaching we should keep in our mind alongside the previous seminal statements of the Magnificat (1:46-55) and the Nazareth Manifesto (4:18,19) as key passages of what Jesus is all about.

The teaching which Luke narrates Jesus giving here in the rest of Chapter 6 has great similarities to Jesus' Sermon on the Mount in Matthew 5-7. Luke's version is much shorter and concentrates on two elements, love and true discipleship. They are also initially spoken directly to the disciples rather than to the crowd as in Matthew. Because Jesus has returned to level ground, Luke's version is sometimes called, 'the sermon on the plain'. The mountain still looms large, however, as the picture here reminds us of Moses returning from Mount Sinai to deliver the Law from God to his people. This is teaching for the new Israel. 'Sermon' is not the most apt word to describe Jesus' teaching here, and we are well wide of the mark if we hear Jesus' opening words as literal laws. They are provocations, invitations, flashes of lightning across a dark sky!

THE LIFE OF THE KINGDOM

The teaching begins with four beatitudes, 'blessings,' immediately followed by four parallel 'woes'. We can think of them as invitations into life in God's kingdom. Jesus is saying, 'Here's what being a disciple is like, here's what trusting God's promises is like, here's what life in my company is like'. There's something subtle and important to notice. Jesus is not saying, 'This is what you *must do* to be my disciple.' He says, 'This is what being a disciple *is*.' Being a disciple always means staying close to Jesus, knowing his living voice and trusting his risen presence. The discipleship journey is not a solitary assault course of the spirit; it's a way we take knowing there is a hand to bear us up, even when we experience ourselves, like Peter, drowning in our attempts to follow.

Jesus says, 'Here's what the transformed life looks like. Do you recognise yourself? Does it make sense to you? These "blessings" of mine, they look odd to begin with: they're completely the opposite to the way the world thinks. Do you see what I'm getting at, or is it too absurd, just nonsense? If it's like that, maybe you need to go deeper, look again.' Jesus is a good teacher, and the mark of the good teacher is not to give ready-made answers which close things down, but to encourage the asking of the right questions. Jesus' words here ask questions, they open the world up, open our lives up and invite us to go further. 'Blessed' means 'happy', and the *GNB* is not incorrect in translating in this way. It means more than 'happy'; it also means, 'fruitful', 'productive'. Blessing is more than a state of mind, it's about the good life God gives. Remember also that these are Messianic words, and a key promise of the Messiah's coming was the invitation to the great universal feast of life and plenty (Isaiah 25:6-9) where all would be filled with good things. Hear then Jesus' words as the gateway to that feast.

'Happy are you poor; the Kingdom of God is yours!' (6:20) The word is 'poor' without qualification, embracing both material and spiritual poverty. Remember Luke's special concern for the poor and Jesus' announcement of 'Good news to the poor' (4:19). Richard Rohr well expresses the mystery of this first beatitude. 'Right now, if you can be free to be economically poor, to be psychologically disarmed, emotionally vulnerable, spiritually naked, socially without reputation - without these things that protect you, give you power, and exalt you - you are in the kingdom' (Rohr 1997, p. 111). In other words, if you can learn to live with loss, let go with grace, if you are prepared to embrace loss for the sake of God and neighbour, then the doors of the kingdom swing open wide.

'Happy are you who are hungry now; you will be filled!' 'Happy are you who weep now; you will laugh!' (6:21) How are hunger and tears to be counted as blessings? It's satisfaction and laughter we prize. In praising what we avoid, Jesus is confronting us with questions about what we value and how we realise our values. He invites us to change the way we look at the world, to find our meaning by looking at the world from the bottom up, through his eyes of compassion and hope.

'Happy are you when people hate you, reject you, insult you, and say that you are evil, all because of the Son of Man! Be glad when that happens, and dance for joy, because a great reward is kept for you in heaven. For their ancestors did the very same thing to the prophets' (6:22,23). The final beatitude looks backwards and forwards. In the mention of the prophets we are reminded that suffering for the cause of truth has a long and honourable history in the human story and the record of faith. Jesus' words point forward, as both his own disciples and the early church came to know the realities of suffering and persecution of which he speaks. We can hardly call ourselves a persecuted minority, though if we look at ourselves honestly we probably have to admit that we are none too good at accepting criticism, valid or otherwise. We have to struggle to be less prickly and less easily wounded by others. If we take these words together with its corresponding woe, 'How terrible when all people speak well of you' (6:26), together these words say powerfully that it's not what other people call you, think of you or do to you that really matters in life. God has named you and called you to life through Jesus. Let that grace define your sense of self...

Which takes us briefly to the four woes. They do speak of a redistribution out of fairness, out of the justice of God. Cumulatively they say to our inner selves, 'Beware of being secure and satisfied, content and smug.' The self-contained life is death. Discipleship is a movement. The kingdom life with Jesus is restless, the road out and on ever beckoning. There's too much pain in the world for us to settle for an easy life, too much truth out there to settle with our present answers.

Just before we leave these words of Jesus, hear this again. The beatitudes and woes are not answers and are certainly not rules. They do not belong to the world of 'musts' and 'oughts' of which we Christians are prosaically fond. They are provocations, invitations to go deeper: deeper into what Jesus and his kingdom are all about, and what and who we really are, as persons. We are being invited to see neither our own needs or drives, nor the way we see the world as it is, as the reality which claims us; there is a bigger picture, a vision of the whole, which is forever beckoning to us, freeing us from selling out to the present age and settling down with our lesser selves. In John's gospel, Jesus calls himself the door, the gateway into life, eternal life, life in its fullness. Jesus' words here are an invitation to walk through the strait gate, the narrow door, which opens out into a broad vista, the widening road of grace, which leads us ever onward.

A church conference recently explored the theme 'God in Ordinary' - God in our daily life. Dr Phil Hanlon, Professor of Public Health at Glasgow University and one of the guest lecturers, from his background in the worlds of faith and public health offered a picture of human development which went like this. We begin in chaos, as babies; slowly we learn a world of order with rules, answers, boundaries - a world which socialises us and gives us security - then as we enter adult life we discover that world is too small for us, it doesn't do justice to the complexity and scope of the world outside, and so we enter a phase of questioning. Hopefully we then arrive at a fourth stage which has four characteristics:

- a real inner life, of reflection and prayer, an inner reality which allows us to be ourselves and not be blown about by every whim and fashion of the moment;

- a commitment to care and social justice, which speaks for itself;

- a mellowness of spirit, which enables acceptance and allows us neither to be too puffed up by success or cast down by failure (though as someone pointed out, the world has reason to be grateful for the contributions of some pretty cantankerous and driven people);

- finally, a willingness to enter into life in community, where our goals and needs and ambitions and aims are always tempered and balanced by the reality of the others in that community.

It's a picture, not a straitjacket. And, as we all know, sometimes chaos breaks through even in our so-called maturity. Sometimes what we need as adults is a period of order and stability. That fourth stage - of a robust inner life, a commitment to people and justice, a mellow spirit, and life in community, all in interaction with one another - is not too distant from life in the kingdom of God, arrived at from a very different angle. Again though, such a life is not something we simply achieve, or make for ourselves. It's something which hopefully grows through our experience and encounters over the years. And it never stops evolving, as we meet new experiences, new people, new struggles, new truths, new challenges, new encouragements on the way. Maybe it's not a bad way to think of the kingdom life, in our daily life in the world.

THE NEW WAY

After the cryptic, tantalizing words of the beatitudes and the woes, Jesus goes on to teach of the discipleship way of abundant and overflowing forgiveness and generosity. The way is introduced by the words of challenge, 'But I tell all who will listen to me: love your enemies...' (6:27). The following words amplify the challenge. The Greek language has three words for love, which enable us to distinguish Christian love (*agape*) from passionate devotion (*eros*) and warm affection (*philia*). Jesus did not tell us his disciples to fall in love with their enemies or to feel for them as they felt for their families and friends. *Agape* is a gracious, determined, and active interest in the true welfare of others, which is not deterred even by hatred, cursing, and abuse, not limited by calculation of desserts or results, based solely on the nature of God. Love does not retaliate (6:27-31), seeks no reward, (6:32-36), is not censorious (6:37,38).

> The men who were bidden to love their enemies were living in enemy-occupied territory, where resentment was natural and provocation frequent. They were not just to submit to aggression, but to rob it of its sting by going beyond its demands.
> (Caird 1963, p 103-4)

This love of enemies, put into active practice and honed by prayer, is anything but passive and negative. It is outgoing and positive, a non-violent response to violence. Remember the situation in which these words are spoken; they are spoken to poor people who lived with a daily experience of powerlessness in the face of forces much stronger than them. Making the responses Jesus invites, 'turning the other cheek', 'giving away your shirt,' is to shift from passive endurance of injury to an active, creative, if certainly risky, response. It is an unexpected response of 'more' which both reflects God's generosity (6:35) and gives the initiative back to the injured. It is also the only way to break the poisonous, seductive, charmed circle of enmity and violence.

> It is not a matter of accepting circumstances passively, but of changing the situations produced by violence by the creation of a new situation.
> Violence is countered by productive imagination, leading to situations which make it possible for the other person to understand himself as a partner and no longer as an opponent. The disciple of Jesus is encouraged to develop modes of action which interrupt the chain of violence and counter-violence, which bring out the absurdity of injustice in such a way that the other person is invited to show solidarity. What is asked for here is the practice of love of the enemy which seeks the end of enmity, but not the end of the enemy.
> (Klaus Wengst 1987, p. 69)

'Do for others just what you want them to do for you' (6:31). These words of Jesus are often called 'the golden rule,' and something like this rule appears in most religions and ethical systems. Very often, however, it is cast negatively, 'Don't do to others, what you don't wish done to you'. Jesus' invitation is positive, reflecting a 'positive and unlimited benevolence' (Caird 1963, p. 104).

The call for an outgoing benevolence is continued and expanded. The disciple's generosity reaches out far beyond the closed and reciprocal circle of friendship (6:32). It extends to money matters. 'Don't just lend to those you know can and will pay you back,' says Jesus (6:34). Is this yet another echo of Jubilee economics? The call to love enemies and lend without stint is repeated (6:35). This time the reward and the reason is attached. Living in this way shows you are children of God, since you will be mirroring the way God acts. God is good to the ungrateful and the wicked (6:35). It's God's forgiveness, God's generosity, God's grace which are boundless.

'DON'T JUDGE'

Actions spring from attitudes. Jesus asks, 'Are our attitudes generous, reflecting the generosity of God? Do we look at people with God's eyes, or only from our limited horizontal human perspective?' (6:37,8) How graciously do we judge others? How do we avoid the trap of being soft on ourselves and hard on others, as the memorable hyperbolic saying about specks and logs asks us? (6:41-42) Again the bottom line is generosity, of heart and action.

OF TREES AND HOUSES

The chapter ends with a saying about knowing a tree by its fruits (6:43-45), and a parable about building on a sure foundation (6:46-49). The tree saying reminds us that disciples are called to be fruitful, and that fruitfulness begins in our inner selves. The parable about foundations, beloved of children's choruses, reminds us that it is staying close to Jesus, living in his company, devouring his words and following his actions which founds us on the rock that does not fail.

Jesus prefaces his parable about the foundations with a question. 'Why do you call me, "Lord, Lord," but don't do what I say?' (6:46) Older members of the Iona Community will hear a voice in their ear, imperiously repeating that question. The voice is that of the Community's founder, George MacLeod who always complemented the question by telling us that 'Lord' came from an Old English word meaning, 'Warden of the loaf', 'the keeper of the bread.' We're back to the kingdom economics of generous sharing again.

STUDY

BY YOURSELF

Along with the Magnificat (1:46-55) and the Nazareth Manifesto (4:18,19), the words of Jesus from Luke 6:20-42 are central to who Jesus is and what his way is about. Spend time with them, until you know them and they become part of your mental and spiritual furniture.

For the next week, recall them in the morning, in the middle of the day and in the evening. Reflect on what they are saying to your life in the midst of your daily activity.

Think of times when you have been challenged by these provocative and radical words of Jesus.

Dear Luke... If 'Theophilus' is one of the 'comfortable' rather than one of the 'afflicted', you might like to write a letter to Luke giving your response to the Beatitudes and Woes.

FOR GROUP WORK

'Most Christians don't live by the gospel of the sermon on the plain but by the gospel of prudent common sense.' Make two lists on a sheet of paper/white board - one for gospel values, one for prudent common sense values.

With these, explore together where you hear Jesus challenging you, in your own life and in the life of the church.

chapter 10

The centurion and the widow

LUKE 7:1-17

Jesus Heals a Roman Officer's Servant
(Mt 8:5-13)

When Jesus had finished saying all these things to the people, he went to Capernaum. A Roman officer there had a servant who was very dear to him; the man was sick and about to die. When the officer heard about Jesus, he sent some Jewish elders to ask him to come and heal his servant. They came to Jesus and begged him earnestly, "This man really deserves your help. He loves our people and he himself built a synagogue for us."

So Jesus went with them. He was not far from the house when the officer sent friends to tell him, "Sir, don't trouble yourself. I do not deserve to have you come into my house, neither do I consider myself worthy to come to you in person. Just give the order, and my servant will get well. I, too, am a man placed under the authority of superior officers, and I have soldiers under me. I order this one, 'Go!' and he goes; and I order that one, 'Come!' and he comes; and I order my slave, 'Do this!' and he does it."

Jesus was surprised when he heard this; he turned round and said to the crowd following him, "I tell you, I have never found faith like this, not even in Israel!"

The messengers went back to the officer's house and found his servant well.

Jesus Raises a Widow's Son

Soon afterwards Jesus went to a town called Nain, accompanied by his disciples and a large crowd. Just as he arrived at the gate of the town, a funeral procession was coming out. The dead man was the only son of a woman who was a widow, and a large crowd from the town was with her. When the Lord saw her, his heart was filled with pity for her, and he said to her, "Don't cry." Then he walked over and touched the coffin, and the men carrying it stopped. Jesus said, "Young man! Get up, I tell you!" The dead man sat up and began to talk, and Jesus gave him back to his mother.

They were all filled with fear and praised God. " A great prophet has appeared among us!" they said; "God has come to save his people!"

This news about Jesus went out through all the country and the surrounding territory.

A PAIR OF HEALING STORIES

The stories of Jesus' healing of the Roman officer's servant and his raising of the son of the widow of Nain complement one another and belong together. They both demonstrate Jesus' compassion and his power to heal and give life, but to two very different people. There is a huge contrast between the officer of the Roman army, secure in status and position, well used to a place of authority and power over others, and the widow of Nain, threatened with destitution. Widows were in a very vulnerable place in society at the time of Jesus, since their rights and security lasted only as long as their husband was alive. On his death, though there were some responsibilities in the extended family, the widow's main hope would lie with her children, and particularly her sons. The Old Testament lays great stress on the care of widows and orphans because of their special vulnerability to poverty and lack of provision. What unites the powerful officer and the powerless widow, bereft of her only son, is their position as outsiders, frequent objects of Luke's attention and Jesus' close care.

THE OFFICER'S SERVANT

Jesus has returned to Capernaum. A deputation of the elders of his own people come to meet him with a strange request. The fact that a group of elders come to seek Jesus out, as shortly will Jairus, an official of the local synagogue (8:41ff), shows that the opposition to Jesus from established religious authority was far from complete. The elders come on behalf of their unusual friend. A Roman officer billeted in their town has behaved towards the local synagogue with interest and benevolence. He has been anything but the stereotypical alien enemy. Is he an example of someone who has put into practice Jesus' teaching in 6:27-36? He has become friends of the local people and has built a synagogue for them. It's of interest to note that not all officers in the army of the empire were Roman, the army drew its recruits from a wide range of subject peoples. Maybe this man had a particular interest in the Jewish faith, like the Godfearers who appear in Acts.

This worthy man has a real concern for his sick servant. He genuinely cares about him in a way that suggests he had replaced the master/servant relationship with one of reciprocal caring humanity. His army training and experience have ensured that he understands the practice of command and authority. In very short compass, Luke has sketched the picture of a good man with wide sympathies and real faith.

Jesus sets out for the officer's house, but before he gets there, the officer sends some of his friends to meet him. They have come to tell Jesus that the officer humbly considers that he doesn't need to go out of his way to come to the house: 'Just say the word, and my servant will get well' (7:7). Tellingly, Luke says that Jesus was surprised when he heard this - a real role reversal as Luke has frequently stated how astonished and surprised people were at Jesus. 'I tell you,' he says, 'I have never found faith like this, not even in Israel' (7:9). It's a compliment to the officer, and perhaps a reproach to those who were expected to show faith. Meanwhile, back at the house, the servant is well again! The grace of God through Jesus' healing power is extended to the officer's servant, probably a pagan. The road is wide indeed!

THE WIDOW'S SON

Again Jesus and his disciples with an accompanying crowd are on the move. Away from the lake we find them at Nain, about five miles from Jesus' home town of Nazareth. Maybe he was known to the people of Nain and they to him. On entering the town gate, they meet the funeral procession of the recently dead son of a widow, her only hope. Jesus is here called by the title of 'the Lord' (7:13) for the first time in the gospel. Of the synoptic writers, it is only found in Luke, though it is frequently used in Acts and later in the New Testament as a title for the risen and exalted Jesus, where it emphasises the uniqueness of his relationship to God. Its use in this context suggests the power of the risen Christ (Evans 1990, p 347-8). We have been alerted to the reality of Jesus' powerful authority by the words of the Roman officer in the previous story (7:8ff). However the characteristic which 'the Lord' displays before the funeral procession is not initially power, but pity. Jesus is profoundly moved by what he sees and feels. The Greek word for 'filled with pity' indicates strong emotion. Jesus' power only operates once his compassion is aroused. He asks the woman to dry her tears and then he goes over to the bier and touches it. Remember that the healing of the officer's servant has been accomplished at a distance, without any human contact, let alone touch. By touching the bier of a dead man, Jesus becomes ritually unclean; that doesn't stop him. He addresses the body directly, 'Young man! Get up, I tell you!' (7:14) The dead man sits up and talks, and the poor widow has her son and hope restored. The people are amazed and say, 'God has come to save his people!' (7:16)

Stories of great and holy men raising people from the dead were not uncommon in the ancient world. The more specific background is found in the raising of the son of the widow of Zarephath by Elijah in 1 Kings 17:8-24, and Elisha's raising of the son of the Shunemite woman in 2 Kings 4:8-37. (There is another echo of Elisha in the previous story which recalls the healing of the Syrian commander Naaman in 2 Kings 5:1-27.) In this act of liberation from death and destitution, Jesus inherits the mantle of these great prophets. It was the people's expectation that the one whom God would send to save his people would be the Messiah. The news spread, Luke tells us, like wildfire.

STUDY

BY YOURSELF
One active exercise, one contemplative.

Outward: The example of Jesus' ministry of healing and his injunction to heal the sick has inspired the church over the years. Healing ministry today means many things and involves a huge number of people, working in the NHS, carers at home, the work of chaplains, spiritual healers. Find out more about this ministry. A good starting point is the book *The Christian Healing Ministry* by Morris Maddox, published by SPCK.

Inward: Reflect on your own life. Are there areas of your life in need of reviving, having new life breathed into them? Bring them before Jesus and ask for the breath of his Spirit.

chapter 11

Answering John

LUKE 7:18-35

The Messengers from John the Baptist
(Mt 11:2-19)

When John's disciples told him about all these things, he called two of them and sent them to the Lord to ask him, "Are you the one John said was going to come, or should we expect someone else?"

When they came to Jesus, they said, "John the Baptist sent us to ask you if you are the one he said was going to come, or should we expect someone else."

At that very time Jesus cured many people of their sicknesses, diseases, and evil spirits, and gave sight to many blind people. He answered John's messengers, "Go back and tell John what you have seen and heard: the blind can see, the lame can walk, those who suffer from dreaded skin diseases are made clean, the deaf can hear, the dead are raised to life, and the Good News is preached to the poor. How happy are those who have no doubts about me!"

After John's messengers had left, Jesus began to speak about him to the crowds: "When you went out to John in the desert, what did you expect to see? A blade of grass bending in the wind? What did you go out to see? A man dressed up in fancy clothes? People who dress like that and live in luxury are found in palaces! Tell me, what did you go out to see? A prophet? Yes indeed, but you saw much more than a prophet. For John is the one of whom the scripture says: 'God said, I will send my messenger ahead of you to open the way for you.' I tell you," Jesus added, "John is greater than anyone who has ever lived. But the one who is least in the Kingdom of God is greater than John."

All the people heard him; they and especially the tax collectors were the ones who had obeyed God's righteous demands and been baptized by John. But the

Pharisees and the teachers of the Law rejected God's purpose for themselves and refused to be baptized by John.

Jesus continued, "Now to what can I compare the people of this day? What are they like? They are like children sitting in the market place. One group shouts to the other, 'We played wedding music for you, but you wouldn't dance! We sang funeral songs, but you wouldn't cry!' John the Baptist came, and he fasted and drank no wine, and you said, 'He has a demon in him!' The Son of Man came, and he ate and drank, and you said, 'Look at this man! He is a glutton and a drinker, a friend of tax collectors and other outcasts!' God's wisdom, however, is shown to be true by all who accept it."

A SERIOUS QUESTION

What was the relationship between the new movement begun by Jesus' ministry and the ministry of his forerunner, John the Baptist? This section of Luke explores that question. It has a two-fold importance. It is relevant to the gospel story itself, and particularly to Luke's gospel, which gives such a prominent place to John in the opening chapters. John's gospel suggests that there were interlinks even in the time of Jesus' own earthly ministry; it describes Andrew and Peter as having been originally disciples of John who moved over to the following of Jesus (John 1:35-43). The relationship between the two groups of disciples continued to be an issue in the early years of the post-resurrection church (see Acts 19). Perhaps it's for that reason that Luke lays down this marker here.

The story begins with some of John's disciples reporting to him on Jesus' ministry to date. In Matthew's account of this incident, John is already in prison. Luke doesn't mention this fact here, he may simply assume readers know this from 3:20, or he may consider it not important enough to mention. John's disciples would be able to report on healings, signs and wonders; they would also be reporting aspects of Jesus' ministry very different from the stern preaching of the ascetic John. There was room for the question to be asked. 'Are you the coming one, or should we be looking elsewhere?' (7:20)

AN INTERESTING ANSWER

The response of Jesus is interesting. He doesn't answer the question of the disciples directly. How often Jesus doesn't answer questions directly. A direct answer can close a conversation down, an indirect answer opens things up. 'Go and tell John what you have seen and heard,' he says (7:22). He goes on to list the signs of healing which they could see and the words of liberation to the poor which they could hear, together pointers to the coming one, the Messiah (see Isaiah 35 & 61). And then he adds, 'Blessed are the ones who do not find me a cause of offence' (7:23). The Greek word for cause of offence is the word from which our word 'scandal' is derived. It is the same word as Paul uses in 1 Corinthians 1:23 to nail his colours to the mast about his gospel. 'We preach Christ crucified, to the Jews a cause of offence, to the Greeks foolishness, but to those who are called, the power of God and the wisdom of God.' We can see Jesus' words here not simply as an answer to John's disciples, but as a prophetic word which points forward to the cross. It is not simply by the signs and wonders so far seen that we will find the answer to the crucial gathering question, 'Who is Jesus?'

'A reed bending in the wind?'

After John's disciples leave, Jesus continues to speak about John. He asks the crowd, 'What did you expect to see when you went out to him in the desert? A reed bending in the wind? A man dressed in rich robes?' The obscure reference to the reed in the wind is clarified on learning that the symbol of a reed was often used by the ruler of Galilee, Herod Antipas on his coinage. The question Jesus puts is, 'Were you looking for another, better king, to replace the old order?' - an order which is both invoked obliquely and scorned in the reference to rich robes and royal palaces. Jesus goes on to speak of John as the forerunner who opens up the way. He quotes scripture. The quotation he uses is a hybrid of both Exodus 23:20 and Malachi 3:1. Exodus calls Moses to mind, and the Malachi quotation Elijah. John is portrayed as the inheritor of the mantle of the two greatest of the prophets. Yet Jesus says he is least in the Kingdom of God. He's not demeaning John, rather he is saying that the new age coming to be is qualitatively different from all that has gone before.

Jesus' words are heard by all, but Luke singles out two groups for special mention: the tax collectors who had heeded John's words, turned their lives round and been baptised, and the Pharisees and teachers of the Law who had rejected John's message and refused his baptism. In the unlikely juxtaposition of despised tax collector and the forces of the orthodox, Jesus once more paints a picture of the upside-down kingdom.

Scunnered!

One of the treasures of Scottish speech is the word 'scunnered' - meaning 'sick,' 'fed up.' In the final passage in this section (7:31-35), it is not hard to see Jesus as scunnered by folks' attitude to both his ministry and that of John. 'People today,' he says, 'are like kids playing games who spend their time bickering about what game they should play. If they don't like the game their pals choose, the cry is "I'm no playing!"' 'John was too strict,' they said, 'There must be something wrong with the man from the desert who fasts and doesn't drink wine. And now that Jesus, look at the company he keeps, he's forever got his nose in the trough and his mouth at the bottle. There's nothing very holy about him.' Both our resentments and our lack of commitment can always find excuses. It's easy to criticise, too easy.

The story is often told of the couple who would settle in a church for a time and soon leave having found something wrong with the fellowship they were in, and sure they had found something better. The pattern was repeated until one day someone said to them, 'When you find the perfect church, don't join - you'll spoil it!' This whole passage reminds us that in this world we always live our lives in the midst of ambiguity and imperfection. It's all too easy to project that imperfection onto 'them' out there, and not see the flaws which begin within ourselves (6:37-42). Jesus concludes, 'God's wisdom, however, is shown to be true by all who accept it' (7:35). Those who can, will see.

STUDY

BY YOURSELF
In our own lives we have to discern between the justifiable anger, which is aroused in us by the actions of others and injustice in the world, and the resentments which boil up within us which tell us more about ourselves and our inner pain than they do about others. It might help to list them in two columns. Reflect prayerfully and seek the wisdom to know the difference and be delivered from resentment.

FOR GROUP WORK
Discuss together those things you have identified as causing righteous anger. How are we to deal with them in the light of Jesus' teaching in Luke 6:27-42?

chapter 12

One woman and several

LUKE 7:36 - 8:3

Jesus at the Home of Simon the Pharisee

A Pharisee invited Jesus to have dinner with him, and Jesus went to his house and sat down to eat. In that town was a woman who lived a sinful life. She heard that Jesus was eating in the Pharisee's house, so she brought an alabaster jar full of perfume and stood behind Jesus, by his feet, crying and wetting his feet with her tears. Then she dried his feet with her hair, kissed them, and poured the perfume on them. When the Pharisee saw this, he said to himself, "If this man really were a prophet, he would know who this woman is who is touching him; he would know what kind of sinful life she lives!"

Jesus spoke up and said to him, "Simon, I have something to tell you."

"Yes, Teacher," he said, "tell me."

"There were two men who owed money to a moneylender," Jesus began. "One owed him five hundred silver coins, and the other owed him fifty. Neither of them could pay him back, so he cancelled the debts of both. Which one, then, will love him more?"

"I suppose," answered Simon, "that it would be the one who was forgiven more."

"You are right," said Jesus. Then he turned to the woman and said to Simon, "Do you see this woman? I came into your home, and you gave me no water for my feet, but she has washed my feet and dried them with her hair. You did not welcome me with a kiss, but she has not stopped kissing my feet since I came. You provided no olive oil for my head, but she has covered my feet with perfume. I tell you, then, the great love she has shown proves that her many sins have been forgiven. But whoever has been forgiven little shows only a little love."

Then Jesus said to the woman, "Your sins are forgiven."

The others who were sitting at the table began to say to themselves, "Who is this, who even forgives sins?"

But Jesus said to the woman, "Your faith has saved you; go in peace."

Women who Accompanied Jesus

Some time later Jesus travelled through towns and villages, preaching the Good News about the Kingdom of God. The twelve disciples went with him, and so did some women who had been healed of evil spirits and diseases: Mary (who was called Magdalene), from whom seven demons had been driven out; Joanna, whose husband Chuza was an officer in Herod's court; and Susanna, and many other women who used their own resources to help Jesus and his disciples.

A CHINESE STORY

Every year in the late spring Glasgow hosts an inter-faith event in its St Mungo Museum of Religious Life and Art. In 2001 a group of children and adults acted out a wonderful old Chinese tale well worth the retelling. Here it is:

The Emperor of China was in need of an Empress. He was fed up rattling around alone in the royal palace and he also needed someone to provide him with an heir to the throne. So he made a decree that any young lady who wished to be empress should gather at the royal court on a certain appointed day. Mai Ling was a young girl from the country who was absolutely devoted to the Emperor. She prevailed on her parents to allow her to make the journey to the court. There, with many others, she met the Emperor, who gave to each of those present a seed and a flower-pot; with the instructions that they should plant the seed in the pot, and watch it grow and return to the palace one year hence. On that day the Emperor would examine the plants and he would take as his empress the young lady who held the most beautiful flower.

So, Mai Ling took her seed home and carefully planted it and waited for it to grow. It didn't. Month by month she waited and watched. Nothing happened, no shoot pushed its way through the soil. Right up to time she was due to return to the palace, nothing grew. Mai Ling was desolate. Her parents said, 'Well, there's no point in you making the long journey back to the palace when you've got nothing to show the Emperor.' Mai Ling also thought she would look very foolish with her pot of bare earth among all the flowers which the other girls would bring, but she was still determined to go. And she did. When she met up with all the others, she discovered her forebodings were right, all the others had pots of plants of the most wonderful colours. And she had nothing but her pot of bare earth.

The Emperor arrived, and walked round all the plants which were on show until at last he stood before Mai Ling. He stood and stopped. 'What is your name?' he asked.

'Mai Ling, your majesty.' 'Mai Ling, you shall be my Empress, the Empress of all China. You see, the seeds which I gave out one year ago had been roasted in the oven, they were sterile, they would never grow. None of these flowers grew from the seeds I gave out. You alone had the honesty, the courage and the humility to bring back your pot of bare earth. You shall be the Empress.'

'I WILL GIVE WHAT I HAVE TO MY LORD'

In Luke's picture-gallery of stories, we have stopped to stand before one of the most beautiful and most telling. We savour the scene of the extravagant care which a woman who is a sinner lavishes on Jesus in the house of Simon the Pharisee. Based on this story, John Bell and Graham Maule have written a song with the title, 'I will give what I have to my Lord' (*Wild Goose Songs* 1988, Vol.2 p. 29). It may seem very little, it may seem quite inappropriate, it may expose me to the scorn of others, but... 'I will give what I have to my Lord.' Here we see a woman give abundantly of what she has to her Lord.

This must have been one of the key stories in circulation when incidents from the life of Jesus were being passed on orally, before the gospels were written down. It clearly goes back to an incident in the life of Jesus that was seminal and unforgettable. The kernel of this story appears in all four gospels, situated in different places. The story's heart is the moment when, in the setting of a group meal, a woman lavishly pours out expensive perfume ointment over Jesus. The other men who are present are shocked and scandalised by what they witness, but Jesus praises the woman for her action. That's the core, but the details of the story differ significantly from gospel to gospel. Luke's finely-worked account has the incident occur much earlier in his gospel than the other gospel-writers in theirs. It takes place in the house of Simon, a Pharisee; and he tells it as a tale of forgiveness and grace. In this gospel the woman is indeed passionate in her outpouring, not only of the ointment, but in washing Jesus' feet with her tears, and drying them with her hair. It is a moment of heart-felt intimacy: the woman is a wondrous example of the self-forgetfulness of love. We are reminded that Luke's gospel has been called the gospel of women. They play a prominent part in it and are portrayed throughout with a real sympathy. This passage ends with a reminder that those who journeyed with Jesus included not only his disciples but a considerable company of women. Some of them are described as 'those who had been healed of evil spirits and diseases' (8:2). In other words, they had had their lives liberated by Jesus, like the unnamed woman here. Let's leave the question open whether there was one incident which the gospel writers describe in three different ways or whether there were three (or two) different but similar incidents involving Jesus' anointing by women. The important thing is not whether it happened once, twice, or three times, but that it happened at all and was seen as so significant.

A MOMENT OF GRACE AND FREEDOM

In Luke's account, Jesus has been invited for a meal with Simon, a Pharisee. The woman is an uninvited guest; but there's nothing strange about that, it was the custom of the times to leave the doors of the house open for other friends, strangers, beggars even, to come in when food and fellowship were being shared. Let's be present at this eruption in Simon's house against all the manners and conventions of the time, and sense this moment of intimacy and love, with overtones and undercurrents of sexuality, with also the stench of male censoriousness and judgementalism, set against a fragrant sense of beauty and the wonder of costly giving, both the woman's and Jesus' own. Let its sweet scent flow over us. For this is a precious moment of grace and freedom. It's one of the few occasions in the gospels when someone does something for Jesus, rather than his initiating the action. What others can you think of?... others who invite him for meals, Peter's mother-in-law, Martha, Simon of Cyrene who carried his cross.

This is a moment of freedom as the woman defies all convention to bring her gift. She wets his feet with her tears, dries them with her hair, kisses them and then pours sweet-smelling ointment over them. Once again, there's an element of touch in the story. Jesus should not have been touched by any woman, and certainly not one with a past like hers. The woman's gift, however, in spite of the scorn and disapproval of others, Jesus freely accepts and affirms. And note well, the woman is not only freed from her sins, she is freed for love, she is free to love. Her love has cancelled her sin, *before* Jesus formally says, 'Your sins are forgiven' (7: 47-48).

This is also a moment of grace. What does grace look like? What is it to be gracious, graceful, grace-filled? Here's a picture, an epiphany, of such an action. The woman's response to having her heart kindled by her encounter with Jesus is full of grace. In turn, Jesus graciously receives her response. But the gift is not unambiguous. There's nothing half-hearted or doubtful about this offering, poured from a heart of faith and love, but the gift is dubious. Was it purchased from the woman's immoral earnings? The gift is dubious, but aren't all our gifts dubious - for who of us in these psychological days can ever claim completely pure motivation? The point is, the gift is received, welcomed, cherished by Jesus. As Jesus receives the woman's gift, he is asking a question of all those who witness this event about their understanding of him and their understanding of God.

ASKING THE QUESTION

The question is asked through Simon. As the woman lavishes her love, his face must have been a right picture. Jesus well understands what he's thinking. 'How can he let himself be embraced by a woman with her reputation. Some prophet he is!' In response to Simon's unspoken thoughts, Jesus once again doesn't resort to a straightforward rebuttal or rebuke. He opens up the question as he tells a story about money and debt (7:41-42). 'Two men owed a moneylender, one 500 silver coins, the other 50. Neither could pay, but the moneylender cancelled the debts of both. Who would love the moneylender more?' Simon answered, 'I suppose the one forgiven more...', which gives

Jesus the opportunity to compare the lavish abandon of the woman's love with Simon's rather meagre welcome. Richard Rohr comments, 'As Jesus encounters the woman with the bad reputation and allows her to touch him and wipe his feet, he is forcing his Jewish contemporaries to ask themselves, "Could we possibly have been wrong about God? If the way this man Jesus is relating to her is right, good and from God, then maybe we don't know God. Maybe we need to look again."' (Rohr, 1997 p.119). As Jesus asks the question, he offers all those who see and hear the opportunity to expand their vision, to see this grace in action which overflows the comfortable boundaries of the moral, known and familiar.

The effect is cumulative. In quick succession we have seen Jesus healing a foreigner's servant, unconditionally, with no strings attached, we have seen him prepared to become ritually impure by touching a corpse, which brings new life, and now he has allowed himself to be lovingly touched by a woman with a bad reputation. In the midst of this healing, accepting sequence he has said, 'Blessed are those who do not find me a cause of offence!... who have no doubts about me!' (7:23) In each of these events, Jesus could be seen as a cause of offence. To the rigidly religious he is a threat to their accepted view of the world and other people. This story ends with those at Simon's table murmuring, 'Who is this who forgives sins?' Jesus is asking us to make sure we don't keep the woman in her sins in order to retain our sense of moral certainty. To do so is to deny the vision Jesus is offering us, of expanding horizons and overflowing grace.

The New Testament Lectionary reading which accompanies this gospel is Galatians 2:15-21. Paul says in that passionate letter, 'I have been crucified with Christ, and it is no longer I who live, but it is Christ who lives in me. And the life I now live in the flesh, I live by faith in the Son of God, who loved me and gave himself for me. I do not nullify the grace of God; for if justification comes through the law, then Christ died for nothing' (Galatians 2:20-21 NRSV). In other words, in and through Christ Jesus, Paul says his old life is dead; his old way of looking at himself and the world, of trying to earn or gain God's favour by a scrupulous keeping of the Law and a staying apart from an unclean world, is swept aside. For he knows the Son of God, who first loved him. He lives by faith in him, and therefore knows he is welcomed, accepted, approved.

In the Church of Scotland we've recently been provoked and energised by the report entitled 'A Church without Walls'. What does the church without walls looks like? Ponder on this gospel story with its wonderful moment of grace and freedom. It's a reminder that there's something fundamentally outrageous about the gospel of Christ, something wild in meeting this Jesus whom we all too often within the church seek to domesticate and contain. But his love and vision are uncontainable, and when we're smitten by them, all things are possible for us also. What's the church? It's the community where we are encouraged and encourage one another to give what each of us has, including what we don't know we have, for in the giving we grow. Sometimes we seem like a lot of dry sticks, but the great thing about dry sticks is that they can catch fire, when we are prepared to share Jesus' vision in the opening of our eyes to let the wind of the Spirit blow through. 'I will give what I have to my Lord.'

MORE DISCIPLES

It is clear from reading the gospels that the twelve male disciples named in 6:13-15 were only a small inner core of Jesus' disciples. It is also clear that there were a significant number of women among those who followed who gave a great deal of practical service to Jesus and the band of disciples. Some of these women are vital witnesses and actors at the time of Jesus' crucifixion, burial and resurrection. In that context they are named. But only Luke of the gospel writers names women much earlier in his gospel - here in 8:1-3. They were part of Jesus' ministry of preaching the good news of the Kingdom of God. Apart from learning of the presence of this significant group of women disciples, we noted that the group included women who had been healed and delivered by Jesus. The group also includes Joanna, whose husband was an officer at the court of Herod. She was therefore a person of some rank and means. We see through her naming something of the wide range of those attracted to and welcomed by Jesus, including those who might be thought to be hostile to him. Like the woman in the previous story, we are also told that they give of their own means and resources to support Jesus and the disciples.

STUDY

BY YOURSELF

Take time to be present at this dramatic scene. Use your imagination to enter into it.

• What can you see, hear, smell, taste, feel as you imagine being present at the scene?

• What is the atmosphere like? Inviting, threatening, lively, solemn?

• How are you feeling? Curious? Attracted? Disturbed? Afraid? Excited?

• Do you want to speak to anyone? To the woman? To Simon? To the other guests? To Jesus? What do you want to say? What do you hear being said to you?

• If any part of this story particularly attracted you, go back to it. Without forcing anything, see if you can identify what is attracting you.

chapter 13

Parables and healings

LUKE 8

The Parable of the Sower
(Mt 13:1-9, Mk 4:1-9)

People kept coming to Jesus from one town after another; and when a great crowd gathered, Jesus told this parable:

"Once there was a man who went out to sow corn. As he scattered the seed in the field, some of it fell along the path, where it was stepped on, and the birds ate it up. Some of it fell on rocky ground, and when the plants sprouted, they dried up because the soil had no moisture. Some of the seed fell among thorn bushes, which grew up with the plants and choked them. And some seeds fell in good soil; the plants grew and produced corn, a hundred grains each."

And Jesus concluded, "Listen, then, if you have ears!"

The Purpose of the Parables
(Mt 13:10-17, Mk 4:10-12)

His disciples asked Jesus what this parable meant, and he answered, "The knowledge of the secrets of the Kingdom of God has been given to you, but to the rest it comes by means of parables, so that they may look but not see, and listen but not understand.

Jesus Explains the Parable of the Sower
(Mt 13:18-23, Mk 4:13-20)

"This is what the parable means: the seed is the word of God. The seeds that fell along the path stand for those who hear; but the Devil comes and takes the message away from their hearts in order to keep them from believing and being saved. The seeds that fell on rocky ground stand for those who hear the message and receive it gladly. But it does not sink deep into them; they believe only for a while but when the time of testing comes, they fall away. The seeds that fell among thorn bushes stand for those who hear; but the worries and riches and pleasures of this life crowd in and choke them, and their fruit never ripens. The seeds that fell in good soil stand for those who hear the message and retain it in a good and obedient heart, and they persist until they bear fruit.

A Lamp under a Bowl
(Mk 4:21-25)

"People do not light a lamp and cover it with a bowl or put it under a bed. Instead, they put it on the lampstand, so that people will see the light as they come in.

"Whatever is hidden away will be brought out into the open, and whatever is covered up will be found and brought to light.

"Be careful, then, how you listen; because those who have something will be given more, but those who have nothing will have taken away from them even the little they think they have."

Jesus' Mother and Brothers
(Mt 12:46-50, Mk 3:31-35)

Jesus' mother and brothers came to him, but were unable to join him because of the crowd. Someone said to Jesus, "Your mother and brothers are standing outside and want to see you."

Jesus said to them all, "My mother and brothers are those who hear the word of God and obey it."

Jesus Calms a Storm
(Mt 8:23-27, Mk 4:35-41)

One day Jesus got into a boat with his disciples and said to them, "Let us go across to the other side of the lake." So they started out. As they were sailing, Jesus fell asleep. Suddenly, a strong wind blew down on the lake, and the boat began to fill with water, so that they were all in great danger. The disciples went to Jesus and woke him up, saying, "Master. Master! We are about to die!" Jesus got up and gave an order to the wind and the stormy water; they died down, and there was a great calm. Then he said to the disciples, "Where is your faith?"

But they were amazed and afraid, and said to one another, "Who is this man? He gives orders to the winds and the waves, and they obey him!"

Jesus Heals a Man with Demons
(Mt 8:28-34, Mk 5:1-20)

Jesus and his disciples sailed on over to the territory of Gerasa, which is across the lake from Galilee. As Jesus stepped ashore, he was met by a man from the town who had demons in him. For a long time this man had gone without clothes and would not stay at home, but spent his time in the burial caves. When he saw Jesus, he gave a loud cry, threw himself down at his feet, and shouted, "Jesus, Son of the Most High God! What do you want with me? I beg you, don't punish me!" He said this because Jesus had ordered the evil spirit to go out of him. Many times it seized him, and even though he was kept a prisoner, his hands and feet fastened by chains, he would break the chains and be driven by the demon out into the desert.

Jesus asked him, "What is your name?"

"My name is 'Mob'," he answered – because many demons had gone into him. The demons begged Jesus not to send them into the abyss.

There was a large herd of pigs near by, feeding on a hillside. So the demons begged Jesus to let them go into the pigs, and he let them. They went out of the man and into the pigs. The whole herd rushed down the side of the cliff into the lake and was drowned.

The men who had been taking care of the pigs saw what had happened, so they ran off and spread the news in the town and among the farms. People went out to see what had happened, and when they came to Jesus, they found the man from whom the demons had gone out sitting at the feet of Jesus, clothed and in his right mind; and they were all afraid. Those who had seen it told the people how the man had been cured. Then all the people from that territory asked Jesus to go away, because they were terribly afraid. So Jesus got into the boat and left. The man from whom the demons had gone out begged Jesus, "Let me go with you."

But Jesus sent him away, saying, "Go back home and tell what God has done for you."

The man went through the town, telling what Jesus had done for him.

Jairus' Daughter and the Woman who Touched Jesus' Cloak
(Mt 9:18-26, Mk 5:21-43)

When Jesus returned to the other side of the lake, the people welcomed him, because they had all been waiting for him. Then a man named Jairus arrived: he was an official in the local synagogue. He threw himself down at Jesus' feet and begged him to go to his home, because his only daughter, who was twelve years old, was dying.

As Jesus went along, the people were crowding him from every side. Among them was a woman who had suffered from severe bleeding for twelve years; she had spent all she had on doctors, but no one had been able to cure her. She came up in the crowd behind Jesus and touched the edge of his cloak, and her bleeding stopped at once. Jesus asked, "Who touched me?"

Everyone denied it, and Peter said, "Master, the people are all round you and crowding in on you."

But Jesus said, "Someone touched me, for I knew it when power went out of me." The woman saw that she had been found out, so she came trembling and threw herself at Jesus' feet. There in front of everybody, she told him why she had touched him and how she had been healed at once. Jesus said to her, "My daughter, your faith has made you well. Go in peace."

While Jesus was saying this, a messenger came from the official's house. "Your daughter has died," he told Jairus; "don't bother the Teacher any longer."

But Jesus heard it and said to Jairus, "Don't be afraid; only believe, and she will be well."

When he arrived at the house, he would not let anyone go in with him except Peter, John and James, and the child's father and mother. Everyone there was crying and mourning for the child. Jesus said, "Don't cry; the child is not dead - she is only sleeping!"

They all laughed at him, because they knew that she was dead. But Jesus took her by the hand and called out, "Get up, my child!" Her life returned, and she got up at once, and Jesus ordered them to give her something to eat. Her parents were astounded, but Jesus commanded them not to tell anyone what had happened.

THE GOSPEL CONTEXT

This next section of the gospel from 8:3 to 9:50 consists of material which Luke shares with Mark. Much of it appears in the same order as in Mark's gospel, though there are a number of additions and subtractions and, within each episode, significant editorial alterations by Luke. We have just worked through a section from around Jesus' Nazareth sermon in Luke 4 in which, by word and action, Jesus has announced the good news of the kingdom. We come now to an important parable, the parable of the sower, which offers a moment for reflection on what has gone before and what will come immediately after. The sower parable is followed by four big stories of liberation, from the powers of nature, evil spirits, chronic illness and death (8:22-56). Jesus then sends out his disciples to preach and heal (9:1-6) and feeds a great crowd (9:10-17). The feeding of the 5000 comes immediately before two key stories - Peter's declaration and its aftermath (9:18-27) and the Transfiguration (9:28-36) which ask, and begin to answer, the big question: 'Who is Jesus?'

THE SOWER

Richard Rohr says parables are invitations, not information (Rohr 1997, p. 120). Parables are picture stories which confront us and invite us to see, imagine and decide. Jesus now invites us to look at our world and ourselves through a picture which would have been thoroughly familiar to his first hearers, of a sower working in the field. It may seem on first appearance that the sower, walking up and down the field and working by hand, is pretty careless in the way he casts the seed to left and right. One explanation is that the Palestinian sower of the time sowed the seed before he ploughed the field. The seed was sown and then ploughed in. Perhaps there is no explanation, maybe Jesus is deliberately adding a bizarre feature to a commonplace picture to draw his hearers into the story. The story's punchline is quite clear, however: some seed fails to sprout for a variety of reasons, but the seed which falls on good ground multiplies abundantly. Jesus ends: 'Listen, then, if you have ears!' (8:8)

A DIFFICULT VERSE

The disciples ask Jesus, 'What does this mean?' Maybe that's not the appropriate question. About parables, you either get it or you don't. Verse 8.10 is a puzzling little section because it can mean, and has been taken to mean, that parables are given deliberately to obscure the truth of the Kingdom to those outside the charmed and secret circle. Such an interpretation is quite at odds with the whole thrust of the rest of the gospel. Jesus' words can be interpreted as saying, 'Look, you either see or don't see. Some folk are so ensnared in their present views and vision that nothing will make them see or understand anything new.'

THE SOWER EXPLAINED

Luke, in common with Matthew and Mark, then has Jesus give an explanation of the parable. The effect is to turn the parable into an allegory in which every aspect of it has a meaning. Commentators are doubtful whether the explanation is original to Jesus. Many argue that it is the work of the evangelists for the benefit of the early church. G B Caird remarks, 'an explained parable is as flat as an explained joke' (Caird 1963, p. 118). The parable stands in its own right as a commentary on the work of Jesus shown up to this point, where he has been sowing the seed of faith prodigally to right and left. It also offers encouragement to disciples living in hard times. And it's a timely reminder to us that our task as disciples is to be sowers of the seed, with the same prodigality as Jesus. We so rarely know when the seed of faith is planted, where it will take root, when it will grow. 'Keep sowing, and keep believing, growth will come,' is the message the sower leaves with us.

THREE SAYINGS

As well as the use of parables, another weapon in the armoury of the Hebrew teacher of wisdom was the proverbial saying which, like the usually longer parable, was used as an invitation to think further and deeper. Luke complements the parable of the sower with three short sayings. The link between them is that each relates to hearing and doing the word. First, lamps are for illumination, for letting light shine. You don't put a lamp under an opaque shade, far less under your bed! So, let the light of the word be seen (8:16). Second, that word is not given for you to keep and hide away. The seed of the word is not secret, but for broadcasting. It's not just for me, my group, my church, my nation, but for all. Don't keep the seed locked up in secret; the truth is you can't. The gospel is not to be kept hidden by the 'in' group; it's universal (8:17). Finally, listen well, so that the seed may grow and you may receive more. (This may be a reference back to 8:9.) Come with an attentive and receptive spirit; a vacant mind (as distinct from an open mind) will stay empty.

FAMILY MATTERS

Jesus' mother and brothers come looking for him, but can't get near him for the crowd. In this incident, Luke softens Mark's account where his family have come to take him home as they are concerned for his safety and the state of his mental health (Mark 3:20, 31-35). Luke's punchline - 'My mother and my brothers are those who hear the word of God and obey it.' (8:21) - links in with the preceding stress on hearing and doing the word to be fruitful people. At the same time, Jesus is also pointing out that in the new community he has come to build, the ties of faith are stronger than the ties of family. In a society where blood ties were primary, such a statement shakes the foundations.

CALMING THE STORM

The scene changes. Jesus and his disciples are off again, this time in a boat to cross the lake. Their destination is not given until we find them arriving at Gerasa in the following story (8:26). Gerasa is not only on the other side of the lake, it is outside Israel. This is the first venture of Jesus and his band into Gentile territory. Before there's a storm in the lake, there could well be a storm brewing in the disciples' minds. 'Why are we going over there?' 'What will he lead us into next?'

The one person who is quite unperturbed about the lake crossing is Jesus. He falls asleep in the boat. Behind this naturalistic detail, there are Old Testament echoes. For the Hebrews, the sea was a sign of the abyss and of chaos, the dwelling of threatening monsters and demons. Sleeping in peace in face of terrors would be seen as a sign of faith - though not for Jonah, reluctant missionary to the Gentiles, who was also found asleep in a boat in the midst of a storm (Jonah 1). Perhaps more significant, the disciples' wake-up cry to their master reminds us of instances in the Psalms and Isaiah, when in the face of peril there is a human cry for help to a seemingly sleeping God.

The wind rises, the boat is in danger of being swamped. The disciples wake Jesus up. 'Master, Master! We are about to die!' Jesus wakes up, gets up and orders the wind and the waves. A great calm ensues. This is the same 'ordering' of the natural elements which has cast out demons (4:35) and told a fever to leave (4:39). The story can be read as another instance of Jesus' battle with evil and his freeing of the disciples from the peril produced by demonic power.

In a milder way than in Mark's gospel (cf Mark 4:40), Jesus queries the disciples' lack of faith. They too have a question to ask, in wonder and terror, not at the power of the storm, but at the power of Jesus, so seemingly God-like. 'Who is this man? He gives orders to the winds and the waves, and they obey him!' (8:25) 'Who is this man?' The question will soon intensify.

LIBERATING LEGION

In Luke's picture-gallery, the story of the healing of the Gerasene demoniac could be described as impressionistic, it's told in such a series of vivid and fantastic images. On landing after the storm at sea, Jesus and his disciples are confronted by another storm raging in the heart and mind of the man who calls himself, 'Mob', 'Legion'. It's a story bristling with questions about what really is freedom. The man himself is so strong and also so deranged that he is quite beyond the restraint of his fellow townsfolk. He could be a symbol of ultimate freedom. He isn't, however, because a mob of demons has colonised his mind. He is in the chains of not knowing who he is, at the prey of all the different voices in his head. Maybe we should prefer the alternative translation, 'Legion' for 'Mob'. 'Legion' conjures up the power of Rome's armies, which may have scarred the man in the past, but which may also be symbolic of the malign influence of flesh and blood occupying forces. (Though this may also be less likely to be found in Luke, who at a surface level tends to be less hard on Roman power than Matthew and Mark.) The man himself inhabits a graveyard, a place of uncleanness and, as a place of death, a symbol of ultimate non-freedom.

Also in the cast for this incident are a herd of pigs. The presence of these animals, unclean to the Hebrews, shows we are in Gentile territory. Jesus frees the man from his demons; these enter the pigs, who rush down the hill and are drowned in the abyss. Are the demons back where they belong? This part of the incident has seen Jesus accused of cruelty to animals, a pretty doubtful accusation given that the pigs were going to be slaughtered and eaten anyway. But the pig-herders were, naturally enough, not happy people and they ran off, less than delighted, to tell the neighbourhood. People came out to see what had happened, to be confronted by the former madman, now clothed - he had been naked before - and sitting down with Jesus, and in his right mind. They were not happy either. The man is free from what harmed him, and the townspeople are free from the threat he represented. Still, they are not happy. It's all too new and uncanny for them. 'Jesus, go away!' is their cry. Why do we find it so difficult to believe in the possibility of change and redemption? One of humanity's least attractive features is our willingness to condemn people to remain locked in our perceptions of them from the past. Think how hard it often is for convicted prisoners on release to convince a sceptical public of real change. Think of how often peace processes are stalled or founder in mutual recrimination over past wrongs which need to be left behind. In that context the initiation and work of the Peace and Reconciliation Commission in South Africa after the collapse of the apartheid regime provides a significant model of hope for the future.

Not unnaturally, the man whom Jesus has set free from his inner chains wants to go with him. Jesus says, 'No, the place for you to tell what God has done for you is here at home.' It's a tough task to bear witness among those who are doubly unbelievers, outside Israel's faith, and unsympathetic to the man's healing! It's always in the place where we actually are that faith's responsibilities begin. 'For freedom Christ has set us free', says Paul in Galatians 5:1. The man was a living witness to his freedom in and through Jesus. Are we?

A YOUNG GIRL AND AN OLDER WOMAN

Jesus and the disciples return to Galilee back across the lake to a warm welcome. Among the welcomers is a desperate man, Jairus, an official of the local synagogue. We would expect Jairus in his official position to be at least wary of Jesus' seemingly cavalier attitude to the Law that he, Jairus, is committed to uphold, but Jairus is desperate. His only daughter, twelve years old, on the verge of womanhood, had fallen suddenly and critically ill. His human concern for his daughter outweighs all other considerations. He throws himself at Jesus' feet and begs him come to see her.

This dramatic and moving story is not the story of one woman's healing, but of two (8:40-56). It's a fascinating exercise to look at the story closely and see the similarities and the differences between both the two women who are healed and also between the two older people in the story, Jairus and the woman we are about to meet. Jesus sets off to Jairus' house, but progress is slow, as the crowd is thick and he is buffeted by folk from every side. Among the crowd is a woman who has suffered from continual menstrual bleeding for the same length of time as Jairus' daughter has been alive, twelve years. She carries the burden that her illness has rendered her ritually unclean according to the laws of the time and must not come into physical contact with anyone; therefore she is socially excluded. She is desperate to touch Jesus the healer, and just as desperate that he should not know he has been touched by her in her uncleanness.

She manages the first, she does touch Jesus, and her bleeding stops instantaneously, but he stops at once to ask, 'Who touched me?' The tension rises. Why has he stopped? He's in a hurry, Jairus' daughter is dying. Luke singles out Peter of the disciples to ask the obvious question. 'Why do you ask who touched you when this crowd is all round you? Everyone's bumping shoulders with you.' Jesus' reply is significant. 'Someone touched me,' he says, 'touched me with intent, for I felt power going out of me.' These words suggest on the one hand that Jesus had very highly developed psychic powers of awareness, and on the other that every act of healing he performed was a costly business in terms of the giving of himself. The healing of others, in the multitude of different forms the healing ministry takes, is always costly whether it be the act of intercession, the patient listening to another's pains, the skilled work of a surgical team, or the wider work of reconciliation.

The woman, in so many ways the polar opposite of Jairus, in sex and social and religious standing, comes forward trembling and she, like Jairus, throws herself at Jesus' feet. In front of everybody she tells her story of the long years of her illness and isolation and also of how, the moment she touched his cloak, she was healed. We can picture her, as she meets Jesus' gaze, and finds not disapproving discouragement but warm encouragement, gaining the strength to tell her story, oblivious to the mass of humanity looking on around her. Instead of a rebuke for crossing a forbidden boundary, she is given approval. In the warmest of words Jesus says to her, *'My* daughter, *your* faith has made you well. Go in peace' (8:48). How important are these personal possessive adjectives: Jesus' warm and inclusive 'my' and his affirmation that it was 'your', her own faith which had freed her.

The woman with her chronic condition may be healed, but news now comes that the daughter of Jairus is dead. It's too late, no need to bother Jesus any longer. Jesus is not to be put off, and continues with Jairus to his house. Mourning is in full swing, according to the custom of the day, but Jesus dismisses the mourners who laugh at his assertion that the child is not dead, only sleeping. With his closest disciples, Peter, James and John, and the child's father and mother he goes in to her, takes her by the hand, and says to her, 'Get up, *my* child!' She does, and Jesus says, 'you'd better get her something to eat' (8:55).

Once again in this story, touch is important. The daughter of Jairus, upholder of the purity laws, is only restored to health by the touch of Jesus, who has been rendered unclean by the touch of the older woman. It is an upside-down world Jesus brings. Thank God! A young girl's promise is restored and an older woman is set free from all that harms her and brought back into ordinary human society. We leave the story with a picture of the young girl's astonished parents, and Jesus' instruction to them not to tell anyone what had happened. Did he have much chance of being obeyed?

STUDY

BY YOURSELF

When I was a student for the ministry in Glasgow in the mid 1960s, I lived for two years with some others who were in the same boat, in a student house called, irreverently, 'The Monastery' - we were celibates by circumstance, not conviction. We used a daily liturgy devised by the University Chaplain. It contained the line: 'Teach us, good Lord, to serve you in the place where we are, for the place whereon we stand is holy ground.' That prayer has 'stuck' with me through all the intervening years.

Thinking about the man from Gerasa whom Jesus healed, and instructed to tell his story in 'the place where he was'; reflect on the words of that prayer in relation to your own daily life.

FOR GROUP WORK

Think back over the story Luke has been telling from the time of Jesus' preaching in the Nazareth synagogue. Use your Bibles. Look at the number of times Jesus has reached out to 'touch' those who are unlikely or outsiders. Then explore together what this means for you and your church.

chapter 14

'You are the Messiah'

LUKE 9:1-27

Jesus Sends Out the Twelve Disciples
(Mt 10:5-15, Mk 6:7-13)

Jesus called the twelve disciples together and gave them power and authority to drive out all demons and to cure diseases. Then he sent them out to preach the Kingdom of God and to heal the sick, after saying to them, "Take nothing with you for the journey: no stick, no beggar's bag, no food, no money, not even an extra shirt. Wherever you are welcomed, stay in the same house until you leave that town; wherever people don't welcome you, leave that town and shake the dust off your feet as a warning to them."

The disciples left and travelled through all the villages, preaching the Good News and healing people everywhere.

Herod's Confusion
(Mt 14:1-12, Mk 6:14-29)

When Herod, the ruler of Galilee, heard about all the things that were happening, he was very confused, because some people were saying that John the Baptist had come back to life. Others were saying that Elijah had appeared, and still others that one of the prophets of long ago had come back to life. Herod said, "I had John's head cut off; but who is this man I hear these things about?" And he kept trying to see Jesus.

Jesus Feeds a Great Crowd
(Mt 14:13-21, Mk 6:30-44, Jn 6:1-14)

The apostles came back and told Jesus everything they had done. He took them with him, and they went off by themselves to a town called Bethsaida. When the crowds heard about it, they followed him. He welcomed them, spoke to them about the Kingdom of God, and healed those who needed it.

When the sun was beginning to set, the twelve disciples came to him and said, "Send the people away so that they can go to the villages and farms round here and find food and lodging, because this is a lonely place."

But Jesus said to them, "Your yourselves give them something to eat."

They answered, "All we have are five loaves and two fish. Do you want us to go and buy food for this whole crowd?" (There were about 5000 men there.)

Jesus said to the disciples, "Make the people sit down in groups of about fifty each."

After the disciples had done so, Jesus took the five loaves and two fish, looked up to heaven, thanked God for them, and gave them to the disciples to distribute to the people. They all ate and had enough, and the disciples took up twelve baskets of what was left over.

Peter's Declaration about Jesus
(Mt 16:13-19, Mk 8:27-29)

One day when Jesus was praying alone, the disciples came to him. "Who do the crowds say I am?" he asked them.

"Some say that you are John the Baptist," they answered. "Others say that you are Elijah, while other say that one of the prophets of long ago has come back to life."

"What about you?" he asked them. "Who do you say I am?"

Peter answered, "You are God's Messiah."

Jesus Speaks about his Suffering and Death
(Mt 16:20-28, Mk 8:30-9:1)

Then Jesus gave them strict orders not to tell this to anyone. He also said to them, "The Son of Man must suffer much and be rejected by the elders, the chief priests, and the teachers of the Law. He will be put to death, but three days later he will be raised to life."

And he said to them all, "Anyone who wants to come with me must forget self, take up their cross every day, and follow me. For whoever wants to save their own life will lose it, but whoever loses their life for my sake will save it. Will people gain anything if they win the whole world but are themselves lost or defeated? Of course not! If people are ashamed of me and of my teaching, then the Son of Man will be ashamed of them when he comes in his glory and in the glory of the Father and of the holy angels. I assure you that there are some here who will not die until they have seen the Kingdom of God."

TRAVELLING LIGHT

So far in our story the only voice we have heard announcing God's Kingdom come near has been that of Jesus himself (and to some extent John the Baptist). Now Jesus calls together his twelve disciples, gives them the authority to heal and cast out demons and sends them out to preach the Kingdom of God. 'Kingdom of God' is a frequent and important phrase in the gospel; it occurs 35 times. It refers to an idea common in the apocalyptic thought of the time, that God would suddenly return to rule the earth and summon to judgement the nations. Many scholars think that Jesus and the earliest Christians believed that such a return was imminent. It was when the return did not materialise, the apocalypse didn't happen, that people had to take a longer view. One of the most influential voices shaping that longer view is Luke's own; with the picture he develops through Luke/Acts, of the early church continuing the history of Jesus in the world after he has gone back, exalted, to his place with the Father in heaven. What then does the Kingdom of God mean? It points to the reality that God is not remote, distant, and indifferent to the world God has made, but rather near, close at hand. God's presence and activity can be seen in the works of Jesus, God's 'Christ', God's anointed one, whose very touch heals, and whose words and works point to God working in the world of the everyday, the commonplace. And God's Kingdom will be seen, supremely in the events at the end of Jesus' life, in his cross and resurrection.

That is not yet. For now the disciples are sent out, probably in pairs, (see 10:1 and also Mark 6:7) to make the reality of 'God come near' known by their words and actions. They take as little with them as possible - there are no 4x4s, air miles or credit cards visible - to show that they come defenceless and in poverty, and to help them travel light. They will rely on the hospitality offered to them, village by village. Richard Rohr says, 'He even calls the Twelve to be dependent and needy, so they go as receivers and not just the guys with the answers - a very vulnerable and never very popular notion of ministry. Francis of Assisi was one of the few who took it seriously' (Rohr 1997, p. 122). Very probably their lifestyle in their dispersed mission was very like their lifestyle when they were travelling in the larger caravan of Jesus' disciples. Always they are on the move - and what a powerful symbol of discipleship that is.

The sending out of the twelve and the subsequent sending out of the 72 (10:1ff) speaks of organisation as well as mission. The organisation and practice of Jesus' original disciples stands in marked contrast to the hierarchical (the very word derives from clerical organisation!), bureaucratic structures with which the church in the West creaks. The need for lack of 'baggage' for effective witness and mission is stressed more than once in the gospel. We carry so much deadweight from tradition, doctrine, practice and culture. How are we to let gospel simplicity judge, reform and energise us?

When Pope John Paul II, the travelling pope, goes on one of his visits to another country, his first act is to kneel down and kiss the ground of the country visited, as a mark of love and respect. That papal sign comes to mind when we read of Jesus' instruction to the twelve to shake from their feet the dust of the towns which refuse to receive them. Behind the instruction lies the practice of the Rabbis in thoroughly shaking off any Gentile dust when they returned home from travelling outside their own country. Refusing towns were to be treated like alien territory and condemned.

Off the disciples went, preaching and healing. That two-fold model has served the church well, with its conjunction of concern for the spiritual and the material, body and soul. It's when the gospel gets disembodied, then we're in trouble. And we are in trouble. On the one hand, when thinking about involvement in Christian Aid, Amnesty International, Trident Ploughshares, anti-war protests, housing initiatives, community organisations, political activities, church members ask (and are asked), 'what has that to do with the gospel?' On the other hand, when our church recently carried out a small survey of our parish population, which largely consists of students, asking them what they thought of the church, the most common reply was, 'Oh, it's all right for people who like that sort of thing, but it's not relevant to me'. We're in trouble, because what God joined together, we have taken apart. Preaching and healing belong together, and both belong to the ministry of the whole church, not some hierarchy! So says the original model.

HEROD

Obviously the work of Jesus and the disciples was effective. It got to the ears of the ruler of Galilee, Herod Antipas (9:7-9). Herod we have already met as the ruler who had arrested and beheaded John the Baptist; we will meet him later at Jesus' own trial (23:7ff). With a mixture of curiosity, fear and superstition, Herod sought to meet Jesus. People were saying he was John the Baptist come back to life. We've clearly seen that the ministries of the austere John, and Jesus, with his news of welcoming grace, were very different. Both had enough bite about them, both were creating enough of a stir to have the man in the palace start to worry about his kingdom.

THE MIRACLE OF THE MULTIPLICATION

When the disciples return, Jesus listens to their stories of all that has happened to them and then takes them off to the lakeside town of Bethsaida, at the north east of the sea of Galilee, out of Herod's territory into the comparative safety of the regime of Philip. Crowds follow and the company gathers outside the town - 'this is a lonely place' (9:12) - where Jesus welcomes them and continues his work of healing and announcing the Kingdom. As evening falls, people need to eat and the disciples suggest to Jesus that he send the people away for provision.

Jesus says to the disciples, just returned from their own preaching tour, 'You give them something to eat.' 'There's only five loaves and two fish between us, that's all we've got,' reply the disciples, 'do you want us to go and buy food for this whole crowd?' Jesus tells them to break up the great mass of the crowd by getting everybody to sit down in manageable groups of about fifty - organisation again. This is also a pertinent reminder that churches grow in all sorts of ways when people belong to a small group in which they come to know, trust and share with the others in their company. It may be a prayer group, a study group, an action group, a worship group, a caring group, a group involved in providing some practical service; the dynamic is the same.

When everyone has sat down, Jesus takes the loaves and the fish, gives thanks to God, and gives them to the disciples to distribute. Everybody has enough - what a telling word 'enough' is. When the disciples get round to clearing up what's left over, there's enough for twelve baskets (a significant number, as Israel had twelve tribes). This is almost the final action in Jesus' campaign in and around Galilee. Soon he will set his face toward Jerusalem. This meal with the 5000 has been called 'The Farewell Meal'. It calls to mind the times already in the gospel when Jesus has been seen sitting down to eat with others, in the house of Simon the disciple (4:39), at Levi's party for tax collectors and sinners (5:29), in the home of Simon the Pharisee (7:36), and, perhaps, with the synagogue official, Jairus, and his household when the girl is given something to eat (8:55). This meal also anticipates the meal together with the disciples on the night of his arrest when, in the upper room, he again takes bread, gives thanks, breaks the bread and gives it to those present (22:19). That sequence of actions, taking, blessing, breaking, and giving, is deeply suggestive and significant not only as the pattern at the heart of Communion, but the pattern at the heart of every table, and indeed our common life.

In the light of the immediately previous comment about Herod's interest in Jesus, it's worth thinking about the size of the crowd. It's big enough to be threatening to authority. It looks like people searching for a leader. The temptation to power is very real, indeed in John's gospel Jesus specifically addresses that temptation (John 6:15). Another way is about to be unfolded.

This event has been called 'the miracle of the multiplication'. It's an interesting name, but it misses the point that at no time in this narrative, in any of the four gospels, are we told that Jesus multiplied the bread. There is no description or explanation given of *how* the people got fed, it is simply told *that* the people got fed. And we probably should leave it there, and accept that here we are being invited into the mystery of the Lord's providing. He feeds the hungry crowd, he feeds his people. Trust him, that's enough.

THE CRUCIAL QUESTION

After the costly feeding of the crowd, Jesus is to be found at prayer. It is a time for prayer as a key moment has arrived. It's time for decision, to change direction. The disciples approach Jesus who initiates a conversation with them. 'Who are people saying I am?' (9:18) 'Well, the John the Baptist rumour is strong. But some say you are Elijah returned, and some say you are another of the great prophets come back to life.' 'What about you, what do you say?' asks Jesus. Peter answers, 'You are the Christ, the Messiah, the Anointed One of God' (9:20). Peter has said enough. He has shown he has seen enough for the journey to Jerusalem and the cross to begin.

Luke tells this story of Peter's declaration of faith very simply. It's significant that in his gospel there is no confrontation with Peter immediately following, as there is in Mark 8:31-33. Mark stresses Peter's lack of faith and understanding of the cross, even at this moment of revelation. While for Luke the disciples' lack is not central to the narrative of the second half of his gospel as it is in Mark, it nonetheless appears at crucial moments. Luke also has Jesus move immediately from Peter's confession to lay out what lies ahead...

A CROSS AND CROSSES

'The Son of Man must suffer....' Jesus tells of his trials at the hands of the authorities of Israel, 'elders, chief priests, and teachers of the Law'. He will be put to death, but three days later he will be raised to life. 'Be raised' is significant, it points to the reality that it is God, and God alone who is behind this mighty action. Now, it's the cross that dominates. Having spoken of his own cross, he now introduces the cross life to anyone who would be a disciple. 'Anyone who wants to follow me must forget self, take up their cross *every day*, and follow me' (9:23). That discipleship litany of self-forgetfulness and self-denial will be played out in a number of variations of the single theme as the gospel continues. It is significant that Luke inserts the words 'every day'. The life of discipleship, the way of following Jesus, is a life and a way renewed day by day, throughout our journey. It's a tough choice, but it's the way to life.

Does Jesus' call to discipleship, day by day and daily, shed any light on the promise at the end of this section? 'I assure you that there are some here who will not die until they have seen the Kingdom of God' (9:27). These words have seen many interpretations. Jesus could be referring to a coming 'day of the Lord', an apocalyptic return he expected imminently. He could also have been simply pointing to the experience of his transfiguration which his closest disciples would share 'about a week later' (9:28). The words could look forward to the great day of Pentecost and the coming of the Spirit in Acts 2. They could point to the central event of Jesus' passion and resurrection, where all is changed; and to the continued dynamic of the cross life, the way of self-denial and new life, giving up and receiving again, which we can know in our lives, day by day. For me, that last is first.

STUDY

BY YOURSELF

The sequence of the sending out of the disciples, bereft of baggage, Peter's declaration of faith, and Jesus' announcement of the cross, and the cross way; these all remind us that it's not easy to be a disciple. Look at your life in the light of these stories; listen to what Jesus is saying to you.

• What do you need to leave behind?

• What do you need to affirm?

chapter 15

The transfiguration and its aftermath

LUKE 9:28-62

The Transfiguration
(Mt 17:1-8, Mk 9:2-8)

About a week after he had said these things, Jesus took Peter, John and James with him and went up a hill to pray. While he was praying, his face changed its appearance, and his clothes became dazzling white. Suddenly two men were there talking with him. They were Moses and Elijah, who appeared in heavenly glory and talked with Jesus about the way in which he would soon fulfil God's purpose by dying in Jerusalem. Peter and his companions were sound asleep, but they woke up and saw Jesus' glory and the two men who were standing with him. As the men were leaving Jesus, Peter said to him, "Master, how good it is that we are here! We will make three tents, one for you, one for Moses, and one for Elijah." (He did not really know what he was saying.)

While he was still speaking, a cloud appeared and covered them with its shadow; and the disciples were afraid as the cloud came over them. A voice said from the cloud, "This is my Son, whom I have chosen - listen to him!"

When the voice stopped, there was Jesus all alone. The disciples kept quiet about all this, and told no one at that time anything they had seen.

Jesus Heals a Boy with an Evil Spirit
(Mt 17:14-18, Mk 9:14-27)

The next day Jesus and the three disciples went down from the hill, and a large crowd met Jesus. A man shouted from the crowd, "Teacher! I beg you, look at my son - my only son! A spirit attacks him with a sudden shout and throws him into a fit, so that he foams at the mouth; it keeps on hurting him and will hardly let him go! I begged your disciples to drive it out, but they couldn't."

Jesus answered, "How unbelieving and wrong you people are! How long must I stay with you? How long do I have to put up with you?" Then he said to the man, "Bring your son here."

As the boy was coming, the demon knocked him to the ground and threw him into a fit. Jesus gave a command to the evil spirit, healed the boy, and gave him back to his father. All the people were amazed at the mighty power of God.

Jesus Speaks Again about his Death
(Mt 17:22-23, Mk 9:30-32)

The people were still marvelling at everything Jesus was doing, when he said to his disciples, "Don't forget what I am about to tell you! The Son of Man is going to be handed over to the power of human beings." But the disciples did not know what this meant. It had been hidden from them so that they could not understand it, and they were afraid to ask him about the matter.

Who is the Greatest?
(Mt 18:1-5, Mk 9:33-37)

An argument broke out among the disciples as to which one of them was the greatest. Jesus knew what they were thinking, so he took a child, stood him by his side, and said to them, "Whoever welcomes this child in my name, welcomes me: and whoever welcomes me, also welcomes the one who sent me. For the one who is least among you all is the greatest."

Whoever is not Against You is For You
(Mk 9:38-40)

John spoke up, "Master, we saw a man driving out demons in your name, and we told him to stop, because he doesn't belong to our group."

"Don't try to stop him," Jesus said to him and to the other disciples, "because whoever is not against you is for you."

A Samaritan Village Refuses to Receive Jesus

As the time drew near when Jesus would be taken up to heaven, he made up his mind and set out on his way to Jerusalem. He sent messengers ahead of him, who went into a village in Samaria to get everything ready for him. But the people there would not receive him, because it was clear that he was on his way to Jerusalem. When the disciples James and John saw this, they said, "Lord, do you want us to call fire down from heaven to destroy them?"

Jesus turned and rebuked them.Then Jesus and his disciples went on to another village.

The Would-be Followers of Jesus
(Mt 8:19-22)

As they went on their way, a man said to Jesus, "I will follow you wherever you go."

Jesus said to him, "Foxes have holes, and birds their nests, but the Son of Man has nowhere to lie down and rest."

He said to another man, "Follow me."

But that man said, "Sir, first let me go back and bury my father."

Jesus answered, "Let the dead bury their own dead. You go and proclaim the Kingdom of God."

Someone else said, "I will follow you, sir; but first let me go and say goodbye to my family."

Jesus said to him, "Anyone who starts to plough and then keeps looking back is of no use to the Kingdom of God."

A MOMENT OF GLORY

In Luke's picture gallery we come to the moment when dark glasses are recommended. This next picture shines with a glorious light. Around a week after the announcement of the cross, Jesus takes the inner core of his disciples, Peter, John and James, to a high place, a place of revelation. He goes to pray (once again) and while at prayer, in that time of communion with God, his face becomes alight with splendour and his clothes shine with a dazzling whiteness. In a trice, Moses and Elijah appear to talk with Jesus. Moses and Elijah represent the Law and the prophets, the faith traditions of the past which Jesus inherits and transforms: they were also seen as key figures in the coming judgement, and so they also have a reference forward into the future. As dwellers in the heavenly places, they also point upward.

HIS DEPARTURE

What do they talk about? The *GNB* says that the subject was 'about the way in which he would soon fulfil God's purpose by dying in Jerusalem' (9:31). This is a weak translation. The Greek word which the *GNB* translates 'by dying' is '*exodus*', and is more usually translated in many versions by 'his departure.' The word here has layers of meaning. It can mean Jesus' leaving this world. It can simply be a euphemism for his death, as the

GNB interprets it. The deepest and most suggestive meaning is to retain the thrust of 'exodus' in the sense that through the events at the end of his life in Jerusalem, through his suffering and sacrifice, he enables a new 'exodus', a new journey into freedom for all God's people - the widening road.

In that sense, Jesus goes forward to the cross, and through the cross to glory, as a representative of all humanity. This moment of transfiguration is a foretaste, a brief glimpse before the end itself. Let us stand before this moment of epiphany of the earthly Jesus touched with heavenly glory, telling of the glory which will be completed and consummated in the non-violent submission to the cross. As we stand watching, our post-Hiroshima generation can never forget that it was on the traditional date of the Feast of the Transfiguration that the first atomic bomb was dropped by Allied Forces on a city in Japan, a nation virtually already defeated. It was an act which resulted in 140,000 deaths and untold human misery and introduced a new apocalyptic fear, of human construction, into our contemporary life. The starkness of the contrast between the way of life and the way of death, the way of the cross and the way of power is immediate and continually haunting.

'LISTEN!'

It's interesting and significant that in Luke's account of this story, Peter and the others are sound asleep, and therefore not party to the 'departure' conversation. They wake up just as Moses and Elijah are leaving. Peter, but lately wakeful, would prolong the moment. Luke says however that Peter was a bit confused by the whole thing. While he is still speaking he is cut short by the appearance of a cloud, symbolic of God's presence. From the cloud a voice speaks which largely repeats the words said to Jesus at his baptism (3:22), 'this is my Son, my Chosen One - listen to him!' 'Chosen One' echoes the words at the beginning of one of the servant songs of Isaiah (42:1). Now the disciples are included in this event and their faith is confirmed. We, as readers, are asked to 'listen', to pay particular attention to what will now unfold. Jesus now stands alone: the scene is ended.

This is a hinge story, closely related to the announcement of the cross, but also bound to the following incident of the scene confronting Jesus and the inner core when they come down the mountain next day, back to the trials of ordinary life and continuing discipleship. So, read on.

'THEY COULDN'T DO IT'

A crowd is waiting for them, there's rarely a moment's peace. They are confronted by a man whose son keeps having fits and self-harming. He's taken him to the disciples for the spirit to be cast out of him, but they couldn't do it. Jesus bursts out into an exasperated lament over the disciples' lack of faith. The lament includes the words, 'How long must I stay with you?' (9:41) Jesus knows that his time is now short. He gets the father to bring over the boy. Peremptorily Jesus commands the evil spirit to leave and gives the boy, now healed, back to his father. All are amazed at this demonstration of God's power.

Luke considerably condenses Mark's account of the story. It's interesting that he omits the moment in Mark where Jesus asks the boy's father, 'How long has he been like this?' (Mark 9:21) Tradition has long regarded Luke as a physician, though some modern commentators find the evidence scant. We might expect Dr Luke to pick up this moment when Jesus asks the father to tell the story of his son's affliction. The words of a distinguished contemporary physician are apt: 'First rule in medicine, ask the patient and listen to the patient'.

THE CROSS AGAIN

The people marvel at Jesus' healings, but it is the dark mystery of the cross Jesus seeks to communicate to disciples who are desperately reluctant to understand (9:43-45). For a second time, closely following on the first, Jesus speaks again about his death. The cross casts its shadow over the rest of the gospel's story.

'LOOK TO THE LEAST!'

The depths of the disciples' misunderstanding of the reality of the cross and its meaning is immediately revealed as they squabble among themselves, not for the last time, about which one of them is greatest (9:46-47). Intuiting what's going on, Jesus summarily shames them. He takes a child, symbol in his society of 'nobody', a person without rights and status, and stands the child beside him. He puts the child in the place of honour. By his action he's saying, 'In my kingdom you need to think of this child and all like him or her as the greatest. It's how you care for such as them that matters'. He ends with another variation of the discipleship litany of a reversal of the world's values and the taking of the new way of self-forgetfulness and self-denial (see 9:23), 'For the one who is least of all among you is the greatest' (9:48).

'DON'T BE EXCLUSIVE'

In this section, Luke, following Mark, gives the disciples a hard time. In quick succession they have failed to heal the boy with his convulsions, through their lack of faith (9:37-43); they have been blind to the reality of the cross, through their lack of understanding (9:44-45); in face of the cross they have argued about their own pompous prestige (9:46-48) and now they show up as members of the exclusivist tendency, convinced that they alone have rights to the Jesus franchise (9:49). A man has been working successfully as an exorcist in Jesus' name and they have told him to stop, 'because he doesn't belong to our group'. How these infamous words have bedevilled the history of the church as priest or minister or sect or church has claimed, 'We alone have authority, we alone have the truth, we alone are the true church'. The argument is not about truth at all, it's about power and about keeping it for me and mine. It has caused wars, inquisitions, heresy hunts, schisms... and it still wreaks its havoc, because we will not listen to Jesus, who says something radically different about power and keeps knocking down the barriers and boundaries we erect in our struggles to retain it. 'Why stop the man?' says Jesus, with the softest of answers, 'If he's not against you, he's for you.'

'BURN THEM!'

It gets worse. The next story begins with Luke's telling us that Jesus has made up his mind and fixed his face toward Jerusalem. The Greek says, 'The days for his being taken up were drawing near' (9:51). 'Taken up' suggests both his return to heaven and his lifting on to the cross. It embraces the whole of the passion and strongly echoes the double meaning of Jesus' words in John's gospel. 'I, when I am lifted up from the earth, will draw all people to myself' John 12:32 *NRSV*. The company travel through part of Samaria. Between Jew and Samaritan, close neighbours and originally one people, hate had long poisoned the atmosphere. The village where Jesus would stay refuses him because he is on his way to Jerusalem. The brothers James and John, who are portrayed in the gospels as having an altogether too 'guid conceit o' themselves', self-absorbed in their own importance, ask Jesus whether they should arrange for fire from heaven to destroy this village of insolent heretics. We can picture Jesus sadly, wearily telling them off. They understand so little. Who would say we do any better?

Probably the 'Brothers Grim' in this instance wish to emulate the prophet Elijah who brought down fire from heaven on his enemies in 2 Kings 1:9-16. But Elijah has gone. On the mountain, Jesus stood alone. It is to him that disciples 'listen'. His is another way.

ALL OR NOTHING

We leave these four pictures of disciples stuttering along the Kingdom way. This chapter ends with three related incidents pointing up the cost of following Jesus, of being a disciple. In each Jesus turns up the heat. Remember where he and the disciples are now heading.

'I will follow you wherever you go,' a man says. 'Are you sure?' says Jesus. 'Foxes have holes, and birds have nests, but the Son of Man has nowhere to lie down and rest' (9:58). Are you sure? It's good to have a place and a home, do you really want to take the way of itinerant poverty? Rohr calls it 'the way of the "homeless" one, the way of the little ones, the *anawim*, outside the system' (Rohr 1997, p. 136). Jesus says there is something more important than place and home.

Another says, 'I'll come, but let me go and bury my father first'. Jesus replies, 'Let the dead bury their own dead. You go and announce the Kingdom' (9:60). Family responsibility, especially towards parents, is good, the holy task of burying the dead is important, but there's something more urgent. Jesus here builds a picture of the consuming urgency of the gospel task, something of a dark hole for those who seek to interpret the gospel literally.

A third person said, 'I'll follow, just let me go and say goodbye to my family.' It's only courtesy, and the family matters, but Jesus says, with another hyperbolic flourish which was part of the Jewish teacher's tools for his task, 'Anyone who puts his hand to the plough and keeps looking back is useless to the Kingdom' (9:62). 'The most difficult choices in life are not between the good and the evil, but between the good and the best' (Caird 1963, p. 141). It's significant that in two out of three of these incidents, Jesus says there is something more important than the family. Once again Luke's ambivalence towards the family is seen.

STUDY

BY YOURSELF
Throughout this passage there is a strong contrast between Jesus, shot through with God's glory, and his disciples, so clearly earthbound in their thoughts and actions. The voice from the clouds on the mountain of transfiguration says that the way to bridge that gap is to 'listen' to Jesus. Read this whole passage daily in the coming week, and seek, attentively, imaginatively and prayerfully, to 'listen' to what Jesus is saying to you.

FOR GROUP WORK
The contrast between Jesus' transfiguration where our humanity is glorified on the mountain and the destruction and wasting of our humanity by nuclear weapons is stark. The Church and Nation Committee of the Church of Scotland's General Assembly has produced a new report on Nuclear Weapons (2003), available from the Committee at 121 George Street, Edinburgh EH2 4YN. Use it for group study and ask what you and your church can do to work for peace in this arena.

chapter 16

Mission

LUKE 10:1-24

Jesus Sends Out the Seventy-two

After this the Lord chose another 72 men and sent them out two by two, to go ahead of him to every town and place where he himself was about to go. He said to them, "There is a large harvest, but few workers to gather it in. Pray to the owner of the harvest that he will send out workers to gather in his harvest. Go! I am sending you like lambs among wolves. Don't take a purse or a beggar's bag or shoes; don't stop to greet anyone on the road. Whenever you go into a house, first say, 'Peace be with this house.' If a peace-loving person lives there, let your greeting of peace remain on him; if not, take back your greeting of peace. Stay in that same house, eating and drinking whatever they offer you, for workers should be given their pay. Don't move round from one house to another. Whenever you go into a town and are made welcome, eat what is set before you, heal the sick in that town, and say to the people there, 'The Kingdom of God has come near you.' But whenever you go into a town and are not welcomed, go out in the streets and say, 'Even the dust from your town that sticks to our feet we wipe off against you. But remember that the Kingdom of God has come near you!' I assure you that on Judgement Day God will show more mercy to Sodom than to that town!

The Unbelieving Towns
(Mt 11:20-24)

"How terrible it will be for you, Chorazin! How terrible for you too, Bethsaida! If the miracles which were performed in you had been performed in Tyre and Sidon, the people there would long ago have sat down, put on sackcloth, and sprinkled ashes on themselves, to show that they had turned from their sins! God will show more mercy on Judgement Day to Tyre and Sidon than to you. And as for you, Capernaum! Did you want to lift yourself up to heaven? You will be thrown down to hell!"

Jesus said to his disciples, "Whoever listens to you listens to me; whoever rejects you rejects me; and whoever rejects me rejects the one who sent me."

The Return of the Seventy-two

The 72 men came back in great joy. "Lord," they said, "even the demons obeyed us when we gave them a command in your name!"

Jesus answered them, "I saw Satan fall like lightning from heaven. Listen! I have given you authority, so that you can walk on snakes and scorpions and overcome all the power of the Enemy, and nothing will hurt you. But don't be glad because the evil spirits obey you; rather be glad because your names are written in heaven."

Jesus Rejoices
(Mt 11:25-27, 13:16-17)

At that time Jesus was filled with joy by the Holy Spirit and said, "Father, Lord of heaven and earth! I thank you because you have shown to the unlearned what you have hidden from the wise and learned. Yes, Father, this was how you wanted it to happen.

'My Father has given me all things. No one knows who the Son is except the Father, and no one knows who the Father is except the Son and those to whom the Son chooses to reveal him."

Then Jesus turned to the disciples and said to them privately, "How fortunate you are to see the things you see! I tell you that many prophets and kings wanted to see what you see, but they could not, and to hear what you hear, but they did not."

NUMBERS
Jesus now comes to send out a larger group of disciples, either 70 or 72; some manuscripts have one and some the other. It doesn't really matter which number we decide on, the symbolic significance remains the same. There are two symbolic references; within old Israel, 70 was the number of elders around Moses in Exodus 24:1ff and Numbers 11:16ff. 70 or 72 was also reckoned to be the number of the nations of the Gentiles in Genesis 10. We can take this sending out to speak both of the renewal of Israel and of the gospel for all nations.

PATTERNS FOR MINISTRY AND MISSION
There are many similarities between this second sending out of the 70 and the first sending out of the twelve (9:1-6). What can they tell us about patterns of ministry and

mission? In this second account Luke makes explicit what was probably implicit in the sending of the twelve, viz. that the disciples are sent out in pairs, two by two. We began this section by thinking about numbers: here we note that two is always more than simply one and one. Two means there is a quality of relationship. Each can support the other, each can complement the other. What happens when we concentrate, as we have done, on one person ministry? Listen to Richard Rohr:

> Luke has a theology of twosomes. As far as he is concerned, the gospel of love cannot be communicated by one person, because, in the end, love is something happening between two. If only one disciple is sent, it is likely to make the gospel a merely verbal gospel. As a preacher and teacher I'm always making tapes and standing behind lecterns and pulpits; but this is not where the message is to be found. Neither is the message in a book. In our day, we are comfortable with lecture-method Christianity, verbal Christianity, as if the truth could be an ideology, contained in words... The gospel happens between two or more people... It doesn't happen in your mind... I'd sooner say, if you have sacrificial love for other people, you're saved. That is a much more valid test for the presence of the Spirit than "I am into religion".
> (Rohr 1997, p. 137, 8, 9)

Relationships and relatedness are at the heart of ministry and mission, as are simplicity and an urgent focused attention (10:4). Defenceless simplicity carries with it a real vulnerability, as Jesus' words about lambs and wolves make clear. At the very start of the sending out, Luke says that the 70 are to go out ahead of him to prepare for his coming. Jesus' coming is prepared for by those who go to make contact with strangers, relate to them, get to be at home, at ease, at peace with them (10:5, 7). The task of the sent-out ones remains the same, to preach and to heal, to minister to the whole person, and in and through the twin tasks, to announce the Kingdom's coming (10:8-9; cf also 9:2). This section asks the question, how does the sending of the 70 inform our ministry and our preparation for ministry?

Acceptance won't be universal. If the disciples are not welcomed they are again to perform the dramatic act of shaking the dust of the unwelcoming town or village from their feet. It has brought judgement on itself. Jesus then bewails the unbelief he has found in some of the Galilean towns and villages where he has been at work: Chorazin, Bethsaida (the other one, near Capernaum, not the one outside Galilee to which he took the disciples for decision time - see 9:10), and Capernaum itself. These further 'woes' of Jesus speak of the urgency of the new way, and of how rejection of him sows the seeds of the townsfolk's own self-destruction. In the background is the story of continual intermittent unrest in the whole region, with a series of futile, armed, nationalistic revolts bringing nothing but pain to people, culminating in the disaster of the fall of Jerusalem in 70CE. The old way no longer worked, it was time for the new way.

Satan's fall

The 72 return with joy, reporting great success. The mission of peace has been accomplished and the message of peace heard. Jesus says two things. 'I saw Satan fall like lightning from heaven' (10:18). Although by this time in the popular mind Satan was regarded as the prince of the forces of evil, his original role was as the fierce prosecuting counsel at the heavenly law court (see his role in the book of Job, particularly Chapters 1 and 2, also Zechariah 3:1-5). In that role he demanded judgement rather than mercy. We can interpret Jesus' words as meaning that the success of the work of the 70 has played its part in dethroning the Satan of implacable judgement; now heaven can be seen as the home of peace and the source of all grace. It's not heaven that's important here, it's what's happening on earth; the reality that through the disciples' work the gospel of grace and peace is releasing many people into freedom.

The second word of Jesus is, 'Don't be glad that the spirits obey you: rejoice rather that your names are written in heaven' (10:20). The 72 have returned exulting in their power over the demons. Jesus has confirmed their authority (10:19). Then he says, 'It's not your power that matters, nor your success, nor your gifts; what matters is that you are chosen and precious, that you are one with me, who is one with the Father.' What comes first, always, is not that we're effective, or even good, but that we are loved.

Father and Son

In 1992 the General Assembly of the Church of Scotland approved a new Statement of Faith for worship and teaching. It begins like this:

> We believe in one God:
> Father, Son and Holy Spirit.
> God is love.
> We praise God the Father:
> who created the universe and keeps it in being.
> He has made us his sons and daughters
> to share his joy,
> living together in justice and peace,
> caring for his world and for each other.
> (*Common Order* 1994, inside back cover)

What is interesting is the way these words include a succinct statement of faith within a framework of thanksgiving and praise. It has been said that the giving of thanks, the returning of 'love for love, worship in return for life', in the words of the prayer of preparation for the Lord's Day, is the truest and most profound expression of faith as our hearts are lifted to give thanks for the grace in which we live. In 10:21-24, we are given a unique glimpse in this gospel of Jesus at prayer, alive with joy and thanksgiving. And the prayer of thanksgiving he offers is also a clear statement of his purposes.

Jesus gives thanks to his Father for the truth of the lowly way, that things hidden from the great and good, God has revealed to... the Greek word means 'babies,' 'children' - by extension the 'unschooled,' 'unlearned'. It is to the 'little people' God has made the truth of his humble servant known. Just as Jesus has immediately previously invited the disciples to rejoice that 'your names are written in heaven' (10:20) - in other words in the love of God which enfolds them - so in his prayer, in language strikingly close to the language of John's gospel, Jesus gives thanks for the closeness of his own relationship with his Father, a relationship of father and son. We shouldn't read into this relationship the future developed doctrine of the Trinity: Jesus celebrates here his awareness of being God's anointed servant. To the disciples, in private, he says, 'How glad you are to live in this time of revelation, to see this day; desired by, yet hidden from, many who have gone before you' (10:24).

STUDY

BY YOURSELF

'Be glad because your names are written in heaven' (10:20).

• Hear these words as words of affirmation and promise spoken to you.

• Think about times when you have been aware that life is good and wonderful, and give thanks for these experiences of the reality of God's love and grace.

chapter 17

'Who is my neighbour?'

LUKE 10:25-37

The Parable of the Good Samaritan

A teacher of the Law came up and tried to trap Jesus. "Teacher," he asked, "what must I do to receive eternal life?"

Jesus answered him, "What do the Scriptures say? How do you interpret them?"

The man answered, "'Love the Lord your God with all your heart, with all your soul, with all your strength, and with all your mind'; and 'Love your neighbour as you love yourself.'"

"You are right," Jesus replied; "do this and you will live."

But the teacher of the Law wanted to justify himself, so he asked Jesus, "Who is my neighbour?"

Jesus answered, "There was once a man who was going down from Jerusalem to Jericho when robbers attacked him, stripped him, and beat him up, leaving him half dead. It so happened that a priest was going down that road; but when he saw the man, he walked on by, on the other side. In the same way a Levite also came along, went over and looked at the man, and then walked on by, on the other side. But a Samaritan who was travelling that way came upon the man, and when he saw him, his heart was filled with pity. He went over to him, poured oil and wine on his wounds and bandaged them; then he put the man on his own animal and took him to an inn, where he took care of him. The next day he took out two silver coins and gave them to the innkeeper. 'Take care of him,' he told the innkeeper, 'and when I come back this way, I will pay you whatever else you spend on him.'"

And Jesus concluded, "In your opinion, which one of these three acted like a neighbour towards the man attacked by the robbers?"

The teacher of the Law answered, "The one who was kind to him."

Jesus replied, "You go, then, and do the same."

WORD ALIVE

A couple of years ago I read a curious little item in the newspapers. It was reported that the book most often stolen from public libraries today is the Bible. That's odd. In our churches' current mood of embattled defensiveness we often think the prevailing view in society is that the Bible is old-fashioned and out-of-touch and that people (like me) who speak about it are congenitally boring. Yet, it's still the Bible which gets nicked most from our library shelves. Maybe folk want it as a talisman, a kind of good luck charm. Maybe they turn to it in some time of crisis in their lives; if they do, they join a very long and diverse line of people. Maybe they find what they seek, and maybe they don't. What is true is that the Bible, frequently seen as old and dull by people outside and inside the church - often because it is read with too much familiarity, too superficially, with not enough questions or imagination - still has the capacity to come alive as the wind of the Spirit blows and the word from the page comes alive to grasp the mind and heart of the reader or the hearer. Annie Dillard, the American writer, has a wonderful essay on Luke's gospel. In it she has this to say about the Bible as a whole:

> This Bible, this ubiquitous, persistent black chunk of a best-seller, is a chink - often the only chink - through which winds howl. It is a singularity, a black hole into which our rich and multiple world strays and vanishes. We crack open its pages at our peril. Many educated, urbane, and flourishing experts in every aspect of business, culture, and science have felt pulled by this anachronistic, semibarbaric mass of antique laws and fabulous tales from far away; they entered its queer, strait gates and were lost. Eyes open, heads high, in full possession of their critical minds, they obeyed the high, inaudible whistle, and let the gates close behind them.
>
> Respectable parents who love their children leave this absolutely respectable book lying about, as a possible safeguard against, say, drugs; alas, it is the book that kidnaps the children, and hooks them.
> *'But he... said unto Jesus, And who is my neighbour?*
> *And Jesus answering him said, A certain man went down from Jerusalem to Jericho, and fell among thieves...'*
> (Dillard 1994, p. 266; quotation from *AV*)

We come to an exploding text. Continuing the analogy of Luke's gospel being like a picture gallery, which of his stories would qualify for the accolade of being his Mona Lisa? Certainly the story we now encounter, of the Good Samaritan, would be high on the shortlist. It is both a highly dramatic story in its own right, and also a story with a perennial and contemporary relevance. In a sense we could say that it continues the previous theme of relationships. This time it's about how the relationships of heaven are realised here on earth.

WHO IS MY NEIGHBOUR?

The story illustrates Jesus' teaching methods in almost classic form. He is asked a question. His response is to question the questioner, to ask another question. The questioner answers Jesus' question and presses on with a further inquiry. And Jesus tells a story, which ends with yet another query, 'What do you think?' All the time the conversation is kept going and kept open. Implicitly Jesus is saying, 'It's not just what I think that matters, there's two of us having a conversation here, what do you think?' The lesson for all teachers is clear: don't close people down, encourage them to speak, and listen... carefully listen.

The conversation begins with the arrival of a teacher of the Law, trying to trap Jesus. This isn't an innocent conversation, there's an agenda here. The first question is, 'What do I have to do to receive eternal life, the life of heaven, the life of God, life in all its fullness.' This conversation, which begins on a lofty, heavenly plain, only gets its resolution through a very earthy story about a mugging. Jesus responds, 'You're a man of the Law. You tell me. What does the holy Law teach?' The lawyer answers with the two commandments the gospels link inseparably together. 'Love God with all that is in you' (Deuteronomy 6:5), and 'Love your neighbour as you love yourself' (Leviticus 19:18). 'You're right' says Jesus, 'that's the way to life.' His questioner wants to press his point. There was considerable debate in rabbinic circles about who was or wasn't a neighbour. 'Who is my neighbour? To whom am I obliged?' he asks. Jesus tells him a story...

'A CERTAIN MAN...'

It's about a man, foolhardy enough to be travelling on his own on the road from Jerusalem to Jericho - infamous for robbery - who is set upon by bandits, beaten up, robbed and left looking half dead. Two representatives of the man's own people, and upholders of the very Law the lawyer has just quoted, come by the stricken bundle by the roadside. The first, a priest of the Temple, passes hurriedly by. The second, a Levite, one who belonged to a second order of clergy with lesser tasks in the Temple, stops to look closer at the man in his plight, and also moves on. A Samaritan is also on the road; when he comes on the man, he is moved, deeply (the same Greek verb in 10:33 as used to describe Jesus' feelings for the widow of Nain at her son's funeral procession in 7:13). The Samaritan not only feels, he acts. He stops on the dangerous road to take time to dress and bind up the man's wounds. Then he puts him on his own animal and leads him to an inn, where he stays overnight to look after the wounded man. As he leaves, he gives the innkeeper money to pay for the man's lodgings and treatment, promising to make good any shortfall next time he passes this way.

'Tell me, who do you say acted like a neighbour to the man who was mugged?' asks Jesus. 'The one who was kind to him', answers the lawyer. 'Go and do the same' (10:37).

Who is my neighbour? Samaritans and Jews were certainly neighbours, originally part of the one old Israel, but they were neighbours who had fallen out long ago with deadly and poisonous effect. In rabbinic dialogue about a Hebrew's obligation to the neighbour, Samaritans, like Gentiles, were not included. The shocking twist to this story is not only the appearance of the Samaritan, but the fact that he, the hated and despised neighbour/enemy is the one who feels pity and acts with kindness. The whole question is blown wide open. Boundaries are hugely enlarged. One of the least attractive features of human beings is our seeming endless ability to dehumanise our enemies. Jesus does the opposite. He lets the lawyer see the Samaritan as a human being with at least the same generous instincts of kindness as himself. Being a neighbour is to treat whoever comes across our path with the same humanity we would wish for ourselves. That's the response required by the children of a generous God.

WHO IS MY NEIGHBOUR... NOW?

It's a sad reality that murderous conflict between neighbours who have fallen out remains an obstinately persistent feature of today's world; and I look no further than the sectarian issue in my own city of Glasgow. When we consider the recent history of Ireland, South Africa and the Balkans, there are signs of hope out of past mayhem, but the situation in Jesus' own homeland between Israeli and Palestinian remains intractable. Yet there are moments when the light of the humanity evoked by Jesus shines through. In recent years, when a young Glasgow Jewish student was killed in a suicide bombing in Israel and some of his organs were donated for the saving of the life of a young Palestinian girl, the spirit of the Good Samaritan burst into flame. We pray for the fanning of such a flame in situations where present violence and injustice are compounded by a persistent sense of ancient wrong.

Jesus' parable invites us to do two things; to look into ourselves and examine our deep feelings towards our 'enemy', who may be close by, and to look outward towards people's needs, wherever they are. The difference between our time and the time of Jesus lies in our ability to look outwards. Through the speed of the many means of modern communication, we see neighbours everywhere. The world is our neighbour and there are people everywhere with a claim to our 'pity' and practical action. We can't help them all, as we sadly know when we consign some of the avalanche of charity requests at Christmas to the waste-paper bin. But we can seek to mirror the spirit of Jesus. Tom Wright writes at the conclusion to his reflection on this parable:

> What is at stake, then and now, is the question of whether we will use the God-given revelation of love and grace as a way of boosting our own sense of isolated security and purity, or whether we will see it as a call and challenge to extend love and grace to the whole world. No church, no Christian, can remain content with easy definitions which allow us to watch most of the world lying half-dead in the road. Today's preachers, and today's defenders of the gospel, must find fresh ways of telling the story of God's love which will do for our day what this brilliant parable did for Jesus' first hearers.
> (Wright 2001, p. 129)

STUDY

BY YOURSELF

Find a way to build into your prayer life a regular pattern of prayer for the peoples and needs of the world, on a monthly basis. The World Council of Churches Ecumenical Prayer Cycle, 'With All God's People' is very useful, and there are also considerable resources from Tearfund, CAFOD, Christian Aid and SCIAF.

FOR GROUP WORK

'Jesus' parable invites us to do two things: to look into ourselves and examine our deep feelings towards our 'enemy', who may be close by, and to look outward towards other people's need, wherever they are.' (page 116)

Talk together about where you could see an instance of the Good Samaritan story in our world today. Take time to act it out in role play. In role play it's important to let people choose which role they are prepared to play rather than the leader being directive. Remind people that role play is not about great acting, but about having the opportunity to put themselves into the story.

Then discuss what you have seen and heard and its implications.

PAUSE

'Outsiders.'

It's worth taking a moment to look back at the way we have come and consider for a moment some of those to whom we've been introduced. Here's a list: the contagious leper (5:12-16), Levi, the dodgy tax collector (5:27-31), the Roman officer and his servant (7:1-10), the widow of Nain's dead son (7:11-17), the woman who was a sinner (7:36-50), the man called 'Mob' (8:27-39), the woman with the bleeding who was ritually unclean (8:43-48), the Good Samaritan (10:25-37). Each of these is an outsider in some way or other, either disreputable, considered ritually unclean, a Gentile, an enemy, or dead. Each of them is either healed, welcomed or commended by Jesus. Whole categories of people are treated in the same way, Gentiles (2:32), the poor (4:18), tax collectors and sinners (5:29-32) Samaritans (10: 25-37).

When we gather these two lists together, we begin to feel the cumulative force of Jesus' concern for the outsider, and the gale of inclusive grace which blows from his life and teaching. We stand before the mystery with its clear social implications that the 'chosen one' (9:35), the agent of the only God, has a special concern to include all those whom humans in their inhumanity would marginalise or dehumanise. We should have expected no less from one born outside the house (2:7) and who in his own ministry chose to 'have nowhere to lay his head' (9:58).

chapter 18

'Teach us to pray'

LUKE 10:38-11:13

Jesus Visits Martha and Mary

As Jesus and his disciples went on their way, he came to a village where a woman named Martha welcomed him in her home. She had a sister named Mary, who sat down at the feet of the Lord and listened to his teaching. Martha was upset over all the work she had to do, so she came and said, "Lord, don't you care that my sister has left me to do all the work by myself? Tell her to come and help me!"

The Lord answered her, "Martha, Martha! You are worried and troubled over so many things, but just one is needed. Mary has chosen the right thing, and it will not be taken away from her."

Jesus' Teaching on Prayer
(Mt 6:9-13, 7:7-11)

One day Jesus was praying in a certain place. When he had finished, one of his disciples said to him, "Lord, teach us to pray, just as John taught his disciples."

Jesus said to them, "When you pray, say this:

'Father:

May your holy name be honoured;

may your Kingdom come.

Give us day by day the food we need.

Forgive us our sins,

for we forgive everyone who does us wrong.

And do not bring us to hard testing.'"

And Jesus said to his disciples, "Suppose one of you should go to a friend's house at midnight and say, 'Friend, let me borrow three loaves of bread. A friend of mine who is on a journey has just come to my house, and I haven't got any food for him!' And suppose your friend should answer from inside, 'Don't bother me! The door is already locked, and my children and I are in bed. I can't get up and give you anything.' Well, what then? I tell you that even if he will not get up and give you the bread because you are his friend, yet he will get up and give you everything you need because you are not ashamed to keep on asking.

"And so I say to you: ask, and you will receive; seek, and you will find; knock, and the door will be opened to you. For all those who ask will receive, and those who seek will find, and the door will be opened to anyone who knocks. Would any of you who are fathers give your son a snake when he asks for fish? Or would you give him a scorpion when he asks for an egg? Bad as you are, you know how to give good things to your children. How much more, then, will the Father in heaven give the Holy Spirit to those who ask him!"

MARTHA AND MARY

A story of profound humanity is followed by an incident of profound humanness. This picture is a domestic miniature. Jesus is welcomed into the house of Martha and Mary. As he settles down to teach, Mary comes to listen to him while her sister scutters around with the hundred and one things she has to do as the good hostess. Martha could be a mirror of ourselves. In the contemporary world, busy-ness is the new universal vocation. Don't dare admit you're not busy. We are even busy fitting in our leisure time these days. We sweat for our salvation.

'Tell her off, Jesus. Look at that Mary, sitting there blethering and listening to you when there's work to be done. Don't you want your dinner?' Jesus says, 'Martha, Martha! Your head's full of distractions. They can wait. You sit down and talk to me. Your visitor is more important than his dinner. Concentrate on what matters. Mary has done the better thing'.

This story questions our often inflated sense of our self-importance. Martha is so busy and wrapped up in what she has to do that she's got no time for her visitor, Jesus. It's pretty easy, in the life of the church, to be so engrossed in the tasks we have to do that *my* tasks become more important than my Lord, the one I serve.

Remember the preceding story of the Good Samaritan and the care of our neighbour. 'Loving our neighbour' is not about driven activity, it begins with active listening; hearing and seeing the neighbour's humanity, 'being filled with pity' - opening our hearts and minds to the reality of the neighbour's life. The perennial temptation of 'carers' is to get so caught up in their work of caring that they are not open to the person of the one they care for.

Jesus' visit to the home of Martha and Mary is followed by his teaching about prayer (11:1-13). We can see Mary's attitude as a model for our praying. She represents the prayer of listening, the prayer of silent waiting, more valuable than the prayer of a thousand busy words. Cultivating Mary's attitude of an imaginative attentiveness enables us the better to wait on the living words of Jesus Christ, and listen to the pain and hope, the cries and courage, the needs and the truths of those today who are our neighbours.

'TEACH US TO PRAY'

After Jesus has been at prayer, one of his disciples asks him to teach them to pray (11:1). In response Jesus begins by giving the words which have come to be known as the Lord's Prayer. Luke's gospel gives us the shorter version of that prayer, which may well be the older; the longer version is found in Matthew 6:9-13. The petitions of the prayer would be largely familiar to the disciples as they closely parallel the pattern of contemporary Jewish prayer (cf Evans 1990, p 477-8). Jesus however puts his own stamp upon them from the beginning.

The beginning is the word of address, 'Father.' Seeing God as father was common in Jewish thought, but its main emphasis was on the authority of a father and the demand on his children to obey him. Jesus' great gift was to call God the Father by the name 'Abba', which denotes intimacy, closeness, warmth. His name for the Father speaks not just of God's authority and providing but of his loving concern for his children. He brings God near.

It may seem that with the first petition itself, 'May your holy name be honoured,' what has been brought near is far removed again. The root meaning of 'holy' is 'other', and this petition does remind us of God's 'otherness', 'beyondness'. We need always to remember that the one Jesus invites us to address as 'Father' is the mystery before and behind all life, and not trivialise or sentimentalise the invitation. There's great consolation in this first petition also. Remembering that God is 'other' is remembering that God is real. Today many voices say that God is *only* within us, *just* an inner voice. This petition speaks to us of God, the living ultimate reality who is always beyond us, and comes to us from outside us. Nearness and otherness are not separate things which never shall meet, but two sides of the mysterious reality which is held together in prayer.

'Give us today the food "we" need'. This second petition recalls Jesus' desert temptation (4:1-4) and the time of Israel in the wilderness, when God daily provided his people with bread for their journey, manna from heaven. It reminds us that the company of Jesus are the people of the new Exodus, walking together into freedom. This is a corporate petition, a prayer of the people and for the people. We don't pray simply for our own daily bread, but for bread for all. We are interceders, those who pray that through them God's loving providing might flow on and out into the lives of those in need and into a needy world. This petition leads to action.

'Forgive us our sins, for we forgive everyone who does us wrong.' The two sides of this petition belong inseparably together. We ask forgiveness for our sins; we know our sins are real. Knowing our sins are real gives us a sense of solidarity with those who have sinned against us, in a realisation of our common failings (Romans 3:23). If we simply ask for forgiveness of our sins and refuse to forgive the sins of others against us, we block the grace of God. We are no longer channels of God's peace flowing into the world. The blockage not only affects those whom we refuse to forgive, it affects us. We build up within ourselves dams of bitterness and resentment, poison to the spirit. And we are certainly no longer witnesses to the transforming love and forgiveness at the heart of the coming of Jesus Christ.

'And do not bring us to hard testing.' 'Testing' includes all the trials and temptations of life. We have seen how Jesus' own testing left him the more able for his life's work. It's through times of testing we so often grow. This petition has been well paraphrased, 'Do not bring upon us more than we can bear... of life's trials and temptations'.

Jesus' teaching on prayer begins, 'When you pray.' He doesn't say at what time 'When' would be, but he lived in a society where regular prayer would be assumed as an integral part of life. In our fragmented daily lives we find regular patterns of prayer hard to achieve. The prayer of Cromwell's general, Thomas Fairfax, has its seductive appeal,

> 'Lord, Thou knowest I shall be busy this day.
> If I forget Thee, do not Thou forget me.'

That prayer is a bit of a cop-out. God won't forget us, but we are certainly in danger of forgetting God in the daily round. The genius of the Lord's Prayer is that it provides a simple and inclusive pattern for all our praying. Find a daily anchor spot for prayer and reflection, and find moments in the busy-ness as well, lest we forget.

'WHO'S THAT KNOCKING?'

After the prayer comes a parable which connects particularly with the preceding prayer through the theme of daily bread. It's a parable from low life, ordinary village life. The situation Jesus describes is this. A guest has just arrived at your house and the cupboard is bare, yet the obligation to provide hospitality is very strong. But it's very late. Late or not, at midnight, you creep round to the neighbour's and in trepidation bang on the door. Remember two things in the background. This is a society where people go to bed early and rise early. There's no electric light or late night TV. Everyone sleeps in the one room, so wakening the neighbour means wakening the whole household, which would probably include young children. The neighbour at first tells you to go and get lost; everything's shut up for the night and he or she's not going to walk all over the children to get you a loaf. But you persist. Jesus says that though the neighbour may not give you your loaf out of friendship, the loaf will come through the sheer nuisance value of your persistence. (There's a very funny paraphrase of this parable in a sketch by John Bell and Graham Maule called 'Knocking at the Door' - Bell and Maule 1989, p 20-1.)

Jesus is still teaching about prayer. The outrageous thing about the parable is that the sleeping neighbour in the story is God! What Jesus is saying is that if you can get your earthly neighbour to answer you through your determined persistence, how much more will God respond to your continued petitions.

There is an alternative reading of this parable argued by William R Herzog II in his book *Parables as Subversive Speech*. He calls his chapter on the parable of the friend at midnight, 'The Moral Economy of the Peasant' (Herzog 1994, p 194-215), and in it he argues that Luke has taken it from its original context and spiritualised its meaning to make it an encouragement to persevere in prayer. Herzog says that this is a story from a village community of poor people, all of whom would struggle daily to have enough. (Luke with his urban background may not have picked up the rural nuances.) Herzog sees the parable as demonstrating the solidarity and generosity of a poor community uniting to offer their common hospitality to the stranger who comes into their midst, and in so doing, anticipating the feast of plenty of the Messianic banquet (Isaiah 25:6-8). The ordinary acts of their simple community anticipate the new order of generosity, justice and mutual sharing. In their own way, these acts are real prayer.

'ASK, SEEK, KNOCK'

Returning to Luke's text, Jesus tells his disciples to 'keep asking, you will receive; keep seeking, you will find; keep knocking, the door will be opened to you' (11:9). As parents you wouldn't give your children bad for good, you would always try to do your best by them. 'You know how to give good gifts to your children.' How much more will that be true of God, your Father in heaven. Just as giving good gifts to your children does not mean giving them all they ask for, it means giving them the good they ask for, so God may not give you all you ask for in prayer, but he will give the best, the gift of the Holy Spirit (11:13).

STUDY

BY YOURSELF

The Lord's Prayer is a prayer for all seasons, a corporate prayer that can also be prayed alone. Reflect on the different aspects of the prayer.

- 'Father, may your holy name be honoured' ... giving honour to God, reflecting on God's greatness.

- 'May your Kingdom come'... the disciple's prayer of faith and hope.

- 'Give us day by day the food we need'... a prayer for our daily needs, where 'our' encompasses all people.

- 'Forgive us our sins, for we forgive everyone who does us wrong'... recognising the burden of our sins, accepting the challenge of accepting others.

- 'And do not bring us to hard testing'... asking God never to put us in situations which are more than we can bear.

chapter 19

Conflicts and warnings

LUKE 11:14 - 12:12

Jesus and Beelzebub
(Mt 12:22-30, Mk 3:20-27)

Jesus was driving out a demon that could not talk; and when the demon went out, the man began to talk. The crowds were amazed, but some of the people said, "It is Beelzebub, the chief of demons, who gives him the power to drive them out."

Others wanted to trap Jesus, so they asked him to perform a miracle to show that God approved of him. But Jesus knew what they were thinking, so he said to them, "Any country that divides itself into groups which fight each other will not last very long; a family divided against itself falls apart. So if Satan's kingdom has groups fighting each other, how can it last? You say that I drive out demons because Beelzebub gives me the power to do so. If this is how I drive them out, how do your followers drive them out? Your own followers prove that you are wrong! No, it is rather by means of God's power that I drive out demons, and this proves that the Kingdom of God has already come to you.

"When a strong man, with all his weapons ready, guards his own house, all his belongings are safe. But when a stronger man attacks him and defeats him, he carries away all the weapons the owner was depending on and divides up what he stole.

"Anyone who is not for me is really against me; anyone who does not help me gather is really scattering.

The Return of the Evil Spirit
(Mt 12:43-45)

"When an evil spirit goes out of a person, it travels over dry country looking for a place to rest. If it can't find one, it says to itself, 'I will go back to my house.' So it goes back and finds the house clean and tidy. Then it goes out and brings seven other spirits even worse than itself, and they come and live there. So when it is all over, that person is in a worse state than he was at the beginning."

True Happiness

When Jesus had said this, a woman spoke up from the crowd and said to him, "How happy is the woman who bore you and nursed you!"

But Jesus answered, "Rather, how happy are those who hear the word of God and obey it!"

The Demand for a Miracle
(Mt 12:38-42)

As the people crowded round Jesus, he went on to say, "How evil are the people of this day! They ask for a miracle, but none will be given them except the miracle of Jonah. In the same way that the prophet Jonah was a sign for the people of Nineveh, so the Son of Man will be a sign for the people of this day. On Judgement Day the Queen of Sheba will stand up and accuse the people of today, because she travelled all the way from her country to listen to King Solomon's wise teaching; and I tell you there is something here greater than Solomon. On Judgement Day the people of Nineveh will stand up and accuse you, because they turned from their sins when they heard Jonah preach; and I assure you that there is something here greater than Jonah!

The Light of the Body
(Mt 5:15, 6:22-23)

"No one lights a lamp and then hides it or puts it under a bowl; instead, he puts it on the lampstand, so that people may see the light as they come in. Your eyes are like a lamp for the body. When your eyes are sound, your whole body is full of light; but when your eyes are no good, your whole body will be in darkness. Make certain, then, that the light in you is not darkness. If your whole body is full of light, with no part of it in darkness, it will be bright all over, as when a lamp shines on you with its brightness."

Jesus Accuses the Pharisees and the Teachers of the Law
(Mt 23:1-6, Mk 12:38-40)

When Jesus finished speaking, a Pharisee invited him to eat with him; so he went in and sat down to eat. The Pharisee was surprised when he noticed that Jesus had not washed before eating. So the Lord said to him, "Now then, you Pharisees clean the outside of your cup and plate, but inside you are full of violence and evil. Fools! Did not God, who made the outside, also make the inside? But give what is in your cups and plates to the poor, and everything will be ritually clean for you.

"How terrible for you Pharisees! You give God a tenth of the seasoning herbs, such as mint and rue and all the other herbs, but you neglect justice and love for God. These you should practise, without neglecting the others.

"How terrible for you Pharisees! You love the reserved seats in the synagogues and to be greeted with respect in the market places. How terrible for you! You are like unmarked graves which people will walk on without knowing it."

One of the teachers of the Law said to him, "Teacher, when you say this, you insult us too!"

Jesus answered, "How terrible also for you teachers of the Law! You put loads on people's backs which are hard to carry, but you yourselves will not stretch out a finger to help them carry those loads. How terrible for you! You make fine tombs for the prophets - the very prophets your ancestors murdered. You yourselves admit, then, that you approve of what your ancestors did; they murdered the prophets, and you build their tombs. For this reason the Wisdom of God said, 'I will send them prophets and messengers; they will kill some of them and persecute others.' So the people of this time will be punished for the murder of all the prophets killed since the creation of the world, from the murder of Abel to the murder of Zechariah, who was killed between the altar and the Holy Place. Yes, I tell you, the people of this time will be punished for them all!

"How terrible for you teachers of the Law! You have kept the key that opens the door to the house of knowledge; you yourselves will not go in, and you stop those who are trying to go in!"

When Jesus left that place, the teachers of the Law and the Pharisees began to criticize him bitterly and ask him questions about many things, trying to lay traps for him and catch him saying something wrong.

A Warning against Hypocrisy
(Mt 10:26-27)

As thousands of people crowded together, so that they were stepping on each other, Jesus said first to his disciples, "Be on guard against the yeast of the Pharisees - I mean their hypocrisy. Whatever is covered up will be uncovered, and every secret will be made known. So then, whatever you have said in the dark will be heard in broad daylight, and whatever you have whispered in private in a closed room will be shouted from the housetops.

Whom to Fear
(Mt 10:28-31)

"I tell you, my friends, do not be afraid of those who kill the body but cannot afterwards do anything worse. I will show you whom to fear: fear God, who, after killing, has the authority to throw into hell. Believe me, he is the one you must fear!

"Aren't five sparrows sold for two pennies? Yet not one sparrow is forgotten by God. Even the hairs of your head have all been counted. So do not be afraid; you are worth much more than many sparrows!

Confessing and Rejecting Christ
(Mt 10:32-33, 12:32, 10:19-20)

"I assure you that for those who declare publicly that they belong to me, the Son of Man will do the same before the angels of God. But those who reject me publicly, the Son of Man will also reject before the angels of God.

"Whoever says a word against the Son of Man can be forgiven; but those who say evil things against the Holy Spirit will not be forgiven.

"When they bring you to be tried in the synagogues or before governors or rulers, do not be worried about how you will defend yourself or what you will say. For the Holy Spirit will teach you at that time what you should say."

TOUGH WORDS

On our journey through Luke's gospel, we have been led by Jesus into ever-widening circles of expanding grace, often to our surprise. Jesus has been showing us more and more of a picture of a God who is gracious, far beyond our human tendencies to block, narrow and confine. We might be tempted to think this way is easy, though there have already been enough hints in the story to show its cost. We have already seen how the exercise of grace can lead to conflict. Indeed it is Jesus' putting into words and action his understanding of God's grace which leads to the cross. In the next section we see Jesus involved in a number of conflicts, and handing out a series of warnings. Be prepared for some tough words on the way to Jerusalem. The strength and toughness of Jesus' words in the coming sections raise the important question for us about when and how we should be outspoken in the name of grace. Strong language is often associated with raucous dogmatism; but Jesus shows that it has its time and place. There are times when our faith in the grace and mercy of God leads us to oppose the powers of this world, both human and structural, with vehemence. The temptation to keep quiet in face of wrong is just that, a temptation. Jesus' own example calls us to speak out and speak boldly, with courage and imagination, in spite of the risks involved. Grace and the quiet life do not belong together. Polemic has its role, without however demonising the opposition, as Jesus is demonised in the next section.

THE VERY DEVIL

The section begins with Jesus healing a man's dumbness - Luke says 'driving out a demon that could not talk' (11:14). Once again the crowd are amazed, but some start sniping at him: 'He only casts out demons by the power of the prince of demons'. It's the oldest trick in the book: bad-mouth your opponents, demonise the enemy. Others want Jesus to fall into the trap of the final temptation (4:9-11), to perform some trick miracle to show the stamp of God's approval. Jesus offers a robust reply. 'A kingdom divided against itself must fall. It is the work of the devil to ensnare people in possession and disease. I liberate them, how can that be devil's work? And what about the other exorcists you know, are they the devil's workers also?' He continues, 'If it is by the finger of God that I cast out the demons, then the Kingdom of God has come to you' (11:20 *NRSV*). 'The finger of God', missing in the *GNB* translation, is a reference to Exodus 8:19 (*NRSV*), describing God's actions in preparing for the liberation of the children of Israel from Egypt. In a variation on Mark's parable on the binding of the strong man (Mark 3:27), Luke portrays Jesus as a stronger opponent defeating and neutralising the strong man, Satan.

Jesus continues, 'Anyone who is not for me is really against me; anyone who does not help me gather is really scattering' (11:23). Wait a minute. Have we not heard something very like this before? Yes. In 9:50, again in connection with the driving out of demons, Jesus said to his disciples, 'Whoever is not against you is for you'. These two sayings of Jesus stand in contradiction to one another. The clue to understanding them is to keep them in context. Although the contexts have similarities, they are also different. The words of 9:50 are spoken only to the disciples as an instruction not to be hungry for power and narrow-minded. The words here are spoken to the waverers in the crowd, in the serious and solemn situation where they have to choose between Jesus and the devil. However, the contradictions between the two statements serve as a warning within the Bible's own text against the dangerous practice of wrenching biblical texts from their context to quote as definitive proof of something. Such a practice is simply a misuse of scripture.

Jesus' next words remind us of our proverb, 'nature abhors a vacuum'. He warns that people are spiritually and psychologically vulnerable when they have renounced evil, or have turned their lives round, or been converted. This is when the person must be supported and encouraged until they bed themselves down into their new way of living. Alcoholics Anonymous understands this dynamic very well, and has built up a network of support for the recovering alcoholic which most churches could study with profit, and even copy.

DARKNESS AND LIGHT

'My, you must have had a wonderful mother! She'll be right proud of you! She must be a happy woman!' So shouts a woman from the crowd. Jesus is quick to reply, eschewing her sentimentality and repeating a familiar word, 'The ones who are happy indeed are those who hear the word of God, and obey it!' (11:28)

With the crowds still thick around him, Jesus upbraids them for always looking for the miraculous. The only miracle they will see is like the miracle of Jonah, brought back to life - resurrected? - from the belly of the whale in the deep waters of chaos. Jonah was the angry, narrow and reluctant prophet whom God sent to the people of Nineveh - outsiders and enemies - to call them to repent and escape destruction. The miracle was that they did. The message is clear: stop looking for miracles among yourselves, here at home in the heartland, look outside. After Jonah and Nineveh, Jesus refers to the Queen of Sheba - another outsider - coming to seek the wisdom of Solomon. There is one here who is greater than Jonah, greater than Solomon. Don't stay in the dark. To reinforce his point, three linked sayings about light and seeing follow on (11:33-36). If we understand them as collectively referring to Jesus himself, they make sense. He is saying, use your eyes to see the light that is now shining before you, and you will be in the light.

TROUBLE AT DINNER

Luke now takes us to a meal that went horribly wrong. After speaking to the crowd, Jesus is invited into the home of a Pharisee for a meal. The Pharisee notices that Jesus has not observed the strict rules for washing before eating, and this provokes Jesus into a lengthy diatribe against first the Pharisees and then also the teachers of the Law. G B Caird wisely observes, 'It is unlikely that Jesus ever delivered a single great harangue such as this against the Pharisees, and still more unlikely that he did it while a guest in a Pharisee's house' (Caird 1963, p 158). Through the device of having Jesus as a guest at the Pharisee's table, Luke collects a number of different sayings and puts them together in the form of this speech. We should note two pieces of background. The words collected here may well have been particularly addressed by Luke to his first readers, who were part of the continuing struggle between the early church and the old Israel. Luke always has two 'audiences', those Jesus addressed in the flesh, and those for whom Luke is writing, about half a century later. In thinking about the Pharisees and the teachers of the Law, we shouldn't think of them purely in religious terms, they were influential in the whole life of their society, leaders of public opinion as members of a powerful pressure group (the Pharisees), or part of the legal establishment (the teachers of the Law).

How terrible!

Jesus' angry indignation is initially kindled by the incident of washing before the meal. The Pharisaic obsession with the minutiae of outward observance can mask an inner being full of violence and hate. It can be argued that the Pharisees' concern for the strict observance of the Law reinforced the view of a nation turned in on itself, seething with the frustration and bitterness of centuries of misrule and occupation, which came to a tragic end with the failed uprising of 66CE and the destruction of the Temple in 70. Jesus says that it's not concern for the outside appearance, but a passion for the poor, that makes clean.

He then launches into a series of denunciations. 'You tithe mint and rue, and neglect justice and love' (11:42). The contrast is between the little picture and the big picture. The law of tithing applied to all agricultural products, but maybe including the herb garden was a bit nit-picking. The Pharisees included the herbs, but neglected the sweet savour of justice and love.

Next in the firing-line is their pompous concern for prestige, a concern in our world by no means confined to the religious. Working seriously for justice and love is likely to produce nothing but humility, in the face of our human inadequacy before the size of the task; concentrating on relatively minor duties can produce the kind of petty martinet under whom we have probably all suffered at some point. We've seen already, in the story of the widow of Nain in Chapter 7, that contact with the dead made a person ritually unclean. Because of this, graves were often painted white as a warning. Jesus now likens the Pharisees to unmarked graves; on the surface all seems well because of their pious reputation, but underneath their influence is poisonous (11:44).

When Jesus turns on the teachers of the Law, his criticism is three-fold. First he accuses them of laying far too heavy burdens on people's backs without doing anything to help them (11:46). Second, as guardians of the status quo, both their history and present practice led them into conflict with any prophet who speaks a new word to challenge them. They conveniently neglect their history and honour the tombs of the very prophets they have persecuted, while still opposing the present prophetic word on Jesus' own lips. In the Hebrew scriptures Abel was the first victim and Zechariah the final martyr (11:51). The blood of prophets, past and present, is on their hands. Finally, they are the appointed guardians of the scripture. By concentrating on the minutiae and resisting all change, instead of opening the book they have left it locked and chained (11:52).

Not surprisingly, after all that, Luke reports that those attacked criticised him bitterly and sought to trap him. The conflict is intensifying: between this enclosed, inward-facing, backward-looking society and its authorities, and the one who brings light to those who look to him and look outside.

More warnings

Luke reports that a huge crowd had gathered, again, and Jesus rounds on the Pharisees, again. Once more he contrasts their outward observance with the inner reaches of the soul. Hypocrisy consists of appearing to be one thing, and actually being another. Jesus warns of the day when all will be known. We remember the opening words of the Communion prayer,

> 'Almighty God,
> to whom all hearts are open,
> all desires known,
> and from whom no secrets are hidden.'
> (*Common Order* 1994, p.122)

From the example of the Pharisees, the followers of Jesus are warned not to pretend to be other than they are. Luke may here be writing directly for his readers, well aware of persecution, and tempted to save their skin (12:4-5). It is not other human beings, however threatening, that they are to fear - it is God alone.

Immediately after these savage words come two of the most beautiful and reassuring verses in the gospel, speaking of God's care for two-a-penny sparrows and his infinitely greater care for his children. 'And even the hairs of your head are numbered' (12:6,7). So, don't be afraid.

A FINAL WORD

This section ends with three sayings, loosely connected. First, Jesus says that those who acknowledge him publicly here on earth he will acknowledge in heaven, but those who reject him publicly, he will reject. This is then qualified when he says that those who speak against him can be forgiven, but those who speak against the Holy Spirit will not be forgiven. The Holy Spirit is the bringer of truth: to deny the Spirit is to condemn oneself to live in falsehood in the dark. Finally, Jesus promises the same Spirit will come to the aid of those who are put on trial for their faith. 'Don't worry about what to say', he says, 'the Holy Spirit will prompt you when the time comes' (12:12). Once more these final verses clearly resonate with the situation to which Luke is writing.

STUDY

BY YOURSELF

Who are today's Pharisees and teachers of the Law, the pressure groups, opinion makers, and movers and shapers of our society? What is their influence for good or bad?

Look at Luke's list of 'Woes' from 11:37 onwards. Without getting carried away with your own self-righteousness, draw up a list of 'Woes' for today.

FOR GROUP WORK

Share with the group the work you have done by yourself. Discuss together how to carry forward what you have shared. From your discussion, put together a list of topics for prayer and action for group members and the group as a whole.

chapter 20

On wakefulness

LUKE 12:13 - 13:9

The Parable of the Rich Fool

A man in the crowd said to Jesus, "Teacher, tell my brother to divide with me the property our father left us."

Jesus answered him, "My friend, who gave me the right to judge or divide the property between you two?" And he went on to say to them all, "Watch out and guard yourselves from every kind of greed; because a person's true life is not made up of the things he owns, no matter how rich he may be."

Then Jesus told them this parable: "There was once a rich man who had lands which bore good crops. He began to think to himself, 'I haven't anywhere to keep all my crops. What can I do? This is what I will do,' he told himself, 'I will tear down my barns and build bigger ones, where I will store my corn and all my other goods. Then I will say to myself, Lucky man! You have all the good things you need for many years. Take life easy, eat, drink, and enjoy yourself!' But God said to him, 'You fool! This very night you will have to give up your life; then who will get all these things you have kept for yourself?'"

And Jesus concluded, "This is how it is with those who pile up riches for themselves but are not rich in God's sight."

Trust in God
(Mt 6:25-34)

Then Jesus said to the disciples, "And so I tell you not to worry about the food you need to stay alive or about the clothes you need for your body. Life is much more important than food, and the body much more important than clothes. Look at the crows; they don't sow seeds or gather a harvest; they don't have store-rooms or barns; God feeds them! You are worth so much more than birds! Can any of you live a bit longer by worrying about it? If you can't manage even such a small thing, why worry about the other things? Look how the wild flowers grow: they don't work or make clothes for themselves. But I tell you that not even King Solomon with all his wealth had clothes as beautiful as one of these flowers. It is God who clothes the wild grass - grass that is here today and gone tomorrow, burnt up in the oven. Won't he be all the more sure to clothe you? How little faith you have!

"So don't be all upset, always concerned about what you will eat and drink. (For the pagans of this world are always concerned about all these things.) Your Father knows that you need these things. Instead, be concerned with his Kingdom, and he will provide you with these things.

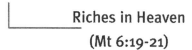

Riches in Heaven
(Mt 6:19-21)

"Do not be afraid, little flock, for your Father is pleased to give you the Kingdom. Sell all your belongings and give the money to the poor. Provide for yourselves purses that don't wear out, and save your riches in heaven, where they will never decrease, because no thief can get at them, and no moth can destroy them. For your heart will always be where your riches are.

Watchful Servants

"Be ready for whatever comes, dressed for action and with your lamps lit, like servants who are waiting for their master to come back from a wedding feast. When he comes and knocks, they will open the door for him at once. How happy are those servants whose master finds them awake and ready when he returns! I tell you, he will take off his coat, ask them to sit down, and will wait on them. How happy they are if he finds them ready, even if he should come at midnight or even later! And you can be sure that if the owner of a house knew the time when the thief would come, he would not let the thief break into his house. And you, too, must be ready, because the Son of Man will come at an hour when you are not expecting him."

The Faithful or the Unfaithful Servant
(Mt 24:45-51)

Peter said, "Lord, does this parable apply to us, or do you mean it for everyone?"

The Lord answered, 'Who, then, is the faithful and wise servant? He is the one that his master will put in charge, to run the household and give the other servants their share of the food at the proper time. How happy that servant is if his master finds him doing this when he comes home! Indeed, I tell you, the master will put that servant in charge of all his property. But if that servant says to himself that his master is taking a long time to come back and if he begins to beat the other servants, both the men and the women, and eats and drinks and gets drunk, then the master will come back one day when the servant does not expect him and at a time he does not know. The master will cut him in pieces and make him share the fate of the disobedient.

"The servant who knows what his master wants him to do, but does not get himself ready and do it, will be punished with a heavy whipping. But the servant who does not know what his master wants, and yet does something for which he deserves a whipping, will be punished with a light whipping. Much is required of the person to whom much is given; much more is required from the person to whom much more is given.

Jesus the Cause of Division
(Mt 10:34-36)

"I came to set the earth on fire, and how I wish it were already kindled! I have a baptism to receive, and how distressed I am until it is over! Do you suppose that I came to bring peace to the world? No, not peace, but division. From now on a family of five will be divided, three against two and two against three. Fathers will be against their sons, and sons against their fathers; mothers will be against their daughters, and daughters against their mothers; mothers-in-law will be against their daughters-in-law, and daughters-in-law against their mothers-in-law."

Understanding the Time
(Mt 16:2-3)

Jesus said also to the people, "When you see a cloud coming up in the west, at once you say that it is going to rain - and it does. And when you feel the south wind blowing, you say that it is going to get hot - and it does. Hypocrites! You can look at the earth and the sky and predict the weather; why, then, don't you know the meaning of this present time?

Settle with your Opponent
(Mt 5:25-26)

"Why do you not judge for yourselves the right thing to do? If someone brings a lawsuit against you and takes you to court, do your best to settle the dispute with them before you get to court. If you don't, they will drag you before the judge, who will hand you over to the police, and you will be put in jail. There you will stay, I tell you, until you pay the last penny of your fine.'

Turn from your Sins or Die

At that time some people were there who told Jesus about the Galileans whom Pilate had killed while they were offering sacrifices to God. Jesus answered them, "Because those Galileans were killed in that way, do you think it proves that they were worse sinners than all the other Galileans? No indeed! And I tell you that if you do not turn from your sins, you will all die as they did. What about those eighteen people in Siloam who were killed when the tower fell on them? Do you suppose this proves that they were worse than all the other people living in Jerusalem? No indeed! And I tell you that if you do not turn from your sins, you will all die as they did."

The Parable of the Unfruitful Fig Tree

Then Jesus told them this parable: "There was once a man who had a fig tree growing in his vineyard. He went looking for figs on it but found none. So he said to his gardener, 'Look, for three years I have been coming here looking for figs on this fig tree, and I haven't found any. Cut it down! Why should it go on using up the soil?' But the gardener answered, 'Leave it alone, sir, just one more year; I will dig round it and put in some manure. Then if the tree bears figs next year, so much the better; if not, then you can have it cut down.'"

'THE MAN'S A FOOL!'

Luke now leads us to two contrasting pictures in quick succession. The first one is sombre. From the crowd a man asks Jesus to arbitrate in a dispute between him and his brother over the estate his father has left. Wealth in Israel at the time of Jesus resided mainly in land. The man may well have been a younger brother who has not received what he considered his due rights, though his elder brother may have wanted to keep the family's land together as a unit and been reluctant to divide it. Jesus, on the way to his trials in Jerusalem, has been talking about the hard road of discipleship and the man's question jars. He isn't interested in getting involved in such a self-absorbed, self-seeking question. He warns about greed, and tells a story, our first picture.

The story has come to be known as the parable of the rich fool. It's about a rich farmer who does so well one harvest time that he decides to pull down his barns and build bigger to hold the harvest. When the work is finished he sits back and says to his soul, his innermost being: 'Now you've got plenty for years to come: relax, eat, drink and enjoy yourself!' But God said, 'You fool! This very night your life will end. What good will all your wealth be then?'

Is he a fool? One distinguished commentator said, 'Everybody knows the man is a fool'. I think he meant that we all know, deep in our beings, that what we accumulate here on earth we do not keep, and that our wealth is not measured by the multitude of our possessions. In today's world, however, or at least in our western capitalist part of it, the farmer might well be the model of the successful business man, sensible yet bold in his investment strategy. Why does God call him a fool?

There are two reasons, not mutually exclusive. Remember Herzog's alternative reading of the parable of the friend at midnight (see p. 122). It should remind us that in the times of Jesus' ministry and the gospel's writing, the vast majority of the population lived lives of what we would call today unremitting poverty - a hairsbreadth away from disaster. The rich farmer's thoughts and actions are totally self-centred; there must have been another way to deal with his surplus apart from hoarding it, he could have distributed it among the rural poor around him who would have welcomed it as a great blessing. He would then have accumulated the right kind of treasure (see 12:33).

The second reason is that the rich man has forgotten that with all his power and wealth, the one thing he doesn't own is the future, not even his own future. Every time I hear this story I think of the true stories of two men. The first learnt that his investment plans had matured so well that he and his wife could look to a comfortable and prosperous retirement. Later that day his wife was diagnosed as having cancer. The other had worked away from home for many years so that he and his wife would have plenty for the future. Then his wife died suddenly, and the years away became the lost years, filled with regret.

There's a word here for our society also. A report was issued in 2001 of progress being made by a group of scientists in controlling our weather, in particular towards banishing clouds, or rather getting them to deposit their moisture before reaching land. Living in the west of Scotland, that often seems like a great idea. No longer will rain stop play in the Test Match, nor covers be on at Wimbledon, nor the Clyde Coast be damp and dreich throughout the Glasgow Fair holidays. The sceptic in me wonders. Because of our collective success through science and technology in using and manipulating the God-given raw material of our world, we are often in danger of thinking we humans are the new masters of the universe. And we aren't. The future, at least, we don't own. With all our achievements, tomorrow is not ours, though of course what we do today influences tomorrow, for better or for worse.

'STOP WORRYING!'

The picture changes to one of reassurance and beauty. Luke inserts here the memorable words and pictures from the Sermon on the Mount in Matthew 6:26ff. The invitation is to look at the birds and see how well they are provided for by the good hand of a generous Creator. How much more will God care for you! God will feed you. Look at the growth of the wild flowers, surpassing the beauty of Solomon clothed in all his wealth. (Solomon's wealth was accumulated at the expense of his people, there may be a veiled criticism here.) If God so bedecks the flowers of the field, here today and gone tomorrow, God will clothe you (12:22-31). 'Stop worrying,' says Jesus, 'about food and clothes, about all these vital, ordinary, daily anxieties.' To a society daily bombarded with inducements and warnings about insuring ourselves to the hilt against all eventualities, these words sound strange. Jesus is not counselling idleness or recklessness. The previous story reminds us that there are some risks we can't insure against. Jesus constantly encourages taking the risks of faith, within a community of mutual care. Always in the gospel background is the assumption of a community of mutual care, whether it be in Luke's early church or the local Galilean village.

Jesus continues. 'I've told you not to worry about your basic needs, don't you worry about the Kingdom either. That's the gift of God the Father, and it will be given' (12:32). The Kingdom and the church are not identical; the Kingdom is always much greater and more mysterious than the church. Let's take these words for a moment and hear them as Jesus' saying to us, 'Don't be anxious about your work of spreading the gospel, don't be anxious about your church work'. In Scotland today, as in much of the Western world, there are a lot of us anxious Christians, worried about the future of our church as we struggle to keep the dwindling little flock, very often housed in a totally inappropriate large late-Victorian pile, from going under. We need to hear this word of Jesus badly.

What does worry do to us? Anxiety makes us defensive, self-absorbed, over-cautious, recriminatory, and therefore unattractive and ungracious. In terms of Luke's gospel, we might well say the demon of anxiety lurking in our midst needs to be exorcised. Anxiety makes us turn inwards, and the Kingdom's out there. We get Pharisaic; preoccupied with the trivial and the material. What if we made verse 33 the programme for our church? Then we would live day by day by faith. Jesus is right. What we do with our 'riches', our money, talents and time is the sure test of what we really value. Listen to Richard Rohr's comment:

> Where do we spend our time and where do we spend our money? That's where our treasure is, we can be sure. The focus of your time and money will tell you what your God is and what is important in your life. As others have wisely said, your chequebook and your calendar [diary] reveal your true belief system.
>
> (Rohr 1997, p. 155)

'KEEP AWAKE!'

The gospels are full of encouragements to wakefulness, alertness. In part, no doubt, this reflects the common belief in the imminent return of the Son of Man. In general the advice given is two-fold; in your state of expectancy don't be misled by the claim of every would-be prophet, but remain expectant, active, watchful. For us this call to alertness is a call to live life to the full, in the here and now, to be as aware as we can be of the life of others and the life of the world around us, and to drink in to the full what each moment brings. Bonhoeffer's call to a life of 'holy worldliness', living fully in the world and taking our share and savour of life's joys and responsibilities, comes to mind.

Two specific historical situations form the background. These words are spoken by Jesus on his way to Jerusalem and the crisis of his passion. They also reflect the turbulent state of Israel in the time of Jesus and the later time of Luke's writing. The parable which follows (12:42-48) reflects the situation in Luke's church when the return of the Son of Man had been delayed longer than expected and the church had to rethink its world-view. The delay has already been hinted at in 12:38 in the lateness of the master's return from the wedding feast. In the period before the master's return, the responsibility for the welfare of the household falls on the principal servant. There is therefore a particular responsibility placed on church leaders for right conduct and the care of their 'household' (12:45-6). This is reflected in many of the New Testament letters. A lesser responsibility is laid on ordinary members of the church community, who do not 'know' so much (12:48).

DIVISION

Tough words intensify. The words of Jesus about bringing not peace but division also have a two-fold reference. They point to his own increasingly imminent trial, and they are written for Luke's young church. In Jesus' words about the baptism which lies ahead of him, his final ordeal in Jerusalem (12:50), the cross casts its shadow. The words of Jesus here also offer counsel and support to those of Luke's readers struggling with the real disruption the gospel message has brought to their own lives, where the taking of the way of Jesus has set children against parents. The divisions Jesus mentions here are generational, between father and son, mother and daughter. This is a society where power and authority lay very firmly with parents. This is another example of the gospel prising loose family ties. Once again Jesus disrupts the status quo and upsets the social apple cart.

WEATHER FORECASTING

Throughout this section, Jesus speaks sometimes to the crowd, sometimes to the disciples. He turns to the crowd once more and complains that while they can forecast the weather from looking skyward they can't read the significance of events on earth. The great sign for which all Israel waited was the coming of the Messiah, but the dominant view of the coming Messiah in Jesus' time was of a narrow nationalistic war hero who would deliver the people from their present oppression and rout their enemies. It was a very understandable view given the injuries and wounds of Israel's history and contemporary state. The trouble was that its inward-looking, self-centredness blinded the people to the living sign in their midst. Their prejudice about the Messiah prevented them hearing the question Jesus' presence was asking them, 'Can you not see that the Messiah God is sending will be different? He will not be the product of your narrow desires for wish-fulfilment, he will be the one whom God sends to bring peace in a way quite unlike your expectations.' Remember Nazareth (4:18-21). Open your eyes. Look to him, and look outside.

OUT OF COURT

Three short passages round off this section, each one pointing to the urgency of the times. First, there's a piece of debt advice (12:57-59). The advice is, if a person is being pursued for debt, usually the plight of the poor, try to settle out of court. Court means trouble. Jesus takes this piece of sound peasant wisdom and gives it the character of a parable. The court can refer either to the high court of heaven, and Israel come to judgement, or to the might of Roman law to which Israel is heading if the futile destructive rebellions don't stop. It can be either, or both.

CHANGE YOUR TRAVEL PLANS?
It was reported to Jesus that Pilate, the Roman governor had killed some Galileans while they were offering sacrifice in the Jerusalem Temple, an act both cruel and blasphemous. Where is Jesus of Nazareth heading? He's on pilgrimage to Jerusalem. Since the start of the second intifada, we have often seen pictures of Bethlehem's Manger Square, devoid of tourists and pilgrims. The dangers of continuing conflict have decided the pilgrims to change their travel plans. Jesus doesn't. He keeps going forward. He is going to Jerusalem.

The question arises from the fate of the Galileans, whether it was their sins which were responsible for the calamity which befell them. Then what about the Jerusalem-dwellers who were killed when a tower in Siloam fell on top of them? Jesus is clear: one lot were the victims of Pilate's cruelty, and the other of an accident. They were no worse than anyone else. He ends with a warning. Unless the whole people of Israel change their direction, death will be commonplace (13:5).

ONE LAST CHANCE
Finally there is a parable about a fig tree, a common symbol for the people of Israel. The fig tree is unfruitful and the owner of the garden instructs the gardener to cut it down; it has been three years barren. The gardener pleads for one last chance; he will nurture it and feed it, and next year if it fruits, well and good, if it doesn't, it gets chopped. Perhaps God is the owner of the garden and Jesus the gardener. Alternatively we can regard Jesus as the owner. The message is the same either way. Israel has failed God, and has one last chance; at this last moment she must change or die.

STUDY

BY YOURSELF

> 'Where do we spend our time and where do we spend our money? Your
> chequebook and your calendar [diary] reveal your true belief system.'
> (Rohr 1997, p. 155)

Do your own personal inventory on the way you spend your money and time. For
a month, keep a diary of all that you spend, under a series of headings like 'food',
'heating', 'leisure', 'the family', 'church'. Make up your own headings. For the
next month keep a careful diary of all your activities. What do you learn from this
exercise about what you value and worship?

FOR GROUP WORK:

• Do a search for the signs of the times, both positive and negative. This is
  homework, either for the whole group or the leader. Either ask each member of
  the group to bring to the meeting cuttings from newspapers and magazines of
  the previous week, or the leader should bring a whole pile of papers and
  magazines to the meeting and ask people to make their own cuttings on the
  spot. The cuttings can be of news items, comment, features or advertising.

• Ask each person to share with the group what they think their cuttings say
  about the values and direction of our society.

• List the cuttings in two columns, one positive and one negative.

• Discuss what you think Jesus would say about each item in each column.

chapter 21

Healing and growth

LUKE 13:10-35

Jesus Heals a Crippled Woman on the Sabbath

One Sabbath Jesus was teaching in a synagogue. A woman there had an evil spirit that had made her ill for eighteen years; she was bent over and could not straighten up at all. When Jesus saw her, he called out to her, "Woman, you are free from your illness!" He placed his hands on her, and at once she straightened herself up and praised God.

The official of the synagogue was angry that Jesus had healed on the Sabbath, so he spoke up and said to the people, "There are six days in which we should work; so come during these days and be healed, but not on the Sabbath!"

The Lord answered him, "You hypocrites! Any one of you would untie your ox or your donkey from the stall and take it out to give it water on the Sabbath. Now here is this descendant of Abraham whom Satan has kept bound up for eighteen years; should she not be released on the Sabbath?" His answer made his enemies ashamed of themselves, while the people rejoiced over all the wonderful things that he did.

The Parable of the Mustard Seed
(Mt 13:31-32, Mk 4:30-32)

Jesus asked, "What is the Kingdom of God like? What shall I compare it with? It is like this. A man takes a mustard seed and sows it in his field. The plant grows and becomes a tree, and the birds make their nests in its branches."

The Parable of the Yeast
(Mt 13:33)

Again Jesus asked, "What shall I compare the Kingdom of God with? It is like this. A woman takes some yeast and mixes it with forty litres of flour until the whole batch of dough rises."

The Narrow Door
(Mt 7:13-14, 21-23)

Jesus went through towns and villages, teaching the people and making his way towards Jerusalem. Someone asked him, "Sir, will just a few people be saved?"

Jesus answered them, "Do your best to go in through the narrow door; because many people will surely try to go in but will not be able. The master of the house will get up and close the door; then when you stand outside and begin to knock on the door and say, 'Open the door for us, sir!' he will answer you, 'I don't know where you come from!' Then you will answer, 'We ate and drank with you; you taught in our town!' But he will say again, 'I don't know where you come from. Get away from me, all you wicked people!' How you will cry and grind your teeth when you see Abraham, Isaac, and Jacob, and all the prophets in the Kingdom of God, while you are thrown out! People will come from the east and the west, the north and the south, and sit down at the feast in the Kingdom of God. Then those who are now last will be first, and those who are now first will be last."

Jesus' Love for Jerusalem
(Mt 23:37-39)

At that same time some Pharisees came to Jesus and said to him, "You must get out of here and go somewhere else, because Herod wants to kill you."

Jesus answered them, "Go and tell that fox: 'I am driving out demons and performing cures today and tomorrow, and on the third day I shall finish my work.' Yet I must be on my way today, tomorrow, and the next day; it is not right for a prophet to be killed anywhere except in Jerusalem.

"Jerusalem, Jerusalem! You kill the prophets, you stone the messengers God has sent you! How many times have I wanted to put my arms round all your people, just as a hen gathers her chicks under her wings, but you would not let me! And so your Temple will be abandoned. I assure you that you will not see me until the time comes when you say, 'God bless him who comes in the name of the Lord.'"

THE BURDENED WOMAN

A long way back in the gospel, Luke told the story of a man being healed on the Sabbath (6:6-11); It is the Sabbath again in this story. Jesus, his disciples and the band of followers are on their way to Jerusalem and Jesus, as usual, is at the local synagogue. As he is teaching, among the women - who would be separate from the men, in the lesser place, probably partly hidden behind a screen - he notices one with a severe back problem, almost bent double. He interrupts his teaching, stops short, and calls the woman out in front of everybody. She comes out, through the assembly of men, up to the teaching place, the most important place in the building, where probably no woman has ever come before. Jesus tells the woman she is free, released from her trouble and then he puts his hands on her: remember again the importance of touch. And at once, the woman who had been bent of back for eighteen long years, straightened up. She was cured, released, and in her thankful joy, in front of the whole assembly, at a place and a time when women were supposed to keep their mouths firmly shut, she began to praise God.

THE ANGRY MAN

This is a story in two parts. We've come to the end of part one. Part two now begins. Stand up the ruler of the synagogue, flushed, angry. 'You shouldn't have done that, Jesus! There's a time and a place for everything and this is neither the time nor the place. This is the Sabbath Day; let me tell everybody here that they can come and be cured on the other six days of the week, but never on a Sabbath.' Jesus will not lie down to the man's rebuke. He answers fire with fire. 'You hypocrites!' he says, 'you're all quite happy to make sure that your cattle and donkeys find release and relief on the Sabbath Day, but this woman, this precious daughter of Abraham, bound by Satan for eighteen years, half a lifetime, why should it not be right for her to be given release as well?' And the hypocrites, the unco-guid, were in a state of confusion, and the people were delighted at what they had seen and heard.

ONE INCIDENT, THREE PERSPECTIVES

This short story is in two parts with three clear sides. There's the woman, bent under her burden, feeling both the weight of her pain and maybe the greater weight of her uselessness. She receives from Jesus a relief and release which has her virtually dancing for joy. She, the forgotten one, in the lesser place, is brought into the centre of the stage and not only receives healing, she also is given the precious dignity of her rightful title as daughter of Abraham, part of the offspring of God's promise. That's what she is, never to be looked or thought on as just a poor, old crippled woman. For the time being, at least, we're glad for her. With the ordinary people, we're delighted for her in the whole new lease of life she's been given through her encounter with Jesus. That simple, uncomplicated, immediate reaction is fine, and to be cherished. With the woman we rejoice, and let's not forget that dominant moment of rejoicing in what comes next.

It is very different. This is a story of healing and conflict, release and uproar, peace and anger; we remember how often that unlikely conjunction occurs in the gospels. Next, there's the angry man, the ruler of the synagogue. Any sympathy for him? He's the man in charge, responsible for preparing the house, ensuring that there is the proper atmosphere for worship, seeing that reverence and good order prevail. And this morning, this stranger has certainly caused a lot of disruption. Is there any sympathy for the ruler of the synagogue? There should be. My experience of church is that anything which disturbs or disrupts people at worship gets them upset. It doesn't take much for usually very tolerant and charitable people to be transformed into their polar opposites. I can remember and bear the bruises of furores over the introduction of new hymn books, uproar over the removal of favourite pews, murmurings when sometimes young children are a bit noisy or restless, and a few more.

But this story is not about a disproportionate reaction to an upsetting situation. Here, the ruler of the synagogue has good reason to be upset. He thinks that the holy Sabbath Law, a keystone in the whole practice of his faith, is being challenged and undermined. It's not just the disturbance in the synagogue that bothers him, upsetting though that is, it's the attack on what he perceives as basic principles. The problem, and it's an enduring one, is, that the precious basic principles of his religion - and we have ours, though not the same ones - are in conflict with yet more basic principles of practical charity and humanity. Jesus is saying, 'The woman is suffering, she needs help now, she can be helped now, I will help her now, and that's a more important demand to fulfil than the demand of the Sabbath Law that on this day no work shall be done'.

Remember the saying that when there's a seeming conflict between God and truth, always choose truth, for God is the God of truth, and we sometimes see in a glass darkly but truth will out. This story reminds us that religion can mess us up, that we too are not immune to the temptations of hypocrisy; which here means letting lesser things obscure greater things, letting the details get in the way of the big picture. What matters in the end is not the practice of our religion but the practice of our humanity; and if in any way the attitudes and practice of our religion makes us less human and less charitable, then these attitudes and practices, however hallowed by time and usage, need to change. It's not hard to sympathise with the ruler of the synagogue, but he's clearly on the wrong side of this argument.

The third perspective is through Jesus' eyes. We've seen his argument. 'The woman is suffering, she needs help now, she can be helped now, I will help her now, and that's a more important demand than the demand of the Sabbath Law that on this day no work shall be done.' Jesus looks on this woman with clear-eyed, uncondescending compassion, and makes her whole; regardless of the flak he has to take, the criticism and conflict he provokes. He will do what is right and compassionate, stand in the open ground and take the consequences. With the eyes of Jesus, let's look again for a moment at this bent and crippled woman. The truth is that we don't know what had crippled the woman, but there are three suggestive possibilities. First, it could have been that her back injury was simply physical. Then Jesus' laying on of his hands can take on an extra dimension, maybe there was a special skill and knowledge in releasing her back. It's interesting that Jesus tells the woman that she is released from her trouble before he lays his hands upon her and that later in the story, in his confrontation with the ruler of the synagogue, Jesus speaks of the woman as a person in bondage to Satan. Maybe the woman's trouble had more than merely physical roots. Perhaps she was suffering from what psychiatry would call a hysterical reaction. Something had happened in her life which had caused her to freeze, to lock rigid: some loss, hurt, guilt. From whatever it was that had bound her, physical, mental or spiritual, through the eyes and the touch of Jesus, she found release. The third possibility is the most elusive and suggestive. It doesn't exclude either of the other two but it goes like this. The Old Testament speaks very little about poverty, but a great deal about the poor. In talking about the poor it uses three different words. The most common is the word 'dal', which comes from a root which means 'bent', 'burdened'; I think a very good Scottish translation would be 'hauden doon.' The description of being bent over is either an allusion to an attitude of subservience, of the slave before the master, the lesser before the greater, or to being huddled over by the sheer weight of the burden of care and oppression carried. There's not much doubt that whatever other burdens this woman was carrying she would also be bearing the burden of poverty. So, it's this poor, pained woman, in the lesser, forgotten place, that Jesus sees and releases, with no little cost to himself, on the way to Jerusalem. As we rejoice in her healing we remember that we are the ones entrusted with being the eyes and hands of Jesus, in our world now.

THE CHALLENGE

One of the early poems of Sorley Maclean, is called 'The Highland Woman'.

> Hast Thou seen her, great Jew,
> who art called the One Son of God?
> Hast Thou seen on Thy way the like of her
> labouring in the distant vineyard?

> The load of fruits on her back,
> a bitter sweat on brow and cheek,
> and the clay basin heavy on the back
> of her bent poor wretched head.

> Thou hast not seen her, Son of the carpenter,
> who art called the King of Glory,
> among the rugged western shores
> in the sweat of her food's creel.

This Spring and last Spring
and every twenty Springs from the beginning,.
she has carried the cold seaweed
for her children's food and the castle's reward.

And every twenty Autumns gone
she has lost the golden summer of her bloom,
and the Black Labour has ploughed the furrow
across the white smoothness of her forehead.

And Thy gentle church has spoken
about the lost state of her miserable soul,
and the unremitting toil has lowered
her body to a black peace in a grave.

And her time has gone like a black sludge
seeping through the thatch of a poor dwelling:
the hard Black Labour was her inheritance;
grey is her sleep tonight.
('The Highland Woman' in Maclean 1989, p. 27-8)

The poem is full of pity for the woman and bitterness and anger towards Jesus. Sorley Maclean grew up in the intensely religious atmosphere of the island of Raasay, early last century. It was a community of many virtues, but for the poet it obscured rather than bore witness to the Jesus we have encountered in today's gospel. A passion for the minutiae of abstract doctrinal debate and a stress on the distance between the righteous God and sinful humanity induced in Sorley Maclean a picture of a Christ who was stuck up on a pedestal, fawningly worshipped by his followers but indifferent to the back-breaking lot of real people in the real world. Can you think of a greater travesty of the gospel or a more pertinent warning to us? Luke tells us that Jesus has seen, cares, heals and releases. Does our church and our witness make that clear?

KINGDOM GROWTH

Luke follows the healing story with two short parables about the mystery and abundance of growth in the Kingdom of God (13:18-21). He speaks of the grain of mustard seed which in time produces a tree big enough for birds to nest in and the leaven of a tiny quantity of yeast working away unseen to bring the whole batch of dough to rise. As an antidote to Sorley Maclean's poem of great bleakness, R S Thomas' poem 'The Kingdom', bubbles with hope.

It's a long way off, but inside it
There are quite different things going on;
Festivals at which the poor man
Is king and the consumptive is

Healed; mirrors in which the blind look
At themselves and love looks at them
Back, and industry is for mending
The bent bones and the minds fractured
By life. It's a long way off, but to get
There takes no time and admission
Is free, if you will but purge yourself
Of desire, and present yourself with
Your need only and the simple offering
Of your faith, green as a leaf.
('The Kingdom' in Thomas 1993, p. 233)

NARROW DOOR, WIDENING ROAD

Jesus continues on his way to Jerusalem teaching in towns and villages. He is asked the perennial question, 'Sir, will just a few people be saved?' (13:23) The answer Jesus gives is not general, but specific. It refers to the particular historical situation in which he finds himself. The thrust of the whole passage is that following the narrow road of discipleship now is the way to being 'saved', into freedom. Neither membership of the nation of Israel, nor association with Jesus guarantees entrance. The master of the house, who may be either God or Jesus will shut the door on those who are not committed to the way. But the door will be open to those who come from every point of the compass to sit down at the feast of the Messiah. To stress the discipleship way and the reversal of the old order in the new Kingdom, the passage ends with a variation on these themes, 'Then those who are now last will be first, and those who are now first will be last' (13:30). The theme of this whole section is repeated. Israel's favoured status no longer holds if it persists in its present ways; people must take the new way.

JERUSALEM, JERUSALEM!

The road becomes progressively more dangerous. Some Pharisees come to warn Jesus that Herod Antipas, the ruler of Galilee and beheader of John the Baptist is out to kill him. Again we see that the opposition of the Pharisees is not monolithic. Jesus dismisses Herod with contempt. 'Go and tell that fox..' (13:32), hardly the words of an other-worldly saviour. He goes on to say that his work of battling with the powers of evil continues today and tomorrow and that on the third day he will finish his work, a clear reference to the resurrection. Yet he must keep going, his end will not be at the hands of Herod; a prophet's end must be in Jerusalem.

Jesus then produces a poignant and beautiful picture as he laments over Jerusalem. His real feeling for the city and its people is clear, but he is also clear that in both past history and present times the people have not listened to the prophetic voice calling them to change their ways, rather they have killed the messengers. Then comes the picture, when he compares himself to a mother hen trying to gather her chicks under her wing for safety, while the chicks, oblivious to danger, scurry to and fro avoiding her protecting. In Luke's gospel Jesus uses feminine imagery more often than masculine. Tom Wright tells of how, after a farmyard fire, a blackened mother hen has been found dead, with her chicks still alive under her wing (Tom Wright 2001, p. 171). Jesus longs to save not just Jerusalem but all Israel from the baptism of fire which surely awaits if change does not come. But they would not have it so.

STUDY

BY YOURSELF

The story of the healing of the crippled woman is dramatic. Use the technique described in Chapter 12 to be present at the scene and spend time in it. Use your imagination to enter into it, and the characters in it.

- What can you see, hear, smell, taste, feel as you imagine being present at the scene?

- What is the atmosphere like? Inviting, threatening, lively, solemn?

- How are you feeling? Curious? Attracted? Disturbed? Afraid? Excited?

- Do you want to speak to anyone? To the woman? To the ruler of the synagogue? To a member of the congregation? To Jesus? What do you want to say? What do you hear being said to you?

- If any of the scenes particularly attracted you, go back to it. Without forcing anything, see if you can identify what is attracting you.

- What sort of burdens cripple women today?

chapter 22

Healing and hospitality

LUKE 14

Jesus Heals a Sick Man

One Sabbath Jesus went to eat a meal at the home of one of the leading Pharisees; and people were watching Jesus closely. A man whose legs and arms were swollen came to Jesus, and Jesus asked the teachers of the Law and the Pharisees, "Does our Law allow healing on the Sabbath or not?"

But they would not say anything. Jesus took the man, healed him, and sent him away. Then he said to them, "If any one of you had a son or an ox that happened to fall in a well on the Sabbath, would you not pull them out at once on the Sabbath itself?"

But they were not able to answer him about this.

Humility and Hospitality

Jesus noticed how some of the guests were choosing the best places, so he told this parable to all of them: "When someone invites you to a wedding feast, do not sit down in the best place. It could happen that someone more important than you has been invited, and your host, who invited both of you, would have to come and say to you, 'Let him have this place.' Then you would be embarrassed and have to sit in the lowest place. Instead, when you are invited, go and sit in the lowest place, so that your host will come to you and say, 'Come on up, my friend, to a better place.' This will bring you honour in the presence of all the other guests. For all those who make themselves great will be humbled, and those who humble themselves will be made great."

Then Jesus said to his host, "When you give a lunch or a dinner, do not invite your friends or your brothers or your relatives or your rich neighbours - for they will invite you back, and in this way you will be paid for what you did. When you give a feast, invite the poor, the crippled, the lame, and the blind; and you will be blessed, because they are not able to pay you back. God will repay you on the day the good people rise from death."

The Parable of the Great Feast
(Mt 22:1-10)

When one of the men sitting at table heard this, he said to Jesus, "How happy are those who will sit down at the feast in the Kingdom of God!"

Jesus said to him, "There was once a man who was giving a great feast to which he invited many people. When it was time for the feast, he sent his servant to tell his guests, 'Come, everything is ready!' But they all began, one after another, to make excuses. The first one told the servant, 'I have bought a field and must go and look at it; please accept my apologies.' Another one said, 'I have bought five pairs of oxen and am on my way to try them out; please accept my apologies.' Another one said, 'I have just got married, and for that reason I cannot come.'

The servant went back and told all this to his master. The master was furious and said to his servant, 'Hurry out to the streets and alleys of the town, and bring back the poor, the crippled, the blind, and the lame.' Soon the servant said, 'Your order has been carried out, sir, but there is room for more.' So the master said to the servant, 'Go out to the country roads and lanes and make people come in, so that my house will be full. I tell you all that none of those who were invited will taste my dinner!'"

The Cost of Being a Disciple
(Mt 10:37-38)

Once when large crowds of people were going along with Jesus, he turned and said to them, "Those who come to me cannot be my disciples unless they love me more than they love father and mother, wife and children, brothers and sisters, and themselves as well. Those who do not carry their own cross and come after me cannot be my disciples.

"If one of you is planning to build a tower, you sit down first and work out what it will cost, to see if you have enough money to finish the job. If you don't, you will not be able to finish the tower after laying the foundation; and all who see what happened will laugh at you. 'This man began to build but couldn't finish the job!' they will say.

"If a king goes out with ten thousand men to fight another king who comes against him with twenty thousand men, he will sit down first and decide if he is strong enough to face the other king. If he isn't, he will send messengers to meet the other king, to ask for terms of peace while he is still a long way off. In the same way", concluded Jesus, "none of you can be my disciple unless you give up everything you have."

Worthless Salt
(Mt 5:13, Mk 9:50)

"Salt is good, but if it loses its saltiness, there is no way to make it salty again. It is no good for the soil or for the manure heap; it is thrown away. Listen, then, if you have ears!"

ANOTHER SABBATH HEALING

Yet again Jesus is in the house of a Pharisee, having accepted an invitation to a meal. The house belongs to one of the leading Pharisees and Luke reports both that it was on a Sabbath and that Jesus was being closely watched. The atmosphere of suspicion and opposition is heightened. A man ill with dropsy is present and Jesus pointedly asks (again) the representatives of the authorities present, 'Does our Law allow healing on the Sabbath or not?' It's a tough question for them to answer: if they say 'yes' they can be accused of being lax, if they say 'no' they seem callous. They say nothing. The silence is deafening. Jesus heals the man and bids him go away and get on with his life - this is the fourth Sabbath healing Luke recounts. Jesus asks a further question, a more specific one. 'If your child or ox fell into a well on the Sabbath, wouldn't you pull them out at once?' Surely your human concern for your child or animal would prevail? In a question of humanity over and against the niceties, humanity must overcome. Again there is silence.

THE BEST SEATS

The atmosphere in the house is now distinctly frosty. Luke doesn't quite portray Jesus as the guest from hell at the Pharisees' table, as in 11:37-54, but Jesus remains an uncomfortable guest. The Sabbath healing was disruptive, and Jesus' unanswerable questions would further ruffle feathers. Now Jesus observes how the other guests are making sure that they get themselves well placed in the seats of honour near their host.

Questions of hospitality are very important in Luke's gospel. At least ten times we meet Jesus sharing table fellowship. He shares with people as diverse as Pharisees and teachers of the Law, tax collectors and sinners, a hungry crowd, and his closest disciples. At table, time and again, in one way or another, Jesus pushes out the boundaries as he confounds expectations, dismantles barriers, meets needs, expands horizons. He not only sits at table, he talks about it; as we are about to see in the following parables. Richard Rohr sees Jesus using table fellowship as 'visual sermon, cultural critique and social protest' (Rohr 1997 p. 160). Always in the background is the picture of the Messianic banquet (Isaiah 25:6-9), with its message of the abundance of God's grace being given for all.

Jesus made the new fellowship of his table central to his teaching because the roles and rules of table fellowship were extremely important in his society. The table was at the centre of family life, and family life with its obligations and loyalties at the centre of society. Rules surrounding the table were very important to the Pharisees, as we have seen (5:30, 11:37-8). One's place at the table, in a society much more formal and stratified than ours, spoke volumes about status, power and wealth; and these themes, already encountered in the gospel, are particularly prominent in the following chapters.

Returning to the text; Jesus, having noticed the dinner party's seating arrangements, now speaks. 'Suppose you're invited to a wedding. Don't sit at the top table. You'll get a right red face if the host politely asks you to move down. You're far better to start at the bottom and then you'll feel really good if the host asks you to move up.' I can imagine Jesus speaking these words, very much tongue-in-cheek. He's being wryly critical of the scramble for the best seats. The advice he offers is at one level simple common sense, but underlying his words is a call for humility. Genuine humility isn't just about feeling good, it's about being humble. Luke calls Jesus' words here a parable: underneath what seems like sensible social advice is a deeper question about how we see ourselves before God. If we think we're better than others, think again. Jesus ends his talk about the seating arrangements with a serious word in yet another version of the discipleship reversal litany. 'For all who make themselves great will be humbled, and those who humble themselves will be made great' (14:11).

He then speaks to his host directly. He describes to him Kingdom hospitality. 'Don't invite friends, family or rich neighbours to your dinner party, they'll only pay you back. No, invite the poor, the handicapped, those who can offer nothing in return for your hospitality. God will reward you.' Reversals continue.

A FULL HOUSE

One of the guests at the table hears what Jesus is saying and remarks piously, or perhaps sanctimoniously, 'How blessed will those be who sit down at the feast in the Kingdom of God!' (14:15) Jesus' reply is to offer a wonderful picture of low life in one of his most uproarious parables, which hugely challenges the man's assumptions of what the Kingdom feast will be like. Here's the story.

A man of substance is organising a great feast with many guests. He sends out the invitations. 'Please come, I've got everything ready!' One by one the guests make excuses. 'I'm too busy.' 'I'm too busy.' 'I'm too busy.' Translating their excuses into our world, they could sound like, 'I've got new property to attend to, sorry, I can't come.' I've got a new car, sorry, I can't come.' 'I've just got married, sorry, I can't come.' Property, wealth and family; these are more important priorities.

The host is furious. He sends his servant out again. 'Hurry, go into the back lanes and alleys of the town and bring in the poor, the crippled, the blind, the lame.' They come, but still there's room for more. 'Go out again, out into the country, to the roads and lanes. Make people come. I want my house to be full. As for those who were invited, none of them will taste my dinner!' (14:16-24) Picture the great man's house packed full with the ragged folk's banquet. It's a moment of chaotic, overflowing grace.

It's a parable told against Jesus' own people. They have now become so preoccupied with themselves and their concerns that they shut themselves off from the invitation to the feast. It's a parable about the width and scope of the new way, downwards to the poor, outwards beyond the city to the Gentiles. We ask ourselves, 'Are we like the refuseniks, too preoccupied with ourselves, our property, our wealth, our relationships, to hear and heed the invitation to the feast of life?'

THE HARD ROAD

Jesus is next found with the crowds around him again. The open invitation is immediately followed by some very tough words. Jesus talks of the cost of discipleship. He says 'You cannot be my disciples unless you hate father, mother, wife and children, brothers and sisters, yes, and even life itself.' (14:26 - the *GNB* softens Jesus' words.) Ouch! Here's the cost being driven up, with a vengeance. The use of hyperbole, exaggeration, was part of the stock and trade of the rabbinic teacher. It's used to give folk pause, draw them up short, make them stop and think. Jesus is asking questions again about priorities. He asks the question in a society which is male-dominated to the extent that in the Old Testament the basic relationship is that of father and son, to ensure family continuity. His questions lever us loose from ourselves and those close ties which can so easily mask self-interest.

> Jesus proclaimed an utterly different view. He made the basic relationship
> not that of father and son but that of man and woman, husband and wife.
> He declared that this was God's purpose in creation: that God from the
> beginning had made them male and female. By so doing he not only put
> marriage in quite a new light: he also made woman a person on an
> equality with man. And we see the effect of this in his treatment of women
> and in the fact that women were among those who followed him. Those
> who followed him had to deny themselves. They had also to deny the use
> they made of their families - their parents, their wives, their children. For a
> man can make his love of his family merely a respectable form of self-love.
> What he does for his family he really does for himself. Family self-love can
> be selfishness on a large and respectable scale. In a peasant society a
> man's care of his wife may be for her economic usefulness: his desire for
> sons his need of labourers. Jesus gave so different a conception of the
> relationship of men and women that he was prepared to use the very
> opposite of love to emphasise how diametrically opposed his teaching was
> to the conventional ideas of his day. If what men were doing was love, then
> the only word that could describe his teaching was 'hate.' He taught that a
> man could not call his life his own. Equally he must not call his wife, his
> children, his family his own. He had to leave all the old conceptions. He
> had to deny all that he was accustomed to call his own. That was the
> beginning of the new commandment that men should love each other as
> he had loved them.
> (Ralph Morton 1956, p. 52-3)

There's more to Christian faith and practice than 'family values!' It is worth noting again Luke's radicalism about the family. In the book of Acts almost all the pioneers in the young church are single. Luke's positive radicalism springs from his fascination with the Christian community as a new kind of kinship group, which cuts across the old family ties to forge its own enduring ties of mutual care.

It's not only the strong language he uses to bid us re-examine our family relationships that's shocking, the call to pick up the cross would be equally disturbing for the first hearers. It's to the cross Jesus is heading, and we must remember the context as Jesus goes on to counsel would-be disciples to think very carefully and reckon up the cost of following. You don't plan a building unless you've worked out the cost and are sure you've enough to finish it. Kings don't plan to fight battles against superior numbers unless they're sure they're strong enough to face the foe. So, you'd better know that the cost of being my disciple is, simply, everything. There's a starter for ten.

The chapter ends with Jesus' call for his disciples to be like the hidden work of salt in their world. Salt was a vital commodity in the ancient world, with three key uses: as a preservative in a hot climate, as a seasoning to give taste, and also as a fertiliser to produce a good harvest. It was full of uses to preserve, enhance, and multiply life; such was the role of the disciple. Only good salt, however, is useful. The worthless is thrown away.

STUDY

BY YOURSELF

• Give thanks for the invitation to the great inclusive feast of life.

• Think how you can be a living invitation to that feast.

• Use this prayer:

> Round your table, through your giving
> show us how to live and pray
> till your kingdom's way of living
> is the bread we share each day;
> bread for us and for our neighbour,
> bread for body, mind, and soul,
> bread of heaven and human labour -
> broken bread that makes us whole.
> (Leith Fisher, in *Common Ground* 1998, no. 35)

FOR GROUP WORK

Arrange to have a meal together. We're now more than halfway through Luke's gospel; round the table, share what has struck you so far in the journey.

• What stories or sayings have you found most memorable?

• What new insights have you received?

• What questions do you have to ask?

• What questions is Luke's gospel asking you about who belongs and who is missing in your table fellowship?

chapter 23

Lost and found

LUKE 15

The Lost Sheep
(Mt 18:12-14)

One day when many tax collectors and other outcasts came to listen to Jesus, the Pharisees and the teachers of the Law started grumbling, 'This man welcomes outcasts and even eats with them!' So Jesus told them this parable.

"Suppose one of you has a hundred sheep and loses one of them - what do you do? You leave the other ninety-nine sheep in the pasture and go looking for the one that got lost until you find it. When you find it, you are so happy that you put it on your shoulders and carry it back home. Then you call your friends and neighbours together and say to them, 'I am so happy I found my lost sheep. Let us celebrate!' In the same way, I tell you, there will be more joy in heaven over one sinner who repents than over ninety-nine respectable people who do not need to repent.

The Lost Coin

"Or suppose a woman who has ten silver coins loses one of them - what does she do? She lights a lamp, sweeps her house, and looks carefully everywhere until she finds it. When she finds it, she calls her friends and neighbours together and says to them, 'I am so happy I found the coin I lost. Let us celebrate!' In the same way, I tell you, the angels of God rejoice over one sinner who repents."

The Lost Son

Jesus went on to say. "There was once a man who had two sons. The younger one said to him, 'Father, give me my share of the property now.' So the man divided his property between his two sons. After a few days the younger son sold his part of the property and left home with the money. He went to a country far away, where he wasted his money in reckless living. He spent everything he had. Then a severe famine spread over that country, and he was left without a thing. So he went to work for one of the citizens of that country, who sent him out to his farm to take care of the pigs. He wished he could fill himself with the bean pods the pigs ate, but no one gave him anything to eat. At last he came to his senses and said, 'All my father's hired servants have more than they can eat, and here I am about to starve! I will get up and go to my father and say, Father, I have sinned against God and against you. I am no longer fit to be called your son; treat me as one of your hired workers.' So he got up and started back to his father.

"He was still a long way away from home when his father saw him; his heart was filled with pity, and he ran, threw his arms round his son, and kissed him. 'Father,' the son said, 'I have sinned against God and against you. I am no longer fit to be called your son.' But the father called his servants. 'Hurry!' he said, 'Bring the best robe and put it on him. Put a ring on his finger and shoes on his feet. Then go and get the prize calf and kill it, and let us celebrate with a feast! For this son of mine was dead, but now he is alive; he was lost, but now he has been found.' And so the feasting began.

"In the meantime the elder son was out in the field. On his way back, when he came close to the house, he heard the music and dancing. So he called one of the servants and asked him, 'What's going on?' 'Your brother has come back home,' the servant answered, 'and your father has killed the prize calf, because he has got him back safe and sound.'

"The elder brother was so angry that he would not go into the house; so his father came out and begged him to come in. But he answered his father, 'Look, all these years I have worked for you like a slave, and I have never disobeyed your orders. What have you given me? Not even a goat for me to have a feast with my friends! But this son of yours wasted all your property on prostitutes, and when he comes back home, you kill the prize calf for him!' 'My son,' the father answered, 'you are always here with me, and everything I have is yours. But we had to celebrate and be happy, because your brother was dead, but now he is alive; he was lost, but now he has been found.'"

DISTURBING GRACE

With the picture of the free, open, generous invitation to the great feast still in our mind's eye, we draw near to another of the huge moments in Luke's gospel, in the parable which has been variously called, 'the prodigal son', 'the lost son', 'the two sons,' and 'the waiting father'. Luke prepares us for that story with an introduction to set the scene, and follows it with two more short parables. In the introduction, gathered around Jesus are the two antithetical groups with whom Luke is much concerned. A large company of tax collectors and other outcasts are listening to Jesus while, at a distance, there are Pharisees and teachers of the Law grumbling away at the company Jesus is keeping. Once again the charge is that Jesus is much too free, too 'prodigal' in those with whom he associates. The authorities' verdict is the doubtful one of 'Guilty, by association'. They find Jesus' freedom undermining their own cherished beliefs, and disturbing for the general well-being of their society. How can a prophet keep such company?

JOY IN HEAVEN

Jesus answers with two parables, of the lost sheep and the lost coin (15:4-10), using two striking images from everyday life thoroughly familiar to his hearers. Imagine a shepherd has lost a sheep which has forsaken its usual gregariousness and wandered off in search of fresh pasture. He will leave the flock and go and search for the one that is lost, by now dangerously isolated. When he finds it, he will hoist it on his shoulders and bring it home amid scenes of general rejoicing. It would not be lost on the audience that sheep straying from the good path was a well-known symbol for the people's waywardness.

A poor woman, in her dark low-roofed home, loses one of her only ten silver coins. Is she now short with the vital rent money? She lights her lamp and carefully sweeps the earth floor until she finds the coin, and tells her friends and neighbours of her relief and delight. Both stories are about the loss of something precious. They both end with a scene of communal rejoicing in the most ordinary of earthy circumstances; the scene is echoed by the angels in heaven. They unite to tell how much God cares, not just for the good, but for the sinner, who also is precious in God's sight. When the sinner is 'found' and returns to the good way, then there is joy in heaven!

THE PRODIGAL

We come now to the parable of the father and the two sons, living on what was at least a comfortable estate. Remember that the father-son relationship was the crucial relationship in Jesus' society. It was the critical relationship for ensuring the continuity of property and family life. Most wealth was to be found in land rather than money. This parable begins with the younger son asking his father for his share in the family inheritance now, while the father is still alive. Most commentators agree that such a request was not unknown. It has been suggested that for the younger son to ask for his inheritance of his still-living father was the equivalent of saying, 'I wish you were dead!' If that were the case, the charge of extreme callousness can be added to the younger son's reckless carelessness. The young man takes his allotted third of the property and with indecent haste sells it off and leaves home. He puts as much distance as he can between himself and the paternal household, and in the far country quickly gets through the family silver in spendthrift living. At this stage in the story we are not told how he wasted his money; later on, his elder brother hazards a pretty mean guess (15:30). So far it is pretty hard to have much sympathy for the prodigal, as he pursues his own selfish and headstrong agenda.

The good times don't last. Soon the prodigal is on his uppers, with his plight compounded as famine sweeps the land. He is reduced to working for a foreigner who gives him a task anathema to a Hebrew, the feeding of a herd of pigs. He's so hungry he is desperate to eat the pigs' food, but even that is denied him. At last he gets to thinking. He'd be better off as one of his father's labourers; their bellies are always full at least. He decides to go home to meet his father face-to-face, and confess he has sinned against both him and God, admit he failed to be worthy of being a son, and beg to be treated just like a day labourer. Is he genuinely repentant, just hungry, or both? He sets off homeward but while he's still a long way from the front door...

The running father

...his father comes running out to meet him. A moment ago we noted that the younger son, with his thoughtless request for his share of the family wealth and his subsequent wastefulness doesn't easily command our sympathy, though his story is far from unique. We look from the outside in: it looks different from the inside, from the perspective of the father's heart. All established practice suggests that the last action expected of the father was for him to pick up his skirts and go running to meet the lost son. He should have waited until the son came and made his abject apology. He doesn't, because - once again we encounter that word for strong emotion - 'his heart was filled with pity.' The father runs, and enfolds the son in an embrace of welcome *before* the son can say a word. The son then makes his speech of pleading repentance, but the sense we get from the story is that the father is too overcome with joy even to hear him. ' Hurry! Get the best robe to cover his rags,' says the father, 'put a ring on his finger and shoes on his feet' (shoes symbolising that the father gives him back the status as son, not that of a barefoot labourer). 'Kill the fatted calf and let's have a feast!' (15:22-4). The father ends his speech by comparing the son's return to a resurrection, new life. 'This son of mine was dead, but now he is alive: he was lost, but now he's found.' We began with the prodigal son, now we have the prodigal father, greeting his boy's return with an exuberance, a grace and a welcome which truly bursts the bounds. God, as seen in and shown by Jesus, is the waiting, running father. And once again we see and hear him calling us to a feast, a party!

The elder son, for and against

Now the third person in the story makes his appearance. After yet another hard day's work in the fields, the elder brother comes home to be confronted by the sounds of music and dancing, evidence of a great party in the family home. When he discovers the feast is in honour of his younger brother's return he is furious, so angry he won't go into the house. Once again the father comes out to meet one of his sons - what a telling moment that is - and begs him join in. The elder brother's seething resentment of what he sees as years of being taken for granted for his loyal work at home breaks through. He complains he's had no recognition from his father, and he puts the worst of interpretations on his brother's fall from grace. Once more the father answers gently. 'My son, you are always with me, and what's mine is yours. But we had to celebrate, your brother is alive again; the lost one is found' (15:32).

This is an intensely 'feeling' parable; throughout it the appeal to our emotions is strong. What do we feel for the elder brother? Maybe we think, what a boorish stick-in-the-mud; is this the best he can do in face of his brother's return and his father's joyful generosity? His response is so grace-less. On the other hand, can we say in all honesty that we've never had occasions when we felt rather like the elder brother? Has he a case to make? Isn't there something unjust in the father's welcome of the prodigal? He's had his share already, and blown it; all the elder brother has had from his share is work, work and more work. We'll come back to the question of forgiveness and justice in a moment. Before we leave the elder brother, we need to hear his father's gentle answer to him. 'All that I have is yours, my son.' Throughout this chapter Jesus is countering the Pharisees' complaint that he is too liberal in the company he keeps, too free with God's grace. There is a particular religious temptation, not exclusive to the Pharisees by any means, which in essence denies the goodness of God. The elder brother's sin - and sin it is, as it cuts him off from grace - is that he also takes the father's generosity for granted. It is there for him, by day and daily, but he will not or cannot see it.

GRACE UPON GRACE

Jesus tells this story that we might see. A central moment in the story occurs when the father clasps his son in warm and welcoming embrace. It is the theme of a wonderful late painting by Rembrandt, full of the painter's evocative use of light and shade, and his own life experience. At the painting's centre is the younger son, kneeling, being received into his father's breast, with his father's hands around his shoulders. Rembrandt has painted the father's hands as different, with the left hand distinctly male, and the right a female hand, as if to say, all the qualities of good parenting, masculine and feminine, of strength and gentleness are found in the father's embrace, which is the embrace of God. Henri Nouwen was captivated by Rembrandt's painting. After long contemplation of it in relation to his own life, he wrote a short book called, *The Return of the Prodigal Son; a Story of Homecoming*. In it he explores the warm and tender mercy of God, which for him overflows both the parable and the painting to become his life's centre. He challenges us to make it the centre of our Christian lives also.

> Perhaps the most radical statement Jesus ever made is: "Be compassionate as your Father is compassionate" (6:36). God's compassion is described by Jesus not simply to show me how willing God is to feel for me, or to forgive me my sins and offer me new life and happiness, but to invite me to become like God and to show the same compassion to others as he is showing to me. If the only meaning in the story were that people sin but God forgives, I could easily begin to think of my sins as a fine occasion for God to show me his forgiveness. There would be no real challenge in such an interpretation. I would resign myself to my weakness

and keep hoping that eventually God would close his eyes to them and let me come home, whatever I did. Such sentimental romanticism is not the message of the Gospels.

What I am called to make true is that whether I am the younger son or the elder son, I am the son of my compassionate father. I am an heir... Indeed, as son and heir I am to become successor. I am destined to step into my Father's place and offer to others the same compassion that he has offered me. The return to the Father is ultimately the challenge to become the Father.

(Henri J M Nouwen 1994, p. 123)

What a challenge that is, to become like the father! It is not the challenge of climbing a tough and forbidding moral staircase. It's the challenge of being so aware of God's goodness, generosity and grace, as we see and hear of it in Jesus, that we become more and more changed into his gracious likeness. Being steeped in this prayer of George MacLeod's can help us on that journey of transformation.

Keep us in the constant sense of Thy presence and forgiveness
that, going our way with gladness,
we may come at last to these things
which eye hath not seen nor ear heard
but which Thou hast prepared
for all them that love Thee
from the foundations of the world.
(George MacLeod 1985, p. 160)

FORGIVENESS...AND UNCONDITIONAL FORGIVENESS

Once we begin exploring forgiveness, we find ourselves in a pool of ever-widening circles. In Luke's gospel it is a central theme from beginning to end, from the story of the healing of the paralysed man in chapter 5:17ff, to the word from the cross, 'Forgive them, Father! They don't know what they are doing' (23:34). The theme travels and builds through the words about love of enemies and not judging others in Chapter 6 through to the story of the prodigal. What is compelling about the prodigal story is that the reality of forgiveness is shown in human, face-to-face terms, in the closeness of family relationships. There's a temptation, perhaps particularly Protestant, to think of the forgiveness of sins as mainly to do with our own personal relationship with God. Through the prodigal story, Jesus makes clear that the forgiveness of sins begins in the way we treat each other.

Forgiveness is about keeping life moving, finding ways to start life again when people have been wronged and relationships damaged by others. Some wrongs are slight, and we all work to build up a pattern of acceptance in our lives, particularly with those closest to us, which simply overcomes daily follies and foibles. How do we deal with being wronged? Words like revenge, restitution, recompense, repentance, spring to mind. We know that to get stuck with revenge is to be condemned to a life of bitterness, but there is a link between forgiveness and justice. In criminal justice circles today there is a new interest in restorative justice. Behind the title is the idea of making offenders face up to the consequences of their offence, perhaps make restitution, perhaps be confronted by their victim. Forgiveness conditional on repentance again implies the restoration of the broken, in our relations with one another and with God. But some things which are broken cannot be restored. And some situations are so awful we say they are 'unforgivable'.

It is in the light of the 'unforgivable' that the post-modern philosopher Jacques Derrida has recently written. 'Forgiveness is not, it should not be, normal, normative, normalising. It should remain exceptional and extraordinary, in the face of the impossible: as if it interrupted the ordinary course of historical temporality' (Derrida 2001, p. 33). These words come from an essay by Derrida on forgiveness. In it he states that the notion of forgiveness has outgrown its roots in the Abrahamic religions and particularly Christianity, to become universally recognised on the world stage. He explores many cases where forgiveness is 'conditional' on restitution, repentance, acceptance of guilt, etc., and he then asks about the possibility of 'unconditional' forgiveness. He says it is possible, not as a norm, but almost as a miracle, the impossible possibility which breaks out to allow reconciliation to take place and life to begin again beyond the cycles of injury, hurt and violence.

Is the welcome of the waiting father in our story an instance of 'unconditional forgiveness?' Certainly the father's welcome precedes the son's confession. Is the word from the cross and indeed the word of the cross, not the supreme example of unconditional forgiveness, grace abounding and undeserving, which bring resurrection? Meanwhile our lives go on. There is the daily practice of accepting and forgiving one another in the light of a generous love, there is the deeper exercise of turning the other cheek and breaking the cycle of violence, and the continuing challenge in Nouwen's words to become, be, like the waiting, welcoming, prodigal Father.

STUDY

BY YOURSELF

Find a copy of Rembrandt's painting 'The Return of the Prodigal Son'. You should be able to find either a small individual copy or a poster size from your local Christian bookshop.

• What do you see in it?

• What do the father's hands say to you?

• How can you make your hands like that?

Use George MacLeod's prayer on page 160 during the next week on a daily basis.

FOR GROUP WORK:

Share in your group your thoughts and feelings about Rembrandt's picture. Begin by sharing in the group what you all see in the painting: then move to ask each other what you feel, and finally, reflect on what you think.

Alternatively, role play the parable of the prodigal, and reflect on the feelings and thoughts aroused.

You might also want to study together Henri Nouwen's short book, *The Return of the Prodigal Son: A Story of Homecoming.*

chapter 24

Shrewdness and faithfulness

LUKE 16:1-19

The Shrewd Manager

Jesus said to his disciples, "There was once a rich man who had a servant who managed his property. The rich man was told that the manager was wasting his master's money, so he called him in and said, 'What is this I hear about you? Hand in a complete account of your handling of my property, because you cannot be my manager any longer.' The servant said to himself, 'My master is going to dismiss me from my job. What shall I do? I am not strong enough to dig ditches, and I am ashamed to beg. Now I know what I will do! Then when my job is gone, I shall have friends who will welcome me in their homes.'

"So he called in all the people who were in debt to his master. He asked the first one, 'How much do you owe my master?' 'One hundred barrels of olive oil,'" he replied. 'Here is your account,' the manager told him; 'sit down and write fifty.' Then he asked another one, 'And you - how much do you owe?' 'A thousand sacks of wheat,' he answered. 'Here is your account,' the manager told him, 'write eight hundred.'

"As a result the master of this dishonest manager praised him for doing such a shrewd thing; because the people of this world are much more shrewd in handling their affairs than the people who belong to the light."

And Jesus went on to say, "And so I tell you; make friends for yourselves with worldly wealth, so that when it gives out, you will be welcomed in the eternal home. Whoever is faithful in small matters will be faithful in large ones; whoever is dishonest in small matters will be dishonest in large ones. If, then, you have not been faithful in handling worldly wealth, how can you be trusted with true wealth? And if you have not been faithful with what belongs to someone else, who will give you what belongs to you?

"No servant can be the slave of two masters; such a servant will hate one and love the other or will be loyal to one and despise the other. You cannot serve both God and money."

Some Sayings of Jesus
(Mt 11:12-13, 5:31-32, Mk 10:11-12)

When the Pharisees heard all this, they sneered at Jesus, because they loved money. Jesus said to them, "You are the ones who make yourselves look right in other people's sight, but God knows your hearts. For the things that are considered of great value by human beings are worth nothing in God's sight.

"The Law of Moses and the writings of the prophets were in effect up to the time of John the Baptist; since then the Good News about the Kingdom of God is being told, and everyone forces their way in. But it is easier for heaven and earth to disappear than for the smallest detail of the Law to be done away with.

"Any man who divorces his wife and marries another woman commits adultery; and the man who marries a divorced woman commits adultery."

AN UNLIKELY HERO

After the grace and glory of the red-blooded love we see in the story of the prodigal, the next picture Luke presents to us has the dominant colour of grey, with a splash of light at the end. We are introduced to the foggy, murky world of the economy of Jesus' time, with its considerable complexities and moral ambiguities. The story Jesus tells, and its interpretation, bristle with difficulties which have long engaged scholars, and to some extent we will have to short-circuit them. It has been hard to interpret because of the difficulty of getting a clear view of the social and economic situation in which Jesus sets the parable's action. The story has long been called, 'The Parable of the Dishonest Steward'; as we will see, it is not only the steward in this story whose practice is distinctly dodgy. The parable begins, 'There was once a rich man...' Every time we hear the word 'rich,' or 'wealthy,' in the gospels we should be on our guard - given the consistent link in the Old Testament between wealth and oppression.

The rich man has a steward, a servant; and part of the problem with the parable is that this servant, the parable's hero, is called 'dishonest' (16:8), a villain. It is the unlikeliness of the hero, who is commended rather than condemned, which perplexes. A surface reading of the story could be that the man's a cheat, who's caught cheating, and who then cheats his way out of the mess his own sins have got him into, or rather cheats his way back into his master's favour. There's more underneath. One first probe beneath the surface suggests that we hear Jesus' words as heavy with irony. We're not meant to take seriously the steward's misuse of money as an example. It's a device to catch our attention and spark our imagination. Gustavo Gutierrez, the father of Liberation Theology writes;

> We can read these verses from the perspective of irony. Jesus' followers must not be austere and certainly not unpleasant preachers of the gospel. We have to be imaginative and able to make friends. No one can deny the pertinence or the validity of the advice, especially if we think of the lack of joy that so many Christians manifest and their constant propensity to criticise and to attract attention. The irony consists in proposing someone who has acted badly as a model of conduct, and irony allows us to take advantage of such behaviour. Irony always makes our outlook more complex and sharper.
>
> (Gutierrez 1997, p. 229)

We could say that Jesus is saying to us obliquely in this story, 'Being a disciple means belonging to me rather than this world. But you live in this world. Don't think yourself either apart from it or above it. Neither ignore nor despise it. Learn from it and learn from people, even so-called bad people. Be alert to the gifts, qualities, humour, lessons that can come even from doubtful characters and grim situations. Be at least as astute as the worldly-wise in your work of making the good news of the Kingdom known. Make friends. But be careful about money.'

Voodoo economics

William R Herzog II has made a close and ground-breaking study of the social setting of the parables. Here is a paraphrase of his interpretation of this parable. The steward in the story is in the classic position of the go-between. He is caught between the peasants - or more probably merchants - to whom he lends, and the master whom he serves, and is loved by neither. In the middle he has to make enough for himself. Jewish society forbade usury, lending at interest, but as the monetary economy grew, rich Pharisees in particular sought to find ways round the Law's prohibition. One way was to reckon loans in terms of goods rather than strict money terms (cf oil and wheat, verses 6 & 7). Another was to employ a steward or financial manager to arrange the loans, do the dirty work, so that strictly speaking, the Pharisee remained untainted. Both these methods operate here.

The story begins with the steward being accused of wasting the money of his master. Interestingly, we are not told whether the accusation had any substance: it may be a malicious rumour intended to weaken the steward's position. If so, it does just that, as the master summons him to reckon things up before his dismissal. The steward recognises that his life is at stake; losing his job means he will fall off his economic and social perch into rough waters where he is unlikely to survive. He calls in the debtors and gets them to rewrite the loans minus the interest he is charging for himself and his master, reckoning this will buy him friendship. The master may have lost in the short term, but he still has his clients, he will find other ways to recoup his profits. The master commends his steward's 'shrewdness'; talk of dismissal is no longer heard. Just for a moment, with the writing off of debts, there's a glimpse of Kingdom economics as the grip of the strong on the weak is loosened!

MONEY MATTERS

This parable occurs in the middle of a section of the gospel where Luke has much to say about wealth and poverty, property and money. Let's apply Gutierrez' suggestion and use this space to do a bit of thinking about money in our lives and our society today. It could be argued that in terms of money, Christians exhibit two sharply contrasting faults; we are either too concerned with money, or not nearly concerned enough. Over-concern means we let economic considerations dictate our decisions. Under-concern probably means that, because we are comfortably enough placed not to worry about money in our own lives, we don't make the effort to see the damaging effect our economic system wreaks in the lives of others, particularly the poor. Jesus' parable here invites us to learn and think deeply about the way money works in our world, to jettison any false innocence about money. His closing words in this section, yet another variation on the theme of the discipleship litany, 'You cannot serve both God and money,' remind us of the insidious way our attachment to wealth skews our whole relationship to God and to the rest of life. So, in concluding this section, here are two quotations, or rather provocations, to get us going in some serious personal and corporate wrestling about the place of money in our lives and in our world. Eugen Drewermann says that our worship of mammon has meant that instead of bringing Christian civilisation to the world we have exported a tawdry capitalism:

> One of the iron pillars of our lethargy, which Jesus wanted to shake, was our acceptance of the fact that human relationships are corrupted by mere money. Our entire society is based upon money. The administration of our society in the form of politics is based upon money. Most human relationships are based on money. No, please don't contradict me. We in the West believe in God and have been Christians for fifteen hundred years, more or less. So then explain to me how it is possible that whenever we come in contact with another culture, it learns not about God but about crass materialism. The people learn that there is no value, religious, human, or natural, except money. Obviously the only 'truth' we export is our knowledge of how to destroy nature and humanity and abuse God in the name of money. We cannot destroy God, but we can and do defame and ideologize him.
> (Drewermann 1991, p. 17)

Philip Esler says that nearer home, we have so individualised and domesticated Luke's teaching on wealth that we no longer have a gospel for the poor:

The ingrained disregard among scholars for the social and economic setting of Luke-Acts, and their corresponding enthusiasm for its alleged spiritual and individualistic approach to salvation, originate in a clear middle-class bias. Generations of scholars, in their seminaries and universities, have been so successful in making Luke's message on possessions palatable for bourgeois tastes that its genuinely radical nature has rarely been noticed. Having succeeded in spiritualising the good news announced by the Lucan Jesus to the destitute, the European scholarly establishment should not be too surprised that during the last 150 years the working classes have abandoned the leading Christian denominations in the West in their droves.
(Esler 1987, p. 170)

SOME SAYINGS

Luke reports that when the Pharisees heard what Jesus had been saying, they sneered at his teaching. This may well suggest that they were in part the target of the preceding parable. Once again Jesus contrasts the outward show we put on for the benefit of others with God's seeing into the heart. He continues by contrasting the validity of the Law and prophets up to the time of the coming of the new order, in which the proclamation of the Kingdom opens the gates to all. Jesus goes on to say that it's easier for heaven and earth to disappear than for the merest detail of the Law to be done away with (16:17). Interpreting this verse is difficult. Jesus has just said the Kingdom supersedes the Law. He could be saying the coming Kingdom doesn't put aside the basic thrust of the Law. Certainly in the next verse about divorce, he interprets the Law with full rigour. Another interpretation is possible. Jesus' saying that not even the tiniest detail of the Law can be changed can be read as a statement of weary irony against those who would block the open door of the Kingdom with nit-picking legalism.

The section ends with a further tough word. It contains the only direct statement in Luke on marriage and divorce; a statement also found in Mark 10:11-12 and Matthew 5:31-32 and 19:9 in a wider context. Jewish Law at the time of Jesus was stringent in the prohibition of divorce by women, but increasingly lax in the exceptions allowed for men. What Jesus does here is to level the playing field and insist on the same standards for both men and women. Once again Jesus asks for faithfulness and awareness in our relationships with one another as in our dealings with money. Sex and money always offer temptations to cheat.

STUDY

BY YOURSELF

Two disciplines for the next month:

• Read the financial pages of your newspaper every day

• Keep a complete record of everything you spend, and look at where your money goes in the light of the gospel. Maybe you've already begun with the exercise at the end of Chapter 20.

FOR GROUP WORK

'Most human relationships are based on money' (page 166). If members of the group have kept a financial diary then it will be very profitable to talk together about what you have learnt.

chapter 25

The blindness Of riches

LUKE 16:19-31

The Rich Man and Lazarus

"There was once a rich man who dressed in the most expensive clothes and lived in great luxury every day. There was also a poor man named Lazarus, covered with sores, who used to be brought to the rich man's door, hoping to eat the bits of food that fell from the rich man's table. Even the dogs would come and lick his sores.

"The poor man died and was carried by the angels to sit beside Abraham at the feast in heaven. The rich man died and was buried, and in Hades, where he was in great pain, he looked up and saw Abraham, far away, with Lazarus at his side. So he called out, 'Father Abraham! Take pity on me, and send Lazarus to dip his finger in some water and cool my tongue, because I am in great pain in this fire!'

"But Abraham said, 'Remember, my son, that in your lifetime you were given all the good things, while Lazarus got all the bad things. But now he is enjoying himself here, while you are in pain. Besides all that, there is a deep pit lying between us, so that those who want to cross over from here to you cannot do so, nor can anyone cross over from to us from where you are.' The rich man said, 'Then I beg you, father Abraham, send Lazarus to my father's house, where I have five brothers. Let him go and warn them so that they, at least, will not come to this place of pain.'

"Abraham said, 'Your brothers have Moses and the prophets to warn them; your brothers should listen to what they say.' The rich man answered, 'That is not enough, father Abraham! But if someone were to rise from death and go to them, then they would turn from their sins.' But Abraham said, 'If they will not listen to Moses and the prophets, they will not be convinced, even if someone were to rise from death.'"

OUCH!

The next room in Luke's picture gallery we'd prefer to hurry through. We are confronted by another parable which paints two vivid, shocking pictures, the first heart-rending and the second frightening. Again the story and the pictures are about wealth and poverty. We will not hasten past, for the pictures Jesus paints compel us to linger agonisingly and attentively before the pain and shock they invoke - and the questions they raise, then and now.

THEN, AT THE RICH MAN'S GATE

Jesus tells the parable of the rich man and Lazarus. It is sometimes called the story of Dives and Lazarus, but in the original the rich man has no name - Dives is simply the Latin word for 'rich'. The significant naming of the destitute beggar immediately alerts us. There are some strange and surprising things going on in this story; the conventional wisdom of the time is about to be summarily challenged. The parable uses a basic theme not uncommon in folk tales in Jesus' society, the theme of the reversal of fortunes in the afterlife. Jesus takes the familiar theme and produces a story of subversive power. Because the story is in two halves, with two distinct pictures of life on earth and life hereafter, many commentators have tended to find separate meanings in each half and to concentrate theologically on the second half, with the rich man's conversation with Abraham. We will look at the parable as a whole, arguing that what Jesus joined together, commentators should not pull asunder.

The story begins with our introduction to a rich man, clothed in garments of the richest of dyes and the finest of linen, who lived in extravagant and ostentatious luxury each and every day. Socially and economically secure, he was perched at the top of the pile and he shows it. He belonged to the small number of the privileged elite; possibly a Sadducee, whose belief-system taught that the possession of worldly wealth was a sign of God's favour. In stark contrast, Lazarus, living in the extremity of poverty, was dumped daily at the gate of this man's house, hoping against hope to get the scraps from the rich man's table. The story belongs long before our present disposable society, with wipes for every occasion; the diners at the table of the rich man would clean their hands on pieces of bread and then cast the bread aside. It was these swept up remnants from the floor which Lazarus hoped for, when they got to the gate as garbage. Waiting for the same scraps were the despised and unclean street dogs. It sounds like they got to the scraps first. Lazarus, lower than a dog in his humiliation, lay helpless as they licked the sores on his body, increasing the infection. How did Lazarus get to be the way he was? A nexus of circumstances in that society meant that life was very precarious for the poor. Too many men were chasing too little work. These circumstances suited the rich as wages were depressed, but lack of work meant hunger, followed by illness, leading to only one end. It is no surprise to learn of Lazarus' demise.

THEN, FROM THE BOSOM OF ABRAHAM

Scene two. Not only does Lazarus die, he is followed by the rich man whose burial, an important propriety, is noted - while that of Lazarus goes unremarked. Lazarus is borne by angels to sit with Abraham at the heavenly feast. Note that no moral virtue has been ascribed to Lazarus, it is simply his poverty and need that carries him to the place of honour and care at the bosom of Abraham. The rich man is found in Hades, the interim place of the dead, and in torment. Hades is not Hell as it developed in later Christian thought; there was still a way out. He looks up and sees, in the far distance, Abraham with Lazarus beside him. Old habits die hard. He addresses Abraham in terms of familiar kinship, 'Father Abraham!' He presumes they share a common faith and status: Abraham too was a rich man. He also presumes on the appropriateness of Lazarus being his errand-boy, his servant, who will bring him cooling water to drink. It is interesting that the rich man knows the beggar's name implying some kind of relationship. What is clear is that there has never been any recognition from the rich man of Lazarus as a person. The rich man doesn't personally do any harm or violence to the beggar at his gate; his 'sin' is that of blindness, neglect and inertia. It is the system in which he lives in unquestioning privilege which does Lazarus such cruelty.

Abraham's reply is terse and to the point. 'You've had your good times, my son, now it's Lazarus' turn.' The rich man tries again, pleading now. 'Send Lazarus - just the messenger again - to warn my five brothers so that they may escape this pain.' We can recognise some humanity in the rich man's plea but there is not so much as a glimmer of his breaking out of the bonds of kinship and privilege. Abraham's response is to query why the brothers should need a special messenger; their obligations are made clear in the words of Moses and the prophets. At issue in this answer is the question of how to interpret the Hebrew scriptures. In the Law of Moses and the prophetic tradition, there is a clear obligation of outgoing care for the poor, for 'the needy at the gate' (Amos 5:12 NRSV). The rich man's in-circle preferred to interpret the Law in terms of its formal and ritualistic obligations, and to find justification in the scriptures for their possession of wealth as a sign of blessing from God.

The rich man makes one final attempt to move Abraham. 'That's not enough. If someone goes to them from the dead, then they will repent' (16:30). His request is for the spirit of Lazarus once more to be sent as the errand boy to the brothers. Again he wants special treatment, a special sign; he's so used to privilege, that even in his present state he is blind to its abusive and exclusive nature. Not a word has the rich man spoken of concern, pity or repentance for Lazarus' former state. Even Abraham has failed to reach him, with what Herzog calls his attempts at 'the pedagogy of the oppressor' (Herzog 1994, p. 123). While Abraham was rich, he was thoroughly practiced in the grace of hospitality.

Once again Jesus has thoroughly upset the apple-cart of conventional thinking. He has again set generosity of spirit and purse against an enclosed ritualised religion. He also unravels a vital loose thread. If wealth and riches are *not* the sign of God's blessing, which they clearly are not, what do they mean, and what should our attitude to them be? A whole new way of looking at the world and its people becomes possible. The song Luke's gospel has been singing, from Mary's Magnificat (1:46-55) through the Nazareth Manifesto (4:18-21), comes to full voice.

Now

Questions of wealth, its possession and distribution, remain central both for our lives as Christians and our lives as citizens and fellow members of one small planet. Jesus reminds us here, with great force, that while many of the answers to these questions are structural, involving the way our society and our world organises itself, they are not abstract. They involve real people. The rich man's 'sin' is blindness, and he is blind because he has a view of his world which separates the privileged wealthy from the rest. He simply doesn't 'see' Lazarus as his brother under God. Change in our world, which we work for as part and parcel of our Christian discipleship, begins when we start to see poor people in the reality of the humanity they share with us. Duncan Forrester tells the following story;

> Just a century or so ago, a real-life Dr Dives, Benjamin Jowett, Master of Balliol, used to say to the brightest and best of his students, 'Go and find your friends among the poor.' And they went to the East End of London, and the slums of Manchester and of Glasgow, and they worked in settlements and slum parishes, they established youth clubs, they worked with unemployed people, they helped provide medical care for malnourished children with rickets, they taught in adult education classes. They got to know poor people...
>
> And then, some decades after Jowett, another Master of Balliol, Edward Caird, called three students, three of the brightest and best, and said to them, 'Go to the East End of London, and find out what poverty is, and why in Britain there is so much grinding poverty alongside great wealth, and work out what can be done about it.' The three young men were Richard Tawney, William Beveridge and William Temple. They went to the East End and they worked there. They were appalled by what they found. Their consciences were pricked by poverty, visible, audible, smellable. They grew angry and confused as they began in a little way to share the pain of poverty.
>
> They realized now that there were great *structural* obstacles to friendship. By going out to Lazarus they saw that they must put the poor at the heart of their concern, that they must speak for the dumb, that they must work to make Britain a place where friendship was possible, the forces that corrode, corrupt or impede friendship removed. They went through a kind of intellectual and emotional conversion.
> (Forrester 2001, p. 234)

Tawney, Beveridge and Temple contributed hugely to the inception of the Welfare State in Britain, through their thinking in church and state. They began by going on a journey to be with the poor, see with their eyes, listen to their voice. The road remains vital for discipleship, and those who travel it are surprised not just by pain, but by courage, resilience and joy. Yes! Luke's word: joy.

BEYOND ANGER

How we read stories, and how we see people and situations, depends on where we start from. If this story is read from the perspective of the poor, it could produce a wave of justifiable anger against the entrenched privileged presumptions of the rich. How might this story 'read' for example to a Palestinian Christian living in a refugee camp for a lifetime, who sees his family's grim situation as the direct consequence of the blind exercise of power by the contemporary sons of Abraham? How does he escape a bitterness of soul which can so easily result in destructive violence? How do any of us, involved in a struggle for justice, avoid demonising and dehumanising those on the opposite side of the argument? In a paper written for St George's College Jerusalem and subtitled, 'How can we cry for justice without inciting hatred?' John Barclay makes a persuasive case for the importance of reading the gospel as a whole. He contrasts this parable with its insistent cry for justice with the parable of the Good Samaritan (10:25-37), with its provocation to get beyond our stereotypes and animosities to the shared humanity of the 'neighbour'. He concludes:

> Neither parable is sufficient in itself. The Parable of the Rich Man and Lazarus displays Jesus' unerring and unwavering critique of the inequalities and oppressions which the wealthy and the comfortable prefer not to see, let alone address. But its story of reversal could play rather easily into an ethic of revenge in which the victims eventually win, but only by creating new victims on the other side. The Parable of the Good Samaritan may help us see ways of breaking down the dangerous barricades which our cries for justice can unwittingly support, but it does not issue a strong protest against the banditry and brutality which left the man dying at the roadside in the first place. We need the two together, to complement each other, to awaken our outrage, if awakening it needs, at the cruelties and barbarities which destroy the lives and ruin the hopes of ordinary people, and to steer our minds, our speech and our actions away from the simple stereotyping into which our campaigns for justice can lead. ...I hope they can motivate us to cry for justice - to cry loudly and effectively, to insist on letting the poorest and the weakest hold us answerable to our religious truths, to refuse to let injustice pass unnoticed and unchallenged - but also to keep our cries from adopting the tones of hatred, and to attempt ever new ways of deconstructing human boundaries and discovering means of turning enemies into friends.
> (John Barclay 2003, p. 9)

STUDY

BY YOURSELF

How we read stories and experience life depends on the place we start from. The stories of Tawney, Beveridge and Temple tell of a journey of three privileged people taking time and effort to see the world through the eyes of the poor. Reflect on how you could 'see' better from the perspective of the other. In recent years Church Action on Poverty has invited us to spend the six weeks of Lent living on the National Minimum Wage. Would you take up that challenge?

FOR GROUP WORK

In the light of the two parables, the Good Samaritan and Dives and Lazarus, John Barclay lists three gospel tasks for Christians and churches. Look at the parables again. Here are the tasks:

• to refuse to let injustice pass unnoticed and unchallenged,

• to insist on letting the poorest and the weakest hold us answerable to our religious truths,

• to attempt ever new ways of deconstructing human boundaries and discovering means of turning enemies into friends.

As a way into these tasks, reflect on these questions:
1) What injustices do you want to raise?

2) How do we ensure that voices of the poor and the weak are heard?

3) How do we ensure that our campaigns for justice do not stereotype and demonise the rich, but offer them a challenge to widen horizons?
Discuss the ways your church seeks to take up these tasks, and what more together you could do.

chapter 26

More teaching

LUKE 17

Sin

(Mt 18:6-7, 21-22; Mk 9:42)

Jesus said to his disciples, "Things that make people fall into sin are bound to happen, but how terrible for the one who makes them happen! It would be better for him if a large millstone were tied round his neck and he were thrown into the sea than for him to cause one of these little ones to sin. So watch what you do!

"If your brother sins, rebuke him, and if he repents, forgive him. If he sins against you seven times in one day, and each time he comes to you saying, 'I repent,' you must forgive him."

Faith

The apostles said to the Lord, "Make our faith greater."

The Lord answered, "If you had faith as big as a mustard seed, you could say to this mulberry tree, 'Pull yourself up by the roots and plant yourself in the sea!' and it would obey you.

A Servant's Duty

"Suppose one of you has a servant who is ploughing or looking after the sheep. When he comes in from the field, do you tell him to hurry and eat his meal? Of course not! Instead you say to him, 'Get my supper ready, then put on your apron and wait on me while I eat and drink; after that you may have your meal.' The servant does not deserve thanks for obeying orders, does he? It is the same with you; when you have done all that you have been told to do, say, 'We are ordinary servants; we have only done our duty.'"

Jesus Heals Ten Men

As Jesus made his way to Jerusalem, he went along the border between Samaria and Galilee. He was going into a village when he was met by ten men suffering from a dreaded skin disease. They stood at a distance and shouted, "Jesus! Master! Take pity on us!"

Jesus saw them and said to them, "Go and let the priests examine you."

On the way they were made clean. When one of them saw that he was healed, he came back, praising God in a loud voice. He threw himself to the ground at Jesus' feet and thanked him. The man was a Samaritan. Jesus said, "There were ten men who were healed; where are the other nine? Why is this foreigner the only one who came back to give thanks to God?" And Jesus said to him, "Get up and go; your faith has made you well."

The Coming of the Kingdom
(Mt 24:23-28, 37-41)

Some Pharisees asked Jesus when the Kingdom of God would come. His answer was, "The Kingdom of God does not come in such a way as to be seen. No one will say, 'Look, here it is!' or 'There it is!' because the Kingdom of God is within you."

Then he said to the disciples, "The time will come when you will wish you could see one of the days of the Son of Man, but you will not see it. There will be those who will say to you, 'Look, over there!' or, 'Look, over here!' But don't go out looking for it. As the lightning flashes across the sky and lights it up from one side to the other, so will the Son of Man be in his day. But first he must suffer much and be rejected by the people of his day. As it was in the time of Noah so shall it be in the days of the Son of Man. Everybody kept on eating and drinking, and men and women married, up to the very day Noah went into the boat and the flood came and killed the lot of them. It will be as it was in the time of Lot. Everybody kept on eating and drinking, buying and selling, planting and building. On the day Lot left Sodom, fire and sulphur rained down from heaven and killed them all. That is how it will be on the day when the Son of Man is revealed.

"On that day someone who is on the roof of his house must not go down into the house to get any belongings; in the same way anyone who is out in the field must not go back to the house. Remember Lot's wife! Whoever tries to save his own life will lose it; whoever loses his life will save it. On that night, I tell you, there will be two people sleeping in the same bed: one will be taken away, the other will be left behind. Two women will be grinding corn together: one will be taken away, the other will be left behind."

The disciples asked him, "Where, Lord?"

Jesus answered, "Wherever there is a dead body, the vultures will gather.'"

CHILD PROTECTION
John Knox called Calvin's church in Geneva, 'the most perfect school of Christ since the time of the apostles'. 'Most perfect' it may have seemed to Knox; completely perfect it wasn't, for, as Jesus reminds us here, all our Christian communities are made up of fallible sinners, and things will go wrong. We now come to a short section dealing with the ongoing life of the faith community. It begins with a stern warning to be careful of what we do and say, taking particular care that no actions of ours will cause 'the little ones' to stumble or sin. The 'little ones' may well mean the unprotected children; we can take these words as a serious reminder to have special concern for all who are in any way vulnerable (17:1-3a).

AGAIN AND AGAIN
Vulnerability within the faith community is not to be seen simply as a handicap, it is also a grace. Jesus continues by offering guidance on what we should do when a member of the community wrongs us. We are to deal with the offender with open vulnerability. 'Confront them, let them know their fault, and if they turn from it, forgive them. And if it happens again and again and again, and they keep trying to turn, keep forgiving!' Again we see forgiving acceptance lying at the very heart of the new order.

THE TINY SEED AND THE FLYING TREE
'Lord, increase our faith.' This prayer, first offered by the disciples (17:5), is on our lips daily. Jesus offers in response to the request not a direct answer, but a vivid hyperbolic parable. 'Even if your faith is no bigger than a tiny mustard seed, you could tell the mulberry or sycamore tree, known for its deep-rootedness, to uproot itself and be planted in the midst of the sea.' Faith does not baulk at the impossible; there is nothing that faith cannot do.

'WE HAVE ONLY DONE OUR DUTY'
Jesus continues with another short parable reminding disciples that they are not greater than their Lord. The image of the servant in a master/slave relationship deserving no thanks or special treatment, but simply more work, may strike us as harsh. Is Jesus speaking pointedly to the disciples, warning them against seeking any special place of honour or privilege in the new community? Certainly these words can be read as another encouragement of the grace of humility.

The servant's life is defined by his relationship to his master. Symbolically we are reminded that all disciples live by faith, as Brian Wren's hymn says:

> Great God, in Christ you call our name
> and then receive us as your own
> not through some merit, right or claim
> but by your gracious love alone.
> We strain to glimpse your mercy seat
> and find you kneeling at our feet.
> (Brian Wren, in *Common Ground* 1998, no. 45)

The final two lines of the hymn verse are vital. We are happy to find our vocation in servanthood because, as Jesus himself will remind us at a key moment in the Passion narrative, 'I am come among you as one who serves' (22:27). We are the servants of a servant Lord.

The grateful Samaritan

We come to the last-but-one healing story in Luke's narrative. It's some time since the early days of the ministry in Galilee, when healings came thick and fast as a central part of Jesus' work of liberation; therefore it's appropriate to remember that in Luke's gospel, works of healing, salvation, liberation and freedom are closely related and interrelated. There is no forced and fallacious distinction between the sacred and the secular, the spiritual and the physical. Jesus brings freedom in a host of different ways, each appropriate to the person and the situation he encounters.

Here he is met, on the borderlands between Samaria and Galilee, by a group of ten men united in their affliction of leprosy. One of them is a Samaritan. As we have already seen, Jews and Samaritans did not associate with one another. In this group, the common affliction of leprosy had already overcome the ancient and deep-seated enmity which kept Jew and Samaritan apart. Properly, the lepers keep their distance from Jesus as they cry for his help. Interestingly, they call him 'Master', a title which, apart from this instance, is used throughout the gospel only by the disciples. Jesus sends them to the priests for examination and on their way they discover themselves to be healed, 'clean'.

One of them returns to Jesus, ecstatic with joy and praise, throwing himself at Jesus' feet in thanksgiving. It is the Samaritan. Jesus pointedly asks, 'Where are the other nine? Why is it the foreigner, the outsider, the enemy who has seen and given thanks for this wonder God has done?' (17:18) Once more healing grace overflows the bounds, and it's the outsider who responds. Jesus' final word is, 'Get up, go on with your journey, your life: your faith has saved you, cleansed you, made you well.'

'The Kingdom is among you.'

The two final sections of this patchwork of a chapter are linked by the theme of the coming Kingdom of God. Some Pharisees come to ask Jesus about when the Kingdom of God would come (17:20). Jesus tells them not to look for dramatic, unambiguous signs, for the Kingdom is a hidden presence, 'among you', or better still, 'within your grasp'. The reference is to Jesus' own ministry with its signs of the Kingdom (4:18-21, 7:21-23).

Coming crisis

Jesus moves from speaking with the Pharisees to a conversation with his disciples. The subject is the related one of the coming of the Son of Man. Luke appears to have put a speech here into the mouth of Jesus from a number of sources, and the lines of thought are difficult to follow. Such difficulties have not prevented something of a modern growth industry of books predicting judgement day and the end of the world, an industry about as biblically warranted or genuinely efficacious in predicting the future as reading teacups. In the New Testament world while there was a strong expectation that the final judgement was imminent, there are equally strong warnings about trying to predict the when and where of its coming. That lies in God's hands alone.

We can trace in these verses the story of Jesus' own purpose as the agent of God's judgement. 'The Kingdom of God is within you' (17:21) can refer to Jesus' own present ministry. 'But first the Son of Man must suffer much and be rejected by the people in his day' (17:25), points to the looming cross. The coming day of judgement is found in the verses which peak with 'That is how the Son of Man is revealed' (17:30).

These verses can also be read as yet another warning to Jesus' people to turn from their present ways in order to avoid disaster. His words are thoroughly in the traditions of the Old Testament prophets who see God's purposes being worked out in the social and political realities of their time. The calamities in Jerusalem in 70CE hang over this passage. Once again Jesus repeats his warning, that for people to continue in their present melancholy way of heedless disobedience can only mean calamity, which will strike out of the blue.

The chapter ends with the disciples asking Jesus a very similar question to that of the Pharisees in 17:20. The Pharisees ask, 'When will the Kingdom come?' The disciples' query is, 'Where will the Son of Man be revealed?' Jesus' answer (17:37) is thoroughly enigmatic. Neither Pharisees nor disciples get an answer, unless to say, 'It's the wrong question. Just be alert, and be faithful.'

STUDY

BY YOURSELF
'Lord, increase our faith.' People always think they have too little faith. However we have all known moments and people that have given much-needed faith to us. What people and events have increased your life of faith, stretched the boundaries for you, confirmed or broadened your understanding, challenged or deepened your commitment? Give thanks for them, and ponder how you can build on what they have given you.

chapter 27

Peasants, Pharisees and publicans

LUKE 18:1-14

The Parable of the Widow and the Judge

Then Jesus told his disciples a parable to teach them that they should always pray and never become discouraged. "In a certain town there was a judge who neither feared God nor respected people. And there was a widow in the same town who kept coming to him and pleading for her rights, saying, 'Help me against my opponent!' For a long time the judge refused to act, but at last he said to himself, 'Even though I don't fear God or respect people, yet because of all the trouble this widow is giving me, I will see to it that she gets her rights. If I don't, she will keep on coming and finally wear me out!'"

And the Lord continued, "Listen to what that corrupt judge said. Now, will God not judge in favour of his own people who cry to him day and night for help? Will he be slow to help them? I tell you, he will judge in their favour and do it quickly. But will the Son of Man find faith on earth when he comes?"

The Parable of the Pharisee and the Tax Collector

Jesus also told this parable to people who were sure of their own goodness and despised everybody else. "Once there were two men who went up to the Temple to pray: one was a Pharisee, the other a tax collector.

"The Pharisee stood apart by himself and prayed, 'I thank you, God, that I am not greedy, dishonest, or an adulterer, like everybody else. I thank you that I am not like that tax collector over there. I fast two days a week, and I give you a tenth of all my income.'

"But the tax collector stood at a distance and would not even raise his face to heaven, but beat on his breast and said, 'God, have pity on me, a sinner!' I tell you," said Jesus, "the tax collector, and not the Pharisee, was in the right with God when he went home. For all who make themselves great will be humbled, and all who humble themselves will be made great."

WHICH CONTEXT?

We move to two more picture-stories, linked by Luke's assertion that they are about prayer. Luke says that the first story, the parable of the widow and the judge, is told to encourage disciples to be persistent in prayer and as such it has much in common with the parable of the friend at midnight (11:5-8). We can quickly see that this parable is being addressed to two groups: the original disciples, and Luke's young church half a century later. William R Herzog II has done further detective work, and he puts forward the theory that the kernel of the story Luke uses to encourage our prayer life originally had a different context and meaning.

Like many commentators he is struck and puzzled by the unlikeliness of the corrupt judge as the parable's hero figure. While many argue that this story works by contrast - that it's the antithesis between the unjust judge and the just God which gives it its point - Herzog theorises that this interpretation diverts attention away from the story's real heroine - the widow. The argument is summarised as follows.

THE CORE STORY

We have already seen that widows were in a particularly vulnerable situation in the society of these times. Their vulnerability was recognised in Jewish law and scriptures, which both gave certain rights to widows and put them under society's protection. Then as now it has to be recognised, however, that there was a considerable gap between the ideal workings of the law and the way it was administered in practice at the local ground level. There is a strong possibility that the judge who neither feared God nor respected public opinion was open to being bought for the right price; such practices were not unusual. We've already seen in the gospel the way in which the Law, despite its stress on protection of the poor, had become re-interpreted as a ritual bulwark for the rich and respectable.

The widow in the story is even more vulnerable than most widows, in that she appears to have no male relative who can speak for her, as would be the usual custom. She is in dispute with her husband's family who have either failed to pay her due maintenance from his estate or refused her claim for *ketubah*, the amount her husband had pledged her in the event of his death. Ideally her case should be heard by a tribunal of three judges; but frequently at small town level, cases were heard by only one judge, which made him the more open to chicanery and corruption. In this case the judge, refuses to hear the woman's plea for a hearing and for justice, probably because he is still negotiating with her opponents over the size of his cut from the proceedings. But the woman, who by all convention should remain silent, is doggedly public and persistent. 'In the midst of all the male voices heard at the gate, a domain where men alone are in control, one woman's voice continually cries for justice' (Herzog 1994, p. 229). She challenges the prevailing and dominant system with its deals behind closed doors, and its nods and winks that 'this is just the way of the world, isn't it?' She calls him to be the judge he is meant to be, and administer the Law in the interests of justice. In the end he submits; it's not worth the trouble to stall her any longer, there will be other easier cases coming his way. What the woman has done is to open up a crack in the system, to challenge the abuse of power and strike a blow for freedom, by having the courage to step out of the silent and subordinate social role expected of her. We can almost hear the woman's fellow townsfolk muttering about this shameless pest harassing the judge. But she will not be silenced, she is the heroine; in the light of the rest of Luke's gospel, we can well see why Jesus would tell this story in her honour. We can now hear this story as one with two calls for persistence: to persevere in prayer on the long road of discipleship and to be as persistent and persevering in unmasking the pretensions and corruptions of power, which often operate under a veneer of legality, in the long road for justice.

'To think again'

We come to the second parable which Jesus locates in the Jerusalem Temple. Luke's story of Jesus will soon take us into Jerusalem as it moves to its climax, and much of the action will be centred around the Temple. We will come to see the Temple and all it stands for as hugely ambiguous. On the one hand it was the epicentre of the devotion and hope of the nation, the supreme holy place of pilgrimage and prayer. It was also a bastion of privilege, a source of great wealth to a small urban elite whose wealth was drawn from their much poorer fellows (19:45-7). That wealth was generated through the Temple's sacrificial system, built on the foundation of the elaborate purity regulations which were in the hands of scribe and Pharisee. These regulations were so demanding that the mass of poor people were unable to fulfil them. The result was that the poor, the *am h'aretz*, the people of the land, were despised and disempowered by an elite establishment of pious wealthy, in a classic case of blaming the victim. William Herzog sees this story as the tale of not one, but two toll collectors, arguing that the regulations of the authorities had set up a highly lucrative and effective system of gathering taxes for the Temple from the poor (Herzog 1994, p. 173ff).

We turn to watch the two men come to pray. It is a story of contrasts, almost of a contest, initiated by the Pharisee. He stands apart to pray and lifts his voice aloud. The hearers would identify good things in his prayer, his giving of thanks, his declaration of personal rectitude, his committed fasting, exceeding the Law's demands, and his honouring of the tithe - all expected of the 'good' Pharisee. We know instinctively where it all goes wrong. It's at that moment when he says, 'I am not greedy, dishonest, or an adulterer, *like everybody else*,' and it goes from bad to worse when he further personalises his pious superiority with the words, 'I thank you *that I am not like that tax collector over there*' (18:11). Before God, 'everybody else' is irrelevant, and the cheap attack on the tax collector reveals an arrogant meanness of spirit, from which, however, we are not immune.

The tax collector also stands apart, but in a posture of distress and humility. As the servant of a despised system, and a member of a group of workers seen by the people as cheats and extortioners, he is an easy target for the Pharisee's public denunciation. He doesn't endure it in silence. Beating on his breast, he makes a brief and loud cry, 'God, be merciful to me, a sinner!' He throws himself on the mercy of God, begging God to make the atonement for his sins that he is unable to make.

SURPRISE, SURPRISE

There is an unlikely parallel with the previous parable; the tax collector, like the widow, does not suffer the response from 'authority' in silence. In this instance the tax collector cries out directly to the high court of heaven. The twist in the parable's tale is that Jesus says that it is the tax collector, rather than the Pharisee who goes home 'justified', reconciled with God. Once more expectations are radically and rudely overturned. Luke introduces this parable as addressed to the self-righteous who thought themselves above everybody else. We can certainly 'hear' it as yet another invitation to humility and an ever apt reminder that in our prayers we stand alone before the God who knows our hearts; self-justification is just about the most crass attitude we could take. Before God there is no hierarchy of piety, it is self-examination, not self-justification we bring. Remember 'Holy Willie's Prayer'.

We can also 'hear' this parable as an illustration of the words of the Magnificat, 'he has brought down the mighty from their seats, and has lifted up the lowly' (1:52). The Pharisee and the tax collector represent two groups in society; the Pharisee standing for the self-satisfied, self-appointed guardians of public standards and order, the tax collector the despised poor. Before the high court of heaven, the tables are overturned. Yet another version of the discipleship/reversal litany ends the parable. 'For all who make themselves great will be humbled, and all who humble themselves will be made great' (18:14b). These words end the parable; they don't close the questions, which now pile up thick and fast.

> Jesus' final comment, "this man went down to his home justified" (18:14a)... unleashes a barrage of questions. On what basis? By whose word? How could God speak outside of official channels? If the toll collector is justified by a mercy as unpredictable and outrageous as this, then who could not be included? And if toll collectors and sinners are justified in the very precinct of the Temple itself, then how is one to evaluate a Temple priesthood and its scribes who declare that nothing of the kind is possible?
> (Herzog 1994, p. 192-3)

Remember, the entry into Jerusalem and the challenge to the Temple are imminent. It becomes more and more apparent that the ministry of Jesus is a threat to the established order and the status quo in many different ways. He is a multiple thorn in the flesh. The cross looms large.

STUDY

BY YOURSELF

The parable of the woman and the judge has as its heroine the unnamed, unknown woman who fights for justice in an everyday situation of corruption. Make for yourself a list of women and men who have 'persisted' in the struggle for mercy and justice in their world, against the odds. Think not just about important historical figures, but about people today in your local community and your own experience. Their lives have been their prayer. What can you take from their lives to inspire your prayer and action?

FOR GROUP WORK

The parable of the woman and the judge asks about our experience of those who continue to struggle for justice and mercy. Share your reflections.

chapter 28

ThOse whO hAven't And thOse whO hAve

LUKE 18:15-43

Jesus Blesses Little Children
(Mt 19:13-15, Mk 10:13-16)

Some people brought their babies to Jesus for him to place his hands on them. The disciples saw them and scolded them for doing so, but Jesus called the children to him and said, "Let the children come to me and do not stop them, because the Kingdom of God belongs to such as these. Remember this! Whoever does not receive the Kingdom of God like a child will never enter it."

The Rich Man
(Mt 19:16-30, Mk 10:17-31)

A Jewish leader asked Jesus, "Good Teacher, what must I do to receive eternal life?"

"Why do you call me good?" Jesus asked him. "No one is good except God alone. You know the commandments: 'Do not commit adultery; do not commit murder; do not steal; do not accuse anyone falsely; respect your father and your mother.'"

The man replied, "Ever since I was young, I have obeyed all these commandments."

When Jesus heard this, he said to him, "There is still one more thing you need to do. Sell all you have and give the money to the poor, and you will have riches in heaven; then come and follow me." But when the man heard this, he became very sad, because he was very rich.

Jesus saw that he was sad and said, "How hard it is for rich people to enter the

Kingdom of God! It is much harder for a rich person to enter the Kingdom of God than for a camel to go through the eye of a needle."

The people who heard him asked, "Who, then, can be saved?"

Jesus answered, "What is humanly impossible is possible for God."

Then Peter said, "Look! We have left our homes to follow you."

"Yes," Jesus said to them, "and I assure you that anyone who leaves home or wife or brothers or parents or children for the sake of the Kingdom of God will receive much more in this present age and eternal life in the age to come."

Jesus Speaks a Third Time about his Death
(Mt 20:17-19, Mk 10:32-34)

Jesus took the twelve disciples aside and said to them, "Listen! We are going to Jerusalem where everything the prophets wrote about the Son of Man will come true. He will be handed over to the Gentiles, who will mock him, insult him, and spit on him. They will whip him and kill him, but three days later he will rise to life."

But the disciples did not understand any of these things; the meaning of the words was hidden from them, and they did not know what Jesus was talking about.

Jesus Heals a Blind Beggar
(Mt 20:29-34, Mk 10:46-52)

As Jesus was coming near Jericho, there was a blind man sitting by the road, begging. When he heard the crowd passing by, he asked, "What is this?"

"Jesus of Nazareth is passing by," they told him.

He cried out, "Jesus! Son of David! Take pity on me!"

The people in front scolded him and told him to be quiet. But he shouted even more loudly, "Son of David! Take pity on me!"

So Jesus stopped and ordered the blind man to be brought to him. When he came near, Jesus asked him, "What do you want me to do for you?"

"Sir," he answered, "I want to see again."

Jesus said to him, "Then see! Your faith has made you well."

At once he was able to see, and he followed Jesus, giving thanks to God. When the crowd saw it, they all praised God.

LIKE A CHILD

In the preceding series of parables, wealth and poverty, power and powerlessness, have been recurring themes. In this first section after Luke rejoins Mark, these themes continue. The section begins with one of the most familiar of all pictures from the life of Jesus. Some very young children, mere babes, are brought to Jesus for blessing. The babes in arms stand as a metaphor for those with nothing, humanity at its most vulnerable and defenceless. The disciples' dismissive attitude to the mothers who brought them would be typical of adults of Jesus' time. It is not the attitude of Jesus. He says that he warmly welcomes these little ones. 'Don't ever stop them,' he says, 'the Kingdom of God belongs to such as these' (18:16). He then adds to and strengthens his words when he says that it is only those who receive the Kingdom like a child who will enter it. Remember Luke's readers in the Graeco-Roman world. In that world no trace can be found of the notion that vulnerability, as evidenced in the child, might be a virtue. On the contrary, vulnerability and 'need' of any kind was to be avoided. In this context Jesus' words and action are thoroughly radical; their radical edge still has force against today's ideal of the self-sufficient, self-contained private life.

What does it mean to enter the Kingdom 'like a child'? The context of this saying in Luke is significant. Luke places this story immediately after the parable of the widow and the judge, where the widow with nothing persists in her plea until she is heard, and the parable of the Pharisee and the publican, where it is the publican, who freely acknowledges the poverty of his life before God, who is justified. Immediately following this saying is the story of the rich ruler who has kept the Law's demands but turns away in sorrow from Jesus' invitation to follow him because he can't get loose from his wealth. It is those who come with nothing, who cry for help, who beg with empty hands, who come to God in their humble need, who find the doors of the Kingdom swinging open before their eyes and who know the new life of that new world in their daily lives here and now.

ONE MORE THING

The story moves from those with nothing to the encounter with Jesus of the man who has everything. He is often called the Rich Young Ruler, though Luke makes no reference to the man's age. He comes to Jesus asking what he needs to do to receive 'eternal life', life in all its fullness. 'What do I need to do?' sounds like a very modern question. We like to think of ourselves as great 'doers' these days. Being busy is considered an accolade of great virtue. The rich ruler seems to see entry into the Kingdom as by way of passing a test. Tests, measures, tables, are among the obsessions of our time. We try to 'measure' everything. But entry into God's Kingdom is not like that. The Kingdom's about a radical change in the way we see the world and its people, from the perspective of God.

What better way is there to do that than to walk in the company of the one who has come to his world in the name of God, to come and go with Jesus himself? That's the essence of Jesus' invitation to the rich ruler. He has kept the Law, his life is blameless, but his keeping of the Law hasn't changed him. There is one thing more - only like a child do you begin to enter the Kingdom and the child has nothing. Sell all you possess, give it to the poor, then you will be unencumbered, and not tempted to rely on other things, and come and follow me. The man was greatly distressed. His face fell. He was very rich.

Luke is again painting a picture rather than laying down a law. He is not saying that anyone with wealth must give it all away to follow Jesus, but he is hammering home once again the dangers of wealth in hindering discipleship and the demand of faith to come to Jesus unencumbered by what we think we 'own', whether it be worldly goods, intellectual baggage, or a view of the world and its people skewed by our perceptions and prejudices. If we are to learn the Kingdom way, these things have to be left behind; we have to get loose from them. In his comment after the rich man's rejection, Jesus acknowledges how hard it is for us to get rid of the baggage of our so-called 'riches', in the wonderfully zany picture of the laden camel struggling to get through the needle's eye.

'GOD MAKES THE IMPOSSIBLE POSSIBLE.'

Not unnaturally, for 'hard', the bystanders hear 'impossible'. 'Can anyone be saved?' they ask (18:26). There are two answers to their question. Jesus reminds them that God can and does make possible what seems impossible from a human perspective. The witness of faith declares that in a multitude of lives in a myriad of situations, great and small, those committed to the following of Jesus have discovered that what they thought impossible became possible, that an initial reaction, 'I can never do that!' has been gently answered by their Lord who says, 'You can!....and you will'. The second answer to the question is simply the presence with Jesus of the disciples, who, in Peter's words, have already left all. They are neither saints nor heroes, just disciples; but in their lives and those who have followed them, we see the impossible become possible.

REMEMBERING GEOFF.

In this story, Luke again holds together his interest in both people and structures. Behind the picture of this intensely real and personal encounter with the rich ruler lies Luke's continuing probe into the way wealth is damaging; both for the poor, who are excluded from a place at the table, and for the wealthy, whose view of the world is unrealistically skewed and blinkered by their possessions so that they lack the Kingdom perspective.

Glasgow from the 1950s to the late 1970s was the scene of a remarkable ministry by Geoff Shaw; one which held together in a telling way Luke's conjunction of people and structures. Geoff was the gifted son of a privileged Edinburgh background with the ecclesiastical world at his feet; but after a conversion experience in New York's East Harlem in the same mould as that of Tawney, Beveridge and Temple, he decided with some like-minded others to go and live and work in Glasgow's Gorbals, which was at that time an area in the throes of deprivation and demolition. Round a discipline of shared resources, meeting and worship, members of the group were involved in what might look like secular tasks in the community, and also in local and national political issues. Geoff combined a costly care for young people with a political involvement which led to his election as the first Convener of Strathclyde Regional Council, the biggest local authority in Scotland, from 1974 till his untimely death in 1978. The story of Geoff Shaw and the Gorbals Group is much too significant to be forgotten. When he went to Gorbals, there were many who thought that his gifts and talents were being wasted in an obscure and insignificant ministry. Ronald Selby Wright, minister of the historic Canongate Kirk in Edinburgh put the record straight thus:

> Of course the many were wrong and he was right and the lack of
> encouragement he must have had must sometimes have been rather hard
> to bear. Here was almost a parable of the Rich Young Ruler in reverse - a
> young man with great possessions who had knelt at the feet of Jesus,
> whom, having given up all, he followed.
> (Ronald Selby Wright, quoted in Ron Ferguson 1979, p. 67)

BLIND DISCIPLES AND THE LOOMING CROSS

After the contrasting stories of the visits of the children and the rich ruler to Jesus, this chapter ends with a further pair of contrasts (18:31-43). In verses 31-34, Jesus speaks for a third time about his impending trial in Jerusalem. He seeks to prepare his disciples for his cross and resurrection. He knows what lies before him but the disciples are as yet blind; both in denial about the trials he and they will face, and in ignorance about who he truly is, which will only become fully apparent through the events of the Passion.

While the disciples remain blind, in the final story a blind beggar receives his sight and follows Jesus. He sits by the pilgrim way to Jerusalem and calls on Jesus, 'Son of David, have pity on me!' (18:38) This is the only time in the gospel when Jesus is called 'Son of David'. It prepares us for Jesus' imminent entry into Jerusalem from the Mount of Olives (19:28ff). Just as the disciples had sought to fob off the mothers with their children, so the crowd try to shut the blind beggar up. He only shouts the louder. Jesus stops, calls the man to him and interestingly asks him, 'What do you want me to do for you?' He gives the man a space to make his own request. The beggar goes for it. He passes over the usual beggarly request for money and asks for the big one. 'I want to see again.' 'Then see,' says Jesus, 'your faith has made you well.' He sees and follows, giving thanks to God. This is the final healing, a story of vision restored for the road ahead, and one last instance of discipleship. We too take heart, and follow into the coming storm.

STUDY

BY YOURSELF

'Here was almost a parable of the Rich Young Ruler in reverse - a man with great possessions who had knelt at the feet of Jesus, whom, having given up all, he followed.' (page 189) What is Geoff's story saying to you?

Read the full story of Geoff Shaw by Ron Ferguson (see *Bibliography)*; reflect on its significance for you and for today's church.

FOR GROUP WORK

Share together the reflections from reading the story of Geoff Shaw. The book by Ron Ferguson is in three parts. Three members of the group could be invited to introduce each section, and the questions the section raises for them.

chapter 29

Good Stewardship?

LUKE 19:1-27

Jesus and Zacchaeus

Jesus went on into Jericho and was passing through. There was a chief tax collector there named Zacchaeus, who was rich. He was trying to see who Jesus was, but he was a little man, and could not see Jesus because of the crowd. So he ran ahead of the crowd and climbed a sycamore tree to see Jesus, who was going to pass that way. When Jesus came to that place, he looked up and said to Zacchaeus, "Hurry down, Zacchaeus, because I must stay in your house today."

Zacchaeus hurried down and welcomed him with great joy. All the people who saw it started grumbling, "This man has gone as a guest to the home of a sinner!"

Zacchaeus stood up and said to the Lord, "Listen, sir! I will give half my belongings to the poor, and if I have cheated anyone, I will pay back four times as much."

Jesus said to him, "Salvation has come to this house today, for this man, also, is a descendant of Abraham. The Son of Man came to seek and to save the lost."

The Parable of the Gold Coins
(Mt 25:14-30)

While the people were listening to this, Jesus continued and told them a parable. He was now almost at Jerusalem, and they supposed that the Kingdom of God was just about to appear. So he said, "There was once a man of high rank who was going away to a country far away to be made king, after which he planned to come back home. Before he left, he called his ten servants and gave them each a gold coin and told them, 'See what you can earn with this while I am gone.' Now, his own people hated him, and so they sent messengers after him to say, 'We don't want this man to be our king.'

"The man was made king and came back. At once he ordered his servants to appear before him, in order to find out how much they had earned. The first one came and said, 'Sir, I have earned ten gold coins with the one you gave me.' 'Well done,' he said, 'you are a good servant! Since you were faithful in small matters, I will put you in charge of ten cities.' The second servant came and said, 'Sir, I have earned five gold coins with the one you gave me.' To this one he said, 'You will be in charge of five cities.'

"Another servant came and said, 'Sir, here is your gold coin; I kept it hidden in a handkerchief. I was afraid of you, because you are a hard man. You take what is not yours and reap what you do not sow.' He said to him, 'You bad servant! I will use your own words to condemn you! You know that I am a hard man, taking what is not mine and reaping what I have not sown. Well, then, why didn't you put my money in the bank? Then I would have received it back with interest when I returned.'

'Then he said to those who were standing there, 'Take the gold coin away from him and give it to the servant who has ten coins.' But they said to him, 'Sir, he already has ten coins!' 'I tell you,' he replied, 'that to all those who have something, even more will be given; but to those who have nothing, even the little that they have will be taken away from them. Now, as for those enemies of mine who did not want me to be their king, bring them here and kill them in my presence!'"

ZACCHAEUS

The last picture in Luke's gallery before Jesus arrives in Jerusalem is one much loved by children, and not without its comic elements, with the little man Zacchaeus high on a tree. Jesus has arrived at Jericho, the last stop before Jerusalem. After the story of the blind beggar Bartimaeus, the unlikely follower, Luke tells of one final encounter which results in another surprising disciple, this time the rich tax collector Zacchaeus. The outcome of this story of Jesus' meeting with the crooked Zacchaeus stands in marked contrast to that of his last meeting with a rich man, the virtuous ruler who had kept all the commandments but turned away from Jesus' invitation, 'because he was very rich' (18:23). Again we see grace striking in the strangest of places.

Zacchaeus is described by two defining characteristics. He is physically small. He is also a swindler. As a senior tax collector he had ample opportunities to line his own pockets both at the expense of the population in general and also from the cut he would rake from his own employees. It made him rich financially, and despised and unpopular socially. We can well imagine his efforts to get near enough to see Jesus being thoroughly rebuffed by not a few sharp elbows from the local crowd who would have shown much more consideration for his small stature had he been other than he was. Zacchaeus is a man of resource, however, and a nearby tree provides an adequate if undignified vantage point to see Jesus as he passes by. What's going on in his mind as he waits to catch a glimpse of this prophet from Galilee? Has he heard from other colleagues in his despised but lucrative profession, that this man has time for such as him?

Jesus spots him perched in his arboreal viewpoint. If it was unlikely that Zacchaeus wanted to see Jesus, it's even more astounding that Jesus wants to see him. 'Hurry down, Zacchaeus, because I must stay in your house today' (19:5). The little tax collector is surprised by joy - that Lucan word again - and hurries down to welcome Jesus, while the general populace grumble, 'What's Jesus doing associating with a crook like him?'

REPENTANCE

The answer is that in the accepting, gracious presence of Jesus, the crook is genuinely repentant. It is important to notice in this story that acceptance comes first. It is Jesus' acceptance that leads to Zacchaeus' repentance and not the other way round. Jesus brings out the best in him, a best which has previously been well hidden by his cynical greed. Now the tax collector will turn his life round. Instead of concentrating on getting more and more for himself, he faces in the opposite direction. He looks outward beyond himself, both to those he has robbed and to those whose needs are great. He promises that he will restore four-fold what is due to anyone he has cheated and he will give away half his wealth to the poor. Zacchaeus is a classic example of what the Bible means by repentance. It involves more than feeling remorse, it includes action. Genuine repentance means looking and walking in a new and different direction.

A SON OF ABRAHAM

It is as one who now walks in God's way of justice, that Jesus says to him, 'Health/ salvation has come to this house today, for this man, also, is a descendant of Abraham' (19:9). We remember our last encounter with Abraham was in the parable of the rich man and Lazarus (16:19-31), where Abraham refuses to acknowledge the rich man as his son because of his lack of concern for the poor. We leave Zacchaeus, repentant and reborn through his meeting with Jesus, called, like the Gerasene demoniac in 8:39, to be a continuing witness in the midst of his own people to the transforming power of an encounter with Jesus.

A PUZZLING PARABLE

Before Jesus leaves Jericho he tells a parable, and it's a puzzler. It is so closely related to the parable of the talents in Matthew 25:14-30 that it's clear they share a common source. Luke however adds some other elements to the story in Matthew which serve to confuse us even further. Luke tells the story of the man of high rank who goes away from his estate to a far-off country to be made king. In the preparations for his leaving he gives to ten of his trusted retainers in turn one gold coin each and invites them to earn as much as they can with the money until his return. Having surprisingly mentioned ten servants at the start, Luke then concentrates on only three of them later. Probably the ten is a slip of the pen.

This parable has a curious history of interpretation. Luke says that Jesus told this parable against a context of his disciples expecting the imminent appearance of the Kingdom of God (19:11). At one level then, it is a cautionary tale to Luke's readers in the early church, warning that the Kingdom's appearance is not necessarily imminent, and in the meantime, God's servants should maximise their gifts (remember the connection with Matthew's 'the parable of the talents'). In this context, both Luke and subsequent commentators have no difficulty in vilifying the third servant who takes his one gold coin and simply hides it until the nobleman reappears as king. The servant is variously described as 'lazy', 'wicked,' 'cowardly', 'lacking in moral courage'. More recently the parable has been abused to provide virtually a biblical basis for venture capitalism. The key words in this context come from what appears to be an independent proverbial saying toward the end of Luke's story, 'I tell you, that to all those who have something, more will be given; but to those who have nothing, even the little that they have will be taken away from them' (19:26).

Another longstanding line of interpretation should be mentioned. The third servant who simply hides the coin in the handkerchief has been identified with the keepers of the Jewish Law, the scribes and Pharisees, Jesus' long standing opponents, who were unwilling to see the Law change in any respect in the light of changing circumstances and particularly in the light of Jesus' own teaching. They were unprepared to open up and open out, and, in their diehard conservatism, they are condemned.

However, many commentators display a certain unease about these interpretations. The unease has two principal causes. One is the identification of the absentee nobleman with God. It is clear that the nobleman's dispensation of justice and what we have already seen of God's justice in no way coincide. The second unease centres round a suspicion of the way the retainers earn their money. They look suspiciously like loan sharks, who are unreservedly condemned elsewhere in the biblical record.

FROM THE BOTTOM UP

Herzog once again has turned his considerable forensic skills to this parable and he uncovers an original parable of Jesus at odds with the usual interpretations. If we look at this story from the bottom up, in other words from the perspective of the rural poor, it turns into something very different. The nobleman sounds very like an absentee landlord, and absentee landlords who milked their peasant tenants were the scourge of the rural countryside. However the nobleman would not have been able to continue with his exactions without the help of his retainers, his trusted underlings who both saw that he got his required profits and skimmed off a little for themselves. The way the system worked was that the retainers, in some ways similar to the tacksmen of the old Scottish clan system, would lend to the peasant farmers to allow them to plant their fields, then, when the lean years came and debts could not be repaid, the nobleman could take over the land in repayment of debt and reduce the tenants to virtual slavery.

THE RECKONING

In the parable, when the nobleman returns he calls his retainers to account. In fulsome terms he lavishes praise on the first two retainers who have increased their money ten- and five-fold. The generous praise of the master hides, however, the grimmer reality of how the retainers have earned their profit and at whose expense. Underneath the flattering congratulations lies a reality of gross profiteering at the expense of the vulnerable. When the third retainer appears, what happens? He gives the nobleman back his coin. He has not stolen it, he has kept it safe, he is not unfaithful. If unadventurous, he is certainly no thief. What the servant then does, is to dare to tell the nobleman the truth about himself. 'I know you are a hard man. You take what is not yours and you reap what you did not sow' (19:21). The question Herzog raises and leaves with us is, 'Is it not this third retainer who is the hero of the original parable?' He is the whistleblower, the one who unmasks the corruption of the whole system which the nobleman operates to exploit and disempower his tenants. He acts alone, and he surely puts his head on the block. 'Once shunned by the aristocrat and banished to the role of a day-labourer, the third servant was on a one-way street to extinction. Such was the price for telling the truth. Whistle-blowers usually meet such fates' (Herzog 1994 p. 166).

This story can be read as one of the parables Jesus tells which unmask the world of oppression. What an irony that Luke tells this story immediately before Jesus enters Jerusalem, where he will blow the whistle loudly on the pretensions of the Temple state, and suffer the whistle-blower's fate. Writing at a time when governments on both sides of the Atlantic are suspected of media manipulation in making the case for war on Iraq, when the power of big corporations seems unchecked and too much of the world's media is in too few hands, no less than in the time of Jesus our world urgently needs faithful whistle-blowers, for the pretensions and abuses of power to be unmasked.

STUDY

BY YOURSELF

In the coming week, study the media carefully and look for both abuses of power and the abuse of language to camouflage corruption and sanitise the unacceptable. Can you give examples of 'whistleblowing'?

'In the accepting, gracious presence of Jesus, the crook is genuinely repentant' (page 193). Jesus' acceptance leads Zaccheus to repentance, to turning his life around. Reflect on the significance of acceptance coming first. So often we expect it to be the other way round.

chapter 30

Into Jerusalem

LUKE 19:28-48

The Triumphant Approach to Jerusalem
(Mt 21:1-11, Mk 11:1-11, Jn 12:12-19)

After Jesus said this, he went on ahead of them to Jerusalem. As he came near Bethphage and Bethany at the Mount of Olives, he sent two disciples ahead with these instructions: "Go to the village there ahead of you; as you go in, you will find a colt tied up that has never been ridden. Untie it and bring it here. If someone asks you why you are untying it, tell him that the Master needs it."

They went on their way and found everything just as Jesus had told them. As they were untying the colt, its owners said to them, "Why are you untying it?"

"The Master needs it," they answered, and they took the colt to Jesus. Then they threw their cloaks over the animal and helped Jesus get on. As he rode on, people spread their cloaks on the road.

When he came near Jerusalem, at the place where the road went down the Mount of Olives, the large crowd of his disciples began to thank God and praise him in loud voices for all the great things that they had seen: "God bless the king who comes in the name of the Lord! Peace in heaven and glory to God!"

Then some of the Pharisees in the crowd spoke to Jesus. "Teacher," they said, "command your disciples to be quiet!"

Jesus answered, "I tell you that if they keep quiet, the stones themselves will start shouting."

Jesus Weeps over Jerusalem

He came closer to the city, and when he saw it, he wept over it, saying, "If you only knew today what is needed for peace! But now you cannot see it! The time will come when your enemies will surround you with barricades, blockade you, and close in on you from every side. They will completely destroy you and the people within your walls; not a single stone will they leave in its place, because you did not recognise the time when God came to save you!"

Jesus Goes to the Temple
(Mt 21:12-17, Mk 11:15-19, John 2:13-22)

Then Jesus went into the Temple and began to drive out the merchants, saying to them, "It is written in the Scriptures that God said, 'My Temple will be a house of prayer.' But you have turned it into a hideout for thieves!"

Every day Jesus taught in the Temple. The chief priests, the teachers of the Law, and the leaders of the people wanted to kill him, but they could not find a way to do it, because all the people kept listening to him, not wanting to miss a single word.

THE APPROACH OF THE KING

As Jerusalem approaches, Jesus strides ahead. In Luke's account, the final acts of the gospel drama are now played out entirely in Jerusalem. On the edge of the city, along the spine of the Mount of Olives, Jesus sends two disciples ahead of him to procure an unbroken colt, on which he will approach the city. He plans to enter with a carefully prepared demonstration. Once the young colt has been safely brought to Jesus, his disciples put cloaks on the colt's back for him to ride on, and they spread yet more cloaks on the road. It's as close as they can get to the red carpet treatment. Jesus is deliberately enacting the words of the prophecy in Zechariah about the coming of the Messiah. 'Rejoice, rejoice, people of Zion! Shout for joy, you people of Jerusalem! Look, your king is coming to you! He comes triumphant and victorious, but humble and riding on a donkey - on a colt, the foal of a donkey' (Zechariah 9:9 GNB). The following words of the prophet make it plain that the new king comes in peace (Zechariah 9:10).

The account of Jesus' entry into Jerusalem occurs in all four gospels. It forms the gospel for Palm Sunday, and we probably have a story in our minds which is a conflation of elements from each of the four accounts. If we look closely at Luke's telling of the story, we notice three significant omissions. There are no Hosannas and no palm branches. The explanation for these omissions probably lies in remembering who were Luke's first readers. As Gentiles, they would be unlikely to have come across the word 'Hosanna', meaning, 'God save us', and they would have been equally unfamiliar with the text from Psalm 118:26-27 with its reference to palms. 'May God bless the one who comes in the name of the Lord! From the Temple of the Lord we bless you. The Lord is God; he has been good to us. With branches in your hands, start the festival and march round the altar.'

More significant is the omission of the crowd. Luke has Jesus acclaimed only by his disciples, although he says there were many of them. Neither accompanying pilgrims from Galilee nor welcoming citizens of Jerusalem appear here. It may be Luke wants to stress that in setting up this scene Jesus is taking care not to gather such a crowd as might appear threatening to the authorities. In the eyes of the watching Pharisees he fails (19:39). They bid Jesus tell his disciples to keep quiet, to desist from their acclamation of the one who comes, and the peace he brings.

'This is not the time for silence,' says Jesus. In the words of the Iona Community's morning liturgy, 'If the Lord's disciples keep silence, these stones would shout aloud' (*Iona Community Worship Book* 1988, p. 22). It is very clear that in this action on the edge of Jerusalem, Jesus is deliberately drawing attention to himself and the Messianic claim he makes. Why? Because it is in the events which will unfold in this critical time in Jerusalem, that all will learn who he truly is and what is the nature and the scope of his kingdom. 'Watch closely,' is the message of the man on the donkey. The reference to the stones is prophetic. The heap of rubble to which the Temple was reduced was mute witness to those who had not heeded the words and way of the one who came in the name of the Lord,and rejected the peace he brought.

JESUS WEEPS OVER THE CITY
From the Mount of Olives, Jerusalem stretches out before the arriving traveller. As Jesus draws very near the city, he weeps. There are two instances in the gospels of Jesus weeping, and they are both precious moments. He weeps at the tomb of his friend Lazarus (John 11:35),and he weeps here over his beloved Jerusalem, the city he sees will reject the message of the prophet who comes in the Lord's name. We cherish these moments as signs of Jesus' vulnerable, compassionate humanity. We remember also how often in the preceding parts of Luke's story, Jesus has uttered dire warnings about the fate of Jerusalem, unless the people change their ways. In the picture of Jesus' tears, it is clear that these warnings are not issued in any sense of unfeeling self-righteousness, they are heartfelt and passionate cries for his people's peace. It is in deep sorrow he speaks, as he now bewails the fate of the city and its people. 'How could you not recognise, why did you not see?' he asks in anguish (19:44). It remains part of the church's task to discern and name the destructive forces acting in people's lives and the life of our society today. The way we do that naming remains of crucial importance. On the one hand, the naming needs to be sufficiently imaginative and direct as to command attention; on the other, there is no place for words from a hectoring, judgemental church. We name in tears, the tears of human solidarity. As Tom Wright reminds us, the tears shed by Jesus as he looks over Jerusalem are the tears of the God of love (Wright 2001, p. 233). God's act of solidarity with erring, self-destructive humanity is about to be accomplished, here in Jerusalem.

JESUS CLEANSES THE TEMPLE
In the briefest of compasses, Luke now tells of Jesus' cleansing of the Temple. Luke's account is terse and muted, with no description of Jesus' strenuous exertions and no mention of the confusion caused by the overturning of tables and the release of captive

birds and animals. Is Luke once again trying to minimise Jesus' capacity for causing disturbance? In telling of Jesus driving out the merchants, Luke points up the greed and profiteering at the heart of the holy place, and the whole Temple enterprise. This attack on greed has been a consistent and continuing theme in this gospel. Jesus quotes the scripture, 'My Temple will be a house of prayer'. Significantly, Luke omits the final words from that sentence, 'for all nations' (cf. Mark 11:17). At first glance this may seem a strange omission for Luke, the most universalist of the gospel writers. For Luke however, the nations need not come *to* Jerusalem, as the gospel will go out *from* Jerusalem to all nations (24:47 and in the book of Acts).

THE TEACHER IN THE TEMPLE

Jesus is then shown teaching daily in the Temple. Luke lays great emphasis on Jesus' teaching at the heart of Jerusalem in this final phase of his ministry. The words 'Every day Jesus taught in the Temple' (19:47) show the typical action of Jesus in Jerusalem; they form a counterpoint to verses like 'he preached in the synagogues throughout the country' (4:44), and ' crowds of people came to hear him and be healed of their diseases' (5:15), which describe the ministry in Galilee.

As Jesus teaches, two groups of people are pictured as listening intently. Ranged against him are the forces of power and privilege: the nexus of the high priests' families, the scribes, keepers of the Law, and the other lay members of the Sanhedrin - the highest court in the land and, like most judges for most of history, drawn from the ranks of the wealthy and the privileged. They are looking for a way to dispose of Jesus; threat to their order and position, and disturber of the peace. Their intentions are baulked by the mass of the people who sit at the feet of Jesus in rapt attention. Luke often pictures Jesus being listened to by 'the people', and it becomes the descriptive title of the crowd in Jerusalem who 'hang on his every word' (19:48). For the time being, they are his protection against the threat of the authorities.

> Luke pictures Jesus in Jerusalem and in its heart the Temple as the great divider, whose teaching creates a schism in Judaism between the people, who in their response show themselves to be, at least potentially, disciples, and so members of the true Israel, and its official representatives, who by their rejection of it and him excommunicate themselves.
> (C F Evans 1990, p. 689)

STUDY

BY YOURSELF:

The entry into Jerusalem sees the start of the final drama of Jesus' life. Make this prayer for Holy Week your own.

> Lord God,
> maker and lover of all,
> as we contemplate again
> the pageant of our Lord's betrayal,
> suffering and death;
> may neither the history, ritual
> or sentiment of this season
> in themselves fascinate us.
> Rather may our souls be grasped
> by what our minds alone cannot contain -
> that this was all for us.
>
> And so, Lord, may we be all for you. Amen.
> (*Common Order* 1994, p. 438)

FOR GROUP WORK:

'On the edge of Jerusalem, Jesus is deliberately drawing attention to himself and the messianic claim he makes' (page 198). The entry into Jerusalem is the equivalent of a modern media event, where Jesus uses his visibility to challenge his people to think again, about his way *to* life and their way *of* life - which carried within it the seeds of their destruction.

Brain-storm together: what do group members think are the most destructive forces operating in the lives of people and in our present society? The 'By yourself' question at the end of the last chapter may help.

Jesus' challenge to Jerusalem is made with tears. How should the church address these issues in a way that gains attention and yet is non-censorious and non-judgemental? (You may wish to organise a session of letter-writing to those in authority about the issues which most concern you. Organising such a session encourages people to write who wouldn't do so on their own. And letter-writing is an effective and worthwhile way of raising concerns. Christian Aid has material about the effectiveness of letter-writing.)

chapter 31

Questions, questions, questions

LUKE 20:1-44

The Question about Jesus' Authority
(Mt 21:23-27, Mk 11:27-33)

One day when Jesus was in the Temple teaching people and preaching the Good News, the chief priests and the teachers of the Law, together with the elders, came and said to him, "Tell us, what right have you to do these things? Who gave you this right?"

Jesus answered them, "Now let me ask you a question. Tell me, did John's right to baptize come from God or from human beings?"

They started to argue among themselves, "What shall we say? If we say 'From God,' he will say, 'Why, then, did you not believe John?' But if we say, 'From human beings,' this whole crowd here will stone us, because they are convinced that John was a prophet." So they answered, "We don't know where it came from.'"

And Jesus said to them, "Neither do I tell you, then, by what right I do these things."

The Parable of the Tenants in the Vineyard
(Mt 21:33-46, Mk 12:1-12)

Then Jesus told the people this parable: "There was once a man who planted a vineyard, let it out to tenants, and then left home for a long time. When the time came to gather the grapes, he sent a slave to the tenants to receive from them his share of the harvest. But the tenants beat the slave and sent him back without a thing. So he sent another slave; but the tenants beat him also, treated him shamefully, and sent him back without a thing. Then he sent a third slave; the tenants wounded him, too, and threw him out. Then the owner of the vineyard said, 'What shall I do? I will send my own dear son; surely they will respect him!' But when the tenants saw him, they said to one another, 'This is the owner's son. Let's kill him, and his property will be ours!' So they threw him out of the vineyard and killed him.

"What, then, will the owner of the vineyard do to the tenants?" Jesus asked.

"He will come and kill these men, and hand the vineyard over to other tenants."

When the people heard this, they said, "Surely not!"

Jesus looked at them and asked, "What, then, does this scripture mean?

"The stone which the builders rejected as worthless

turned out to be the most important of all."

"Everyone who falls on that stone will be cut to pieces; and if that stone falls on someone, it will crush him to dust."

The Question about Paying Taxes
(Mt 22:15-22, Mk 12:13-17)

The teachers of the Law and the chief priests tried to arrest Jesus on the spot, because they knew that he had told this parable against them; but they were afraid of the people. So they looked for an opportunity. They bribed some men to pretend they were sincere, and they sent them to trap Jesus with questions, so that they could hand him over to the authority and power of the Roman Governor. These spies said to Jesus, "Teacher, we know that what you say and teach is right. We know that you pay no attention to anyone's status, but teach the truth about God's will for people. Tell us, is it against our Law for us to pay taxes to the Roman Emperor, or not?"

But Jesus saw through their trick and said to them, "Show me a silver coin. Whose face and name are these on it?"

"The Emperor's", they answered.

So Jesus said, "Well, then, pay the Emperor what belongs to the Emperor, and pay God what belongs to God."

There before the people they could not catch him out in anything, so they kept quiet, amazed at his answer.

The Question about Rising from Death
(Mt 22:23-33, Mk 12:18-27)

Then some Sadducees, who say that people will not rise from death, came to Jesus and said, "Teacher, Moses wrote this law for us: 'If a man dies and leaves a wife but no children, that man's brother must marry the widow so that they can have children who will be considered the dead man's children.' Once there were seven brothers; the eldest got married and died without having children. Then the second one married the woman, and then the third. The same thing happened to all seven - they died without having children. Last of all, the woman died. Now, on the day when the dead rise to life, whose wife will she be? All seven of them had married her."

Jesus answered them. "The men and women of this age marry, but the men and women who are worthy to rise from death and live in the age to come will not then marry. They will be like angels and cannot die. They are the children of God, because they have risen from death. And Moses clearly proves that the dead are raised to life. In the passage about the burning bush he speaks of the Lord as 'the God of Abraham, the God of Isaac, and the God of Jacob.' He is the God of the living, not the dead, for to him all are alive."

Some of the teachers of the Law spoke up, "A good answer, Teacher!" For they did not dare ask him any more questions.

The Question about the Messiah
(Mt 22:41-46, Mk 12:35-37)

Jesus asked them, "How can it be said that the Messiah will be the descendant of David? For David himself says in the book of Psalms,

'The Lord said to my Lord:
Sit here on my right
until I put your enemies as a
footstool under your feet.'

David called him 'Lord'; how, then, can the Messiah be David's descendant?"

BY WHAT AUTHORITY?

Soren Kierkegaard, that consistent thorn in the Episcopal flesh of early 19th century Denmark, issued a solemn warning about the dangers of reading the gospels with the doubtful benefit of hindsight. The long centuries of our culture's exposure to the gospels have us taking for granted Jesus' claim of Lordship and the church's confession of him as the Son of God. Kierkegaard prescribed that one essential condition for approaching the gospels was to make every imaginative effort to think oneself into the situation of being a contemporary of Jesus. What did he look like, sound like, to those who first heard him? What was it like as a 1st century Jew to be confronted with the appearance of the man from Nazareth? Not all 1st century Jews were alike, no more than 21st century Scots. There were the "haves", a small minority, and the "have-nots" - the great majority. Most significant among the "haves" were the grouping we met at the end of the last chapter, 'the chief priests and the teachers of the Law, together with the Elders' (20:1). What were they to make of this new arrival in Jerusalem? Doubtless they had had news of his activities both in Galilee - where trouble had come from before - and on the way to Jerusalem. His ability to gather a crowd, the challenging directness of his words, his many previous head-to-heads with scribe and Pharisee, and various rumours about 'Messiahship' would have aroused their suspicion. They had their privileges and responsibilities to keep. The chief priest's circle had to negotiate their uneasy modus vivendi with the Roman authorities, which often involved their seeking to keep a lid on popular, nationalistic feelings of unrest. The scribes as the guardians of the Law, whose interpretation Jesus had frequently challenged, were obviously on their guard. The elders, probably synonymous with 'the leaders of the people' in 19:47, combined with the chief priests to seek to ensure the fragile peace of Jerusalem and preserve their own interests. Now this Jesus had arrived in their midst with a carefully-staged demonstration on the Mount of Olives, and an act of provocation in the Temple courts where he was at this very moment sitting teaching a large crowd. Outraged, it was time to confront him and ask him who he thought he was.

There is no surprise in the question they, the authorities, ask Jesus, the unauthorised teacher from Galilee. 'What is your authority for doing what you're doing? Who gave you this right?' Jesus' response is clever and tangential. In the traditions of rabbinic debate, he asks the questioners a question. At first sight Jesus' question seems obscure. 'Tell me,' he asks, 'did John's right to baptise come from God, or from human beings?' (20:4) The question well serves its purpose, as it throws Jesus' opponents into heated confusion. If they admit that John's authority came from God, they can be accused of failing to acknowledge and support that prophet: if they deny John's authority, they fall foul of the people who have no doubt about John's prophetic credentials. They make the barely credible reply, 'We don't know.' Jesus is off the hook. He says, 'Well, if you're so unsure about John, I'm not going to tell you the nature of my authority either.'

This episode raises two contemporary questions. Both John and Jesus claim their authority from the Spirit of God. Theirs is not the authority of ecclesiastical office. It has its own authentic directness. Obviously they pose a real problem for the existing authorities. There is a long biblical tradition of authentic prophets being cold-shouldered by the powers that be, whether priestly or regal. Reading David Jenkins' account of his years as Bishop of Durham, *The Calling of a Cuckoo*, suggests that the issue of traditional ecclesiastical authority cuts both ways. One of the main concerns which that humane, honest and humorous human being raises, is that the expectations thrust upon him in the donning of his bishop's mitre required him to temper his humanity and honesty for the sake of the tender intelligences and consciences of his flock. His hopes of being a missionary bishop, engaged in an open, spirited dialogue with a largely sceptical world, were blunted by the combined effects of media over-simplification and ecclesial defensiveness. Our times need more free spirits, not less.

There is also something cynical about the authorities' 'Don't know' response to the question of Jesus. Of course they knew. It is not conceivable that they did not have a view about the significant event of the coming of John the Baptist, and the issues he raised for religious and national life. Sadly, many Christians today still hide behind a selectively cynical agnosticism. They will have strong views on doctrinal minutiae and personal morality, but on the big issues which Luke raises about wealth and poverty, the question of violence, an inclusive gospel which transcends boundaries, respects and welcomes outsiders, heads are kept well down. 'What have these matters to do with the full gospel?' they ask. Answer: everything. Behind the question of the powers-that-be about Jesus' authority lies the central claim of Luke's gospel: that Jesus is Lord of all, and that his claim informs and penetrates every aspect of our lives in the world.

HEAD OF THE CORNER

> Israel is the vineyard of the Lord Almighty; the people of Judah are the vines he planted.
> He expected them to do what was good, but instead they committed murder.
> He expected them to do what was right, but their victims cried out for justice.
> (Isaiah 5:7)

These words from Isaiah are a reminder that God's vineyard was a very common symbol of Israel. In the Parable of the Tenants in the Vineyard, Jesus uses this familiar imagery. The owner and planter of the vineyard is God, the tenants are the rulers of Israel and the slaves sent to recover their share of the harvest stand for the succession of prophets who have met rejection at the hands of priest and king. The son is Jesus himself, whose brutal end is tellingly described as occurring outside the vineyard (20:15), echoing the words of Hebrews 13:12, 'Jesus suffered outside the gate'; beyond the in-circle of orthodox religion, outside holiness. In the background to the parable was the usage that if the owner of a property died, the property could be claimed by its tenant farmers.

The story does not end with the son's death. In the hands of Jesus and Luke, it offers the prospect of resurrection. Jesus quotes from the longest of the Hallel psalms - Psalms 113-118 - which were recited in the house at the Passover meal. Changing the imagery to that of a builder's yard, he cites the words of Psalm 118:22. 'The stone which the builders rejected as worthless turned out to be the most important of all'. Jesus is on the attack, pillorying Israel's leaders for their rejection of God's way of peace, and promising his death will be the way the Kingdom's gates open far and wide.

WHAT BELONGS TO CAESAR?

The authorities get the point. The vineyard story is told against them. They would do away with Jesus, but his popular support continues to threaten their plans. Their next plan is to move from a direct question to a more devious approach. They set up a situation in which they hope Jesus will incriminate himself in the eyes of the Roman authorities. Some men are sent with a trick question to trap Jesus. The whole scene has a comic edge to it. Those who are sent are to make play of their sincerity: the unctuous flattery with which they address Jesus must immediately have blown their cover. Their question remains. 'Does God's Law allow us to pay taxes to Caesar, or not?'

If Jesus says, 'Yes,' he forfeits the popular support of the crowd, incensed by their tax burden, and he can be accused of failing to uphold the integrity of Israel's faith. If he says, 'No', he can be accused of inciting the people to civil disobedience, and dragged before Roman jurisdiction. He says neither yea nor nay; instead he asks for the production of the coin with which the Roman poll tax must be paid. His opponents have to produce the coin; the obvious implication is that he hasn't got one. He asks whose face and image the coin bears. The answer is 'the Emperor's'; hidden under that reply is the conviction shared by Jesus, his opponents and the whole Jewish people, that the Emperor's image on the coinage was a blasphemy against the opening commandments.

Laconically Jesus offers the aphorism, 'Well, then, pay the Emperor what belongs to the Emperor, and pay God what belongs to God'. Jesus says neither 'Pay', nor 'Don't pay'. Once again, by implication he would be reminding all who heard that their obligations to God were infinitely more demanding and unconditional than any obligation they had to Caesar. One of the suspicions held about Luke's gospel is that he goes a bit soft on Caesar, since he is writing from the perspective of the gentile mission taking place in the wider Roman Empire, and the young church needed at least Rome's neutrality to be able to flourish. The charge cannot be substantiated here, as Luke largely takes over the same text as used by Mark. There is another powerful irony at work. Very shortly, Jesus himself, who from first to last belongs to God, will be handed over to Caesar by the same authorities who set up this question, and who will twist his answer to incriminate him (23:2). The result will be surprising, to say the least.

MERE SOPHISTRY

We have seen already in the gospel the vital importance of the father/son relationship in Israel. The gift of sons to continue the family line was the greatest of gifts, and to be childless was a great misfortune. So the Law of Moses stipulated that on the death of her husband, a childless widow must marry one of his brothers for the continuance of the family line. It is this law which forms the background to the final confrontation in this section, though there is considerable debate about whether this law was actually still in practice in Jesus' time.

Some Sadducees, the upper class who did not believe in any resurrection and who thought their present worldly wealth was the greatest sign of God's blessing, come with yet another trick question. 'If a woman marries each of seven brothers successively on the death of her previous husband, to whom will she belong at the resurrection?' Cynical, isn't it? Presumably they hope that Jesus in his answer will supply them with further ammunition to rubbish the belief in resurrection, one of their favourite ploys. It is interesting to note the use of the word 'belong' to describe the relations of the woman to her husband. In the patriarchal society of the time, the woman was virtually 'owned'. There is little of the belonging of genuine mutuality.

Jesus' answer is twofold. 'Of course male/female relationships will be very different in the world to come. Don't be so silly and legalistic!' He then goes on the attack. Since the Sadducees have based their question on the law of Moses, in proof of the resurrection, Jesus quotes Moses back to them. From the seminal encounter at the burning bush in Exodus 3 he quotes God's description of himself as 'the God of

Abraham, the God of Isaac, and the God of Jacob'. Since these three patriarchs had long departed life on this earth by the time of God's meeting with Moses at the bush, God's words are signs of their continuing life in God. Jesus ends with that wonderful verse, 'He is the God of the living, not of the dead, for to him all are alive' (20:38). His answer is so convincing that some of the listening scribes, opponents of the Sadducees over the matter of resurrection, are impressed.

JESUS ASKS A QUESTION

Jesus' attack continues. He now has a question to clarify what Messiahship means. He quotes from Psalm 110:1 (*NRSV*), where David calls the Messiah his Lord, and asks how in that case the Messiah can be described simply as the descendant of David. The point he is making, in terms of typical scribal argument, is that the coming Messiah is not to be thought of as a returning clone of David. 'Son of David' is an inadequate and misleading description of Jesus' own messianic role. He will not be confined to the role of a simple nationalistic hero bringing salvation through violent conquest. It is indeed the longing for that model of Messiahship which is bringing the nation to the brink of destruction. The coming one is greater than David, and very different, as we shall see.

The questions are over. Taking them as a whole, we can see in them the gospel in miniature, and a restatement of Jesus' own prediction about his destiny from 9:22 onwards. The question about his authority reminds us that he comes from God, the parable of the vineyard that he will suffer at the hand of the authorities of his own people, the issue of the coin that he will be crucified under Pontius Pilate, and the Sadducees' question gives an intimation of resurrection and reminds us of the promise in 8:22 that after three days, 'he will be raised to life'. In that work of God, the one greater than David will be made known.

STUDY

BY YOURSELF

Find yourself present in the Temple court as the questions fly to and fro. You have heard the story so far: what are the questions you would like to ask Jesus, arising either from this chapter or from the whole gospel. What do you hear him saying to you?

chapter 32

The scribe, the widOw and the Temple

LUKE 20:45 - 21:6

Jesus Warns against the Teachers of the Law
(Mt 23:1-36, Mk 12:38-40)

As all the people listened to him, Jesus said to his disciples, "Be on your guard against the teachers of the Law, who like to walk about in their long robes and love to be greeted with respect in the market place; who choose the reserved seats in the synagogues and the best places at feasts; who take advantage of widows and rob them of their homes, and then make a show of saying long prayers! Their punishment will be all the worse!"

The Widow's Offering
(Mk 12:41-44)

Jesus looked round and saw rich people dropping their gifts in the temple treasury, and he also saw a very poor widow dropping in two little copper coins. He said, 'I tell you that this poor widow put in more than all the others. For the others offered their gifts from what they had to spare of their riches; but she, poor as she is, gave all she had to live on.'

Jesus Speaks of the Destruction of the Temple
(Mt 24:1-2, Mk 13:1-2)

Some of the disciples were talking about the Temple, how beautiful it looked with its fine stones and the gifts offered to God. Jesus said, 'All this you see - the time will come when not a single stone here will be left in its place; every one will be thrown down.'

Beware scribes!

Jesus' question about the Messiah at the end of the last section serves as a timely reminder, as the cross approaches, that the work of the living God is wider, more mysterious and surprising than we think. His words immediately following about the teachers of the Law, the scribes, bring us back down to earth with their description of inturned, self-serving religion. Every Sunday, as I trip over my robes on the way up the pulpit steps, Jesus' picture of the scribes with their long robes comes to mind. They continue to stand as a warning against the unhealthy veneration of the clergy, either by the clergy or by their misguided parishioners. In too many places there is still a kind of neurotic collusion between minister and people, which prevents the genuine flourishing of the ministry of the whole people of God. Jesus does not mince his words about the scribes here. He says they are fakes, and their posturing self-importance a sham. Instead of being servants of the living God, they have usurped the place of God, using their position for their own self-advancement, under the cover of a pompous display of piety. Remind me to keep my prayers short!

Watch the widow

There follows one of the gospel's unforgettable pictures: of the contrast between the ostentatious display of giving by the wealthy, and the truly costly offering of the poor widow, made in quiet simplicity. It is linked to the preceding section by the place in both of widows. The poor woman's offering can remind us of two other poor women from the gospel's beginning: the old woman Anna in the Temple greeting the child Jesus (2:36-38); and the young woman Mary, supreme exemplar of 'his lowly servant' (1:48), whom God has visited, filled with his life and song, and lifted up. The incident of the widow at the temple treasury also points forward: very soon the one who commends her offering, Jesus himself, will give all that he has. It is clear whom God honours.

Jesus is criticising the honouring of the wealthy and the aura of false piety which surrounds them and their giving. His criticism should encourage us to ask sharp questions about those whom our society 'honours' and rewards through honours lists, golden handshakes and directors' share bonuses. Arising from this story, whenever a business boasts of its charitable giving, a very direct question can be asked, 'How much are they paying their cleaners... and the other 'invisible' workers on whom their enterprise depends?' The great contemporary Jewish historian Josephus notes in his history those who had donated gold plating for the Temple doors. Jesus, by contrast, sees and brings to our notice the poor widow. It is good that aid agencies and fair trade organisations, by telling us something of the lives of those they assist or who are their trade partners, encourage us to 'see' something of the lives of real people, far from our doors, who would otherwise remain invisible. Is there a link between the poor widow and Jesus' immediately following prediction of the Temple's doom? It should have been the Temple which was supporting the widow rather than the other way round. If the Temple system no longer offered succour and protection to those entrusted to its care, did it deserve to survive?

THE END OF THE TEMPLE

We live in the aftermath of the moment of destruction and atrocity of September 11th 2001, in the attack on the twin towers of the World Trade Centre in New York. The effects of that moment are still being acutely felt, both in the American psyche and in subsequent events around the world. That attack operated at two levels. It visited destruction, loss and death on the lives of real people in its callous inhumanity: it was also an attack on buildings which were a vital symbol for the American and Western way of life. We could say that the twin towers were secular temples of our age. The Temple in Jerusalem occupied a similar, indeed greater, place in the minds and hearts of Jesus' contemporaries. Huge and beautiful, enriched by many hands over many generations, it dominated the skyline. Its place in the life of the people as the home of their life, longings and relation to God was immense, but at its heart, as Jesus has already insistently warned, its life had succumbed to the temptation which lurks in wait for all human and religious enterprises: it had become inward-looking, self-centred and corrupt. By the year 70CE it would become a heap of rubble, with not one stone left on another. The shock of the Temple's fall was cataclysmic.

The final incident in this short section pictures some of Jesus' disciples viewing the Temple in rapt adoration and commenting on its beauty to Jesus. It is the brusque voice of Jesus the prophet which disturbs their contemplation. 'If this people continues to think and live as they do, the great Temple will soon be a pile of stones.' The question is raised, 'Maybe God is not mainly to be found in the Temple. Are you looking for God in the wrong place?' The New Testament is witness that the place of God-with-us is in Jesus, the new centre of his indwelling. By the presence and activity of the Holy Spirit, through Jesus Christ, God's home is in each of us and all of us together. The focus of our life is therefore not turned inward towards the temple, the citadel, in a defensive, against-the-world, attitude; but outwards towards the world, as the sphere of God's continuing activity, where we are ever open to be surprised by the turn of events and the truth of the stranger.

STUDY

BY YOURSELF
The story of the poor widow has a double edge.

1 Her sacrifice is commended by Jesus. Reflect on your own life, on how you give what you have to your Lord, and on the truth that it is in giving that we do receive.

2 The widow is also the victim of a system which in theory was there for her protection but in reality took from her the little that she had. Sadly, very often our actual practice does not reflect our core values. Think on situations in which you are involved, where practice does not measure up to ideal. How can they be changed?

FOR GROUP WORK
These three short passages can be read as a recall to the essentials of our faith and its practice. Discuss these three questions:

1 From the warning about the scribes (20:45-47) ... How do we avoid self-importance and self-serving in our Christian lives and communities?

2 From the poor widow's offering (21:1-4) ... The core of our faith centres around the sacrifice of Christ. How can our lives reflect his sacrifice?

3 From the prediction of the Temple's doom (21:5-6)... Are we looking for God in the wrong place, enclosed to our building and confined in our fellowship?

chapter 33

Darkness before the dawn

LUKE 21:7-38

Troubles and Persecutions
(Mt 24:3-14, Mk 13:3-13)

"Teacher," they asked, "when will this be? And what will happen in order to show that the time has come for it to take place?"

Jesus said, "Be on your guard; don't be deceived. Many men, claiming to speak for me, will come and say, 'I am he!' and 'The time has come!' But don't follow them. Don't be afraid when you hear of wars and revolutions; such things must happen first, but they do not mean that the end is near."

He went on to say, "Countries will fight each other; kingdoms will attack one another. There will be terrible earthquakes, famines, and plagues everywhere; there will be strange and terrifying things coming from the sky. Before all these things take place, however, you will be arrested and persecuted; you will be handed over to be tried in synagogues and put in prison; you will be brought before kings and rulers for my sake. This will be your chance to tell the Good News. Make up your minds beforehand not to worry about how you will defend yourselves, because I will give you such words and wisdom that none of your enemies will be able to refute or contradict what you say. You will be handed over by your parents, your brothers, your relatives, and your friends; and some of you will be put to death. Everyone will hate you because of me. But not a single hair from your heads will be lost. Stand firm, and you will save yourselves.

Jesus Speaks of the Destruction of Jerusalem
(Mt 24:15-21, Mk 13:14-19)

"When you see Jerusalem surrounded by armies, then you will know that it will soon be destroyed. Then those who are in Judea must run away to the hills; those who are in the city must leave, and those who are out in the country must not go into the city. For those will be 'The Days of Punishment', to make all that the Scriptures say come true. How terrible it will be in those days for women who are pregnant and for mothers with little babies! Terrible distress will come upon this land, and God's punishment will fall on this people. Some will be killed by the sword, and others will be taken as prisoners to all countries; and the heathen will trample over Jerusalem until their time is up.

The Coming of the Son of Man
(Mt 24:29-31, Mk 13:24-27)

"There will be strange things happening to the sun, the moon, and the stars. On earth whole countries will be in despair, afraid of the roar of the sea and the raging tides. People will faint from fear as they wait for what is coming over the whole earth, for the powers in space will be driven from their courses. Then the Son of Man will appear, coming in a cloud with great power and glory. When these things begin to happen, stand up and raise your heads, because your salvation is near."

The Lesson of the Fig Tree
(Mt 24:32-35, Mk 13:28-31)

Then Jesus told them this parable: "Think of the fig tree and all the other trees. When you see their leaves beginning to appear, you know that summer is near. In the same way, when you see these things happening, you will know that the Kingdom of God is about to come.

"Remember that all these things will take place before the people now living have all died. Heaven and earth will pass away, but my words will never pass away.

The Need to Watch

"Be on your guard! Don't let yourselves become occupied with too much feasting and drinking and with the worries of this life, or that Day may suddenly catch you like a trap. For it will come upon all people everywhere on earth. Be on the alert and pray always that you will have the strength to go safely through all those things that will happen and to stand before the Son of Man."

Jesus spent those days teaching in the Temple, and when evening came, he would go out and spend the night on the Mount of Olives. Early each morning all the people went to the Temple to listen to him.

TROUBLE IS NORMAL

We have just heard how the disciples' comment on the wonder of the Temple leads to the prediction of Jesus about its destruction. His prediction in turn provokes the obvious questions, 'When will this happen? Will there be any signs which help us prepare for it?' In response to the questions, Jesus makes a long speech about discerning the signs of the times and what lies ahead. This long speech occurs in each of the first three gospels, in Matthew 24 and Mark 13 as well as here in Luke. It is the last speech of any significant length Jesus makes before his passion, but it is notoriously difficult to interpret. While the speech occurs in each of the gospels mentioned, the gospel editors have their significant differences. One difficulty in its interpretation is that many of Jesus' words here belong to the genre of apocalyptic writing. The apocalypse, which finds its fullest expression in the New Testament in the book of Revelation, was the expected end of all things when God would establish his rule and judgement over earth and heaven. Apocalyptic writing is therefore always an attempt to say the unsayable. It uses highly pictorial language which it is particularly dangerous to take literally. A second strand in understanding these speeches of Jesus is that they speak to two different sets of listeners. More than most other passages in the gospels, the original words of Jesus to his disciples are reinterpreted as a word to the gospel's first hearers, living in a situation at least one generation away from the original context and with their own contextual agenda.

The interpretation of the beginning of Jesus' speech is relatively easy. Jesus says, 'Trouble is normal'. Wars, famines, earthquakes, plagues, strange signs in the sky - these are part and parcel of the daily stuff of a fallen world. Because dangerous and portentous events erupt, there will be no shortage of those who claim to be Messiahs who will save the people. Don't be lured into thinking every sign of disaster is a sign that the end is near, and don't follow those who claim to be the answer to world history with their promise of salvation.

In 21:12, he moves on to speak specifically about the troubles which will face members of the believing community - arrest, persecution, trial before the synagogue and other authorities, imprisonment. These words form a trailer to the events narrated in the book of Acts, with its stories of Peter and Paul and the struggles and growth of the young church. Luke's Jesus says that the very troubles the followers of Jesus will face are opportunities for witness and spreading the Good News. In the time of trial, disciples are not to worry about the account they will give of their faith, Jesus himself through the Spirit will give them the necessary 'words and wisdom' (21:15) to refute their enemies. Not all the trouble disciples will face will come from the authorities; division will begin within families. It will be the disciples' own parents, siblings, relatives and friends who will accuse them. Again Luke's ambiguity about the role of the family crops up. These words are a reminder that, from its beginnings, the gospel has divided as well as united. The section ends with a word of encouragement and an injunction. In face of troubles in store, the gospel insists you will know God's care: through it all 'stand firm' (21:19).

SPECIFICALLY ABOUT JERUSALEM

In the times we live in, we are hugely aware of our global interconnectedness, whether through the range of modern communications, the contents of the supermarket trolley, the fluctuations in the stock market, or the precautions countries take to avoid the spread of terrorism or epidemic. What happens in places far distant from us can impact upon us virtually immediately. While the range and speed of our contemporary intercon-nectedness is an accelerating modern phenomenon with both positive and negative aspects, its reality has long impinged on human life. Part of the peculiar genius of the Hebrew prophet was the ability to make connections between events in the life of their own people, events in neighbouring countries and the will and purpose of God.

Jesus and Luke next speak specifically about the fate of Jerusalem. The events of the years 66-70CE form the background. Frequently through the gospel, Jesus has warned of the consequences for his people and its capital city if they do not change their ways. What the gospel says here is consistent with Jesus' teachings and warnings. It very much appears, however, that Luke was writing his gospel after the fall of Jerusalem in 70CE. The events surrounding that fall show evidence of the interconnectedness mentioned above. Not once, but twice in the Jewish revolt against Rome from 66-70, the iron fist of the Roman legions was stayed in dealing with the rebels in Jerusalem because of events elsewhere in the Empire and, in particular, the struggle over the succession to the Imperial throne, following the suicide of Nero. It proved a false dawn, nemesis did eventually come; it's in the face of these terrible times described in 21:20-24 that the disciples are counselled not to hang around Jerusalem with any sense of misplaced loyalty, but to take to the hills and not return to the city (21:21).

THE COMING OF THE SON OF MAN

The initial question about Jerusalem has now been answered. After the description of the troubles which will beset the inhabitants of Jerusalem, Luke moves on to list a series of cosmic troubles which will befall the inhabited world, the gentile nations. The description of the troubles echoes the prophetic words of Isaiah 13:10, Ezekiel 32:7 and Joel 2:31. It is in the midst of them that the Son of Man will appear (21:27, cf Daniel 7:13). Matthew, Mark and Luke all witness to the appearance of this apocalyptic figure from the book of Daniel, who will come from God to bring hope to a beleaguered people and to establish the judgement of God. Jesus identifies himself closely with the figure of the Son of Man and in Mark's gospel in particular, this prophecy from Daniel is crucial in the disclosure of Who He Is. One significant divergence from Mark is in 21:27, where Luke has Jesus say that the Son of Man will appear coming in a cloud (singular) with great power and glory. Mark uses the plural 'clouds' (Mk 13: 26), and quotes Daniel 7:13 precisely. By changing the plural into the singular Luke recalls the single cloud of the divine glory in the story of the transfiguration (9:34), and anticipates the cloud which will receive Jesus back into heaven at his ascension (Acts 1:9-11), where it is clearly stated to the watching disciples that he will return in the same way to complete his work at the end of all things. The effect of this is to push the return of Jesus into the future, and allow Luke in Acts to develop the significance of the times between the first and second comings and the place of the church as part of the history of salvation.

Jesus' words towards the end of the ensuing parable of the fig tree and the other trees (21:29-33), 'Remember that all these things will take place before the people now living have died' (21:32), seem to contradict what has just been stated about Luke's sense of a time-space between the first and second comings. Various explanations of this are given by different commentators, none of them very satisfactory. 'People now living' is a paraphrase of the Greek word for 'generation'. Perhaps the best interpretation of these words is to take 'all these things' as referring to Jesus' passion and resurrection coupled with the fall of Jerusalem. Luke is therefore communicating to his readers a sense of urgency in the light of the imminent Kingdom. A similar urgency remains for us in our situation, with our task of communicating the coming of the peaceable Kingdom to a world which still will not learn the gospel ways of peace. There is a timeless and enduring word to be spoken to and heard, by each and every 'generation' (21:33).

STRENGTH FOR THE ROAD AHEAD

Jesus' speech ends with the charge to keep alert and watchful. Avoid the worldly twin traps of hedonism or anxiety; remain constant in prayer for the strength from beyond ourselves to endure whatever befalls us. In Luke's context we can read these words as encouragement for the long haul of discipleship, the continuing journey of the long road of which Luke/Acts and the letter to the Hebrews speak. In our church life with its constant temptation to be either backward-looking or to get stuck, Jesus' words here focus us resolutely forward. We go outwards and we press on, until that day when we stand before the Son of Man (21:36).

The section ends with yet another description of Jesus in Jerusalem, teaching in the Temple from early morning (21:37, cf 19:47), and retiring to the Mount of Olives when evening fell. In the pattern of his days in Jerusalem, he himself presents a living model of disciplined alertness in the face of the trials to come.

STUDY

BY YOURSELF

The clash between the world's ways of war and struggle, and the gospel ways of peace, continues in our world. What is your reaction to those who demonstrate against the destructiveness of our weaponry, or the oppressiveness of our economic systems? Ponder this affirmation written by Iona Community members after the peaceful demonstration against the Faslane Trident nuclear missile submarine base, February 2001:

> We believe that God is present in the darkness before dawn;
> in the waiting and uncertainty where fear and courage join hands,
> conflict and caring link arms, and the sun rises over the barbed wire.
> We believe in a with-us God who sits down in our midst
> to share our humanity.
> We affirm a faith that takes us beyond the safe place;
> into action, into vulnerability and into the streets.
> We commit ourselves to work for change and put ourselves on the line;
> to bear responsibility, take risks, live powerfully and face humiliation;
> to stand with those on the edge; to choose life
> and be used by the Spirit for God's new community of hope. Amen.
> (Neil Paynter 2002, p 36-7)

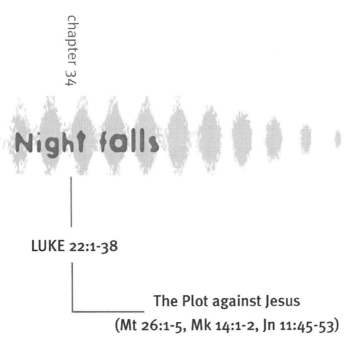

chapter 34

Night falls

LUKE 22:1-38

The Plot against Jesus
(Mt 26:1-5, Mk 14:1-2, Jn 11:45-53)

The time was near for the Festival of Unleavened Bread, which is called the Passover. The chief priests and the teachers of the Law were afraid of the people, and so they were trying to find a way of putting Jesus to death secretly.

Judas Agrees to Betray Jesus
(Mt 26:14-16, Mk 14:10-11)

Then Satan entered Judas, called Iscariot, who was one of the twelve disciples. So Judas went off and spoke with the chief priests and the officers of the temple guard about how he could betray Jesus to them. They were pleased and offered to pay him money. Judas agreed to it and started looking for a good chance to hand Jesus over to them without the people knowing about it.

Jesus Prepares to Eat the Passover Meal
(Mt 26:17-25, Mk 14:12-21, Jn 13:21-30)

The day came during the Festival of Unleavened Bread when the lambs for the Passover meal were to be killed. Jesus sent off Peter and John with these instructions: "Go and get the Passover meal ready for us to eat."

"Where do you want us to get it ready?" they asked him.

He answered, "As you go into the city, a man carrying a jar of water will meet you. Follow him into the house that he enters, and say to the owner of the house, 'The Teacher says to you, Where is the room where my disciples and I will eat the

Passover meal?' He will show you a large furnished room upstairs, where you will get everything ready."

They went off and found everything just as Jesus had told them, and they prepared the Passover Meal.

The Lord's Supper
(Mt 26:26-30, Mk 14:22-26, 1 Cor 11:23-25)

When the hour came, Jesus took his place at the table with the apostles. He said to them, "I have wanted so much to eat this Passover meal with you before I suffer! For I tell you, I will never eat it until it is given its full meaning in the Kingdom of God."

Then Jesus took a cup, gave thanks to God, and said, "Take this and share it among yourselves. I tell you that from now on I will not drink this wine until the Kingdom of God comes."

Then he took a piece of bread, gave thanks to God, broke it, and gave it to them, saying, "This is my body, which is given for you. Do this in memory of me." In the same way, he gave them the cup after the supper, saying, "This cup is God's new covenant sealed with my blood, which is poured out for you.

"But, look! The one who betrays me is here at the table with me! The Son of Man will die as God has decided, but how terrible for that man who betrays him!"

Then they began to ask among themselves which one of them it could be who was going to do this.

The Argument about Greatness

An argument broke out among the disciples as to which one of them should be thought of as the greatest. Jesus said to them, "The kings of the pagans have power over their people, and the rulers claim the title, 'Friends of the People'. But this is not the way it is with you; rather, the greatest one among you must be like the youngest, and the leader must be like the servant. Who is greater, the one who sits down to eat or the one who serves? The one who sits down, of course. But I am among you as one who serves.

"You have stayed with me all through my trials; and just as my Father has given me the right to rule, so I will give you the same right. You will eat and drink at my table in my Kingdom, and you will sit on thrones to rule over the twelve tribes of Israel.

Jesus Predicts Peter's Denial
(Mt 26:31-35, Mk 14:27-31, Jn 13:36-38)

"Simon, Simon! Listen! Satan has received permission to test all of you, to separate the good from the bad, as a farmer separates the wheat from the chaff. But I have prayed for you, Simon, that your faith will not fail. And when you turn back to me, you must strengthen your brothers."

Peter answered, "Lord, I am ready to go to prison with you and to die with you!"

"I tell you, Peter," Jesus said, "the cock will not crow tonight until you have said three times that you do not know me.'"

Purse, Bag and Sword

Then Jesus asked his disciples, "When I sent you out that time without purse, bag or shoes, did you lack anything?"

"Not a thing," they answered.

"But now," Jesus said, "whoever has a purse or a bag must take it; and whoever has no sword must sell his coat and buy one. For I tell you that the scripture which says, 'He shared the fate of criminals,' must come true about me, because what was written about me is coming true."

The disciples said, "Look! Here are two swords, Lord!"

"That is enough," he replied.

CRISIS TIME

The words, 'The time was near...' (22:1), introduce this section. We have come to crisis time. The dark drama of Jesus' betrayal, arrest, trials and death will now be concentrated into the period of less than one full day. While Luke's account of Jesus' passion has many similarities with that of the other gospel writers, particularly Matthew and Mark, he has his own emphasis. In his account, throughout the unfolding events, Jesus continues to be the teacher, both in his words and in the example he shows. He is the exemplary martyr, suffering for good and God. Into the headlong rush of events we now plunge.

CONSPIRACY

The height of the Passover feast approaches. Two groups of people are making preparations. The authorities are plotting Jesus' death, Jesus and his disciples are making plans to keep the feast. The story of the plotting of the authorities is a peculiar amalgam of demonic possession and realpolitik. The Jerusalem authorities continue to have difficulties finding an opportunity to arrest Jesus quietly, away from the eyes of the crowd who still accompany his every word. This certainly suggests that Jesus and his disciples are well aware of the threat to his person and take great care in concealing his movements when he is vulnerably alone. Out of the blue in terms of Luke's narrative, from the inner circle of the disciples Judas Iscariot goes to the authorities and offers to lead them to Jesus at an opportune time. He will betray him (the original Greek says 'hand him over').

Theories proliferate over the motivation of Judas: jealousy, disillusion, his being under suspicion of theft, attempting to force Jesus' hand to make clear who he is. Luke says that whatever Judas' psychological state, there was outside influence: 'Satan entered Judas' (22:3). What do we make of Satan? In the Introduction to *Unmasking the Powers*, the second in his trilogy of books on 'the powers' in the New Testament, Walter Wink writes:

> One of the best ways to discern the weakness of a social system is to discover what it excludes from its conversation... Angels, spirits, principalities, powers, gods, Satan - these, along with all other spiritual realities, are the unmentionables of our culture. The dominant materialistic worldview has absolutely no place for them. These archaic relics of a superstitious past are unspeakable because modern secularism simply has no categories, no vocabulary, no presuppositions by which to discern what was in the actual experiences of people that brought these words to speech. And it has massive resistance even to thinking about these phenomena, having fought so long and hard to rid itself of every vestige of transcendence.
> (Wink 1986, p. 1)

Wink says that our world has great difficulty in thinking about the reality of evil. It is not that we don't know evil, rather, 'the evil of our time has become so gigantic that it has virtually outstripped the symbol and become autonomous, unrepresentable, beyond comprehension' (Wink p. 10). Some Christians have trivialised or domesticated evil, recognising its presence in the psychological states of individuals or in psychic phenomena, but being blind to its presence in such monstrous forces as racism, nuclear arms, the present system of international finance, etc. There has been a blindness to the reality that some of the greatest evils of our time have been perpetrated by those who appear quite rational and self-possessed, and who have indeed been in positions of great power and prestige. Luke's introduction of Satan into the preliminaries of the passion story signals the presence of monstrous evil, and that we are about to witness a cosmic struggle between good and evil. In his chapter on Satan (Wink p 9-40), Wink makes clear the ambiguous character of Satan in the Bible, appearing both as God's servant and God's enemy. Here Satan is the enemy, but the mystery remains that the action of Judas, prompted by Satan, is both malign and necessary on the way to Jesus' victory and our redemption. We are in deep waters indeed.

Passover preparation

We turn to the second set of preparations. Jesus makes careful plans to keep the Passover meal with his disciples. Peter and John are despatched to look for the unlikely sight of a man carrying a water jug, usually a female task. He would show them a large upstairs room made ready for the feast. The careful preparations once again suggest a community under threat, and Jesus showing great care and planning about his movements. They also point to his determination to keep the feast of Passover, the great feast of his people's freedom. Passover was celebrated as a family occasion with all ages present. Who was with Jesus in the large upstairs room? Quentin Quesnell makes a strong argument for the presence of women (and children) in the upper room (Quesnell 1983, p 59-80).

'How have I desired...'

The time for the feast has arrived. Jesus sits down at the table with the disciples. How I love his first words from the King James version (AV), 'With desire I have desired to eat this Passover with you before I suffer!' (22:15) What feeling, what intensity of longing is in these words of Jesus as he sits down to share this precious moment with those closest to him, those who 'have stayed with me all through my trials' (*GNB* 22:28). The intensity is heightened by Jesus' sense that this is the last Passover he will share with them, indeed his last meal with them before the imminent crisis. Jesus' words here convey a powerful picture of the humanity and comradeship he has shared with the disciples and which he continues to treasure. Luke does not have the same sense found in Mark's gospel, of the discipleship community's disintegration in the face of the cross. While they will have their trials and failures through the next few hours, Luke lays more stress on the continuity between Jesus' disciples before and after the passion, as those who have been the companions of his ministry become in turn the first leaders in the church of the apostles.

'Take this and share it...'

Luke's account of the Lord's Supper has distinctive features. The lack of exact correspondence in the words attributed to Jesus at the Lord's Supper by the gospel writers is a reminder that they are writing before the final tradition of this central act of Christian worship has been established. In Luke's version, Jesus first takes the cup before the bread and invites the disciples to share it together without any mention of the wine being his blood. He then speaks of the cup a second time. However, the second mention of the cup in verse 20, 'This cup is God's new covenant sealed with my blood, which is poured out for you', is missing from a number of significant manuscripts, prompting the suggestion that it has been inserted by a later scribe to bring Luke's narrative into line with what had come to be the accepted pattern of the Lord's Supper. The reason for Luke's possible omission of Jesus' reference to the 'blood of the new covenant' can be found in his theology of the cross as G B Caird suggests: 'The explanation is to be sought in Luke's theology: for believing, as he did, that God's saving act was the whole of Jesus' life of service and self-giving, and that the Cross was simply the preordained price of friendship with the outcast, he naturally felt little interest in sayings which appeared to concentrate the whole of God's redemption in the Cross' (Caird 1963, p. 238).

It is nevertheless true that Luke sees this last meal together as a key moment of Jesus' ministry. Meals with others, whether Jesus has been a guest (4:39, 5:29, 7:36,

11:37, 14:1, 19:5), or host as at the feeding of the 5000 (9:10-17) and here, have formed a central part of his ministry and his message of hospitality towards all, particularly the outsider. The new significance Jesus gives to the old feast of freedom, as a sign of costly sharing and continuing presence, gathers up and concentrates the meaning of all these previous meals together. Duncan Forrester writes:

> The strange and complex relation between the meals and the death of Jesus suggests that it is not at all fanciful to see Jesus' meals as a significant part of the work of reconciliation, the breaking down of the dividing wall of hostility, the bringing near of those who were far off, the welcoming of strangers into the commonwealth of Israel, for "He abolished the law with its commandments and ordinances, so that he might create in himself one new humanity in place of the two, thus making peace, and might reconcile both groups to God in one body through the cross, thus putting to death that hostility through it" (Ephesians 2:15,16).
> (Forrester, 2001, p. 206)

The fellowship of the meal is abruptly broken by Jesus' announcement of his imminent betrayal by one of his inner circle of disciples, sharing at the same table. The stark revelation that evil lurks at the very heart of the discipleship enterprise warns against any simplistic division of our world into goodies and baddies, and the recurring temptation to externalise the enemy. Jesus declares that while his betrayal is part of the plan of God, how terrible it is for the one who does the deed, though Luke's gospel says no more about the fate of Judas. The announcement causes confusion among the disciples as they talk and ponder together who among them would do the deed. The embattled community now has to deal with its suspicions at its very heart.

THE NEW COMMUNITY: 'I AM AMONG YOU AS ONE WHO SERVES'

Perhaps to cover their confusion, the disciples now talk nonsense. They have an argument, in the immediate aftermath of the precious moment of the feast of communion, about which one of them is greatest. This episode, which Luke places in this key position in his gospel, is largely similar to Mark 10:42-45. In Mark's gospel the argument occurs at an equally crass moment, immediately after Jesus has forewarned the disciples about his suffering and death for the third time. The passage here in Luke contains a further echo. It ends in verse 27 with words which appear at the end of John's unique account of Jesus washing his disciples' feet (John 13:12-15). 'Who is greater, the one who sits down to eat or the one who serves? The one who sits down, of course. But I am among you as one who serves.'

Jesus contrasts the way of the world, with its pyramidal structures of power, and the way of the new community he creates, with an ethos of mutuality and humble, outgoing, costly service at its heart. It is a way which will find its supreme expression in the event of the cross. It is also the way it is to be among us - the ethos and form of the continuing presence of Christ in the world; in Bonhoeffer's words, 'Christ existing as community'.

This community of mutuality and service is the church. What a constant challenge that is to us! Embodying Christ as community and taking the way of humble service has frequently not been the way of those who would call him 'Lord'. All too often, the church in its historic institutional forms has reduplicated the power structures and domination systems of 'the kings of the pagans', whether it be the courts of medieval Europe or the management structures of today's big corporations. The challenge to the unity of mutual service comes from the event at the heart of our salvation, its evangelical heart. The way of taking, giving thanks, breaking, giving and sharing, which is central to the supper Jesus inaugurates, is not only to be at the centre of a liturgical act, it is to be the living centre of the life of the new community, into which we are called now.

After the call to service in the steps of our servant Lord, Jesus offers warm words of commendation and promise. He praises the disciples for their constancy and he gives them a place of leadership in the new Israel, the new community he creates. It is, of course, a leadership informed and permeated by his immediately preceding words about the servant way.

JESUS AND PETER

Immediately following his praise of the disciples' constant presence, Jesus predicts their desertion in the final, lonely hours of his trial. He speaks directly to Peter as leader and representative of the twelve (22:31 - and in this passage Satan has reverted to his role as accuser at the heavenly court as in Job 1:6-12). Jesus' prediction is not only that Peter will deny Jesus - thrice before the cock crows tonight - but that Jesus' prayer for him will ensure that after his failure and desertion he will turn back to Jesus and be given the task of strengthening the other apostles. This emphasis on Peter's return to Jesus - 'reconversion' is the force of the Greek verb - and his future leadership role, sets Luke's account apart from the other three gospels. It softens the impact of Peter's predicted failure.

ENOUGH!

Turning to the disciples, Jesus reminds how they lacked nothing when they were sent out on their mission without purse, bag or shoes (9:1-6). 'Times are different now,' says Jesus, 'we're a community under threat and you're on your own. Get what you need for your survival.' What is meant by Jesus' instruction to get swords? Is he using metaphorical speech to stress the urgency and danger of the disciples' situation? Is he suggesting that swords are necessary so that at his arrest he will be identified as a criminal, an insurgent? Is that why he quotes the words of the song of the suffering servant in Isaiah 53:12, 'He shared the fate of criminals', and says these words will be fulfilled in him? Is this a sign of the length that Jesus, who has consistently taught and shown a peaceable way of vulnerable non-violence, will go in his identification with sinful, violent humanity? Either interpretation is possible. At any rate, the disciples produce two swords, which are obviously quite inappropriate weapons for the cosmic battle into which Jesus is going. Perhaps this is a sign that Jesus is already in the company of sinful men; a further indication, along with the argument about greatness, that even the disciples, whose faithfulness has just been praised, have not completely left the old ways of death behind. Wearily, Jesus says, 'That's enough!' - which can be interpreted either as 'Let's stop this conversation, you've missed the point, lost the plot', or as a word heavy with irony - for what have swords to do with the sacrificial way immediately ahead?

STUDY

BY YOURSELF
Imagine yourself present in the upstairs room with Jesus and the disciples.
• Watch and listen to the words and actions of Jesus, and of his disciples.

• What's the atmosphere like? Does it change, from episode to episode?

• Is there anything you want to ask Jesus, or Peter, or Judas?

• What do you hear them saying to you?

• Is there a particular moment, word, action which moves, challenges, disturbs you? Return to it and pray through it.

FOR GROUP WORK
Have one person read through this passage slowly, with plenty of pauses; and then share with one another your thoughts, questions and feelings from your contemplation of this passage.

Share together a simple *agape* meal of bread, wine and prayer. Resources can be found in *The One Loaf - an everyday celebration* by Joy Mead, published by Wild Goose Publications.

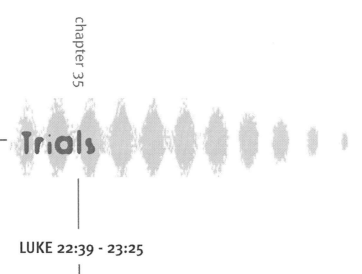

chapter 35

Trials

LUKE 22:39 - 23:25

Jesus Prays on the Mount of Olives
(Mt 26:36-46, Mk: 14:32-42)

Jesus left the city and went, as he usually did, to the Mount of Olives; and the disciples went with him. When he arrived at the place, he said to them, "Pray that you will not fall into temptation."

Then he went off from them about the distance of a stone's throw and knelt down and prayed. "Father," he said, "If you will, take this cup of suffering away from me. Not my will, however, but your will be done." An angel from heaven appeared to him and strengthened him. In great anguish he prayed even more fervently; his sweat was like drops of blood falling to the ground.

Rising from his prayer, he went back to the disciples and found them asleep, worn out by their grief. He said to them, "Why are you sleeping? Get up and pray that you will not fall into temptation. "

The Arrest of Jesus
(Mt 26:47-56, Mk 14:43-50, Jn 18:3-11)

Jesus was still speaking when a crowd arrived, led by Judas, one of the twelve disciples. He came up to Jesus to kiss him. But Jesus said, "Judas, is it with a kiss that you betray the Son of Man?"

When the disciples who were with Jesus saw what was going to happen, they asked, "Shall we use our swords, Lord?" And one of them struck the High Priest's slave and cut off his right ear.

But Jesus said, "Enough of this!" He touched the man's ear and healed him.

Then Jesus said to the chief priests and the officers of the temple guard and the elders who had come there to get him, "Did you have to come with swords and clubs, as though I were an outlaw? I was with you in the Temple every day, and you did not try to arrest me. But this is your hour to act, when the power of darkness rules."

Peter Denies Jesus
(Mt 26:57-58, 69-75, Mk 14:53-54, 66-72, Jn 18:12-18, 25-27)

They arrested Jesus and took him away into the house of the High Priest; and Peter followed at a distance. A fire had been lit in the centre of the courtyard, and Peter joined those who were sitting round it. When one of the servant women saw him sitting there at the fire, she looked straight at him and said, "This man too was with Jesus!"

But Peter denied it, "Woman, I don't even know him!"

After a little while a man noticed Peter and said, "You are one of them, too!"

But Peter answered, "Man, I am not!"

And about an hour later another man insisted strongly, "There isn't any doubt that this man was with Jesus, because he also is a Galilean!"

But Peter answered, "Man, I don't know what you are talking about!"

At once, while he was still speaking, a cock crowed. The Lord turned round and looked straight at Peter, and Peter remembered that the Lord had said to him, "Before the cock crows tonight, you will say three times that you do not know me." Peter went out and wept bitterly.

Jesus is Mocked and Beaten
(Mt 26:67-68, Mk 14:65)

The men who were guarding Jesus mocked him and beat him. They blindfolded him and asked him, "Who hit you? Guess!" And they said many other insulting things to him.

Jesus is Brought before the Council
(Mt 26:59-66, Mk 14:55-64, Jn 18:19-24)

When day came, the elders, the chief priests, and the teachers of the Law met together, and Jesus was brought before the Council. "Tell us," they said, "are you the Messiah?"

He answered, "If I tell you, you will not believe me; and if I ask you a question, you will not answer. But from now on the Son of Man will be seated on the right of Almighty God."

They all said, "Are you, then, the Son of God?"

He answered them, "You say that I am."

And they said, "We don't need any witnesses! We ourselves have heard what he said!"

Jesus is Brought before Pilate
(Mt 27:1-2, 11-14, Mk 15:1-5, Jn 18:28-38)

The whole group rose up and took Jesus before Pilate, where they began to accuse him: "We caught this man misleading our people, telling them not to pay taxes to the Emperor and claiming that he himself is the Messiah, a king."

Pilate asked him, "Are you the king of the Jews?"

"So you say," answered Jesus.

Then Pilate said to the chief priests and the crowds, "I find no reason to condemn this man."

But they insisted even more strongly, "With his teaching he is starting a riot among the people all through Judea. He began in Galilee and now has come here."

Jesus is Sent to Herod

When Pilate heard this, he asked, "Is this man a Galilean?" When he learnt that Jesus was from the region ruled by Herod, he sent him to Herod, who was also in Jerusalem at this time. Herod was very pleased when he saw Jesus, because he had heard about him and had been wanting to see him for a long time. He was hoping to see Jesus perform some miracle. So Herod asked Jesus many questions, but Jesus made no answer. The chief priests and the teachers of the Law stepped forward and made strong accusations against Jesus. Herod and his soldiers mocked Jesus and treated him with contempt; then they put a fine robe on him and sent him back to Pilate. On that very day Herod and Pilate became friends; before this they had been enemies.

Jesus is Sentenced to Death
(Mt 27:15-26, Mk 15:6-15, Jn 18:39 - 19:16)

Pilate called together the chief priests, the leaders, and the people, and said to them, "You brought this man to me and said he was misleading the people. Now, I have examined him here in your presence, and I have not found him guilty of any of the crimes you accuse him of. Nor did Herod find him guilty, for he sent him back to us. There is nothing this man has done to deserve death. So I will have him whipped and let him go."

The whole crowd cried out, "Kill him! Set Barabbas free for us!" (Barabbas had been put in prison for a riot that had taken place in the city, and for murder.)

Pilate wanted to set Jesus free, so he appealed to the crowd again. But they shouted back, "Crucify him! Crucify him!"

Pilate said to them a third time, "But what crime has he committed? I cannot find anything he has done to deserve death! I will have him whipped and set him free."

But they kept on shouting at the top of their voices that Jesus should be crucified, and finally their shouting succeeded. So Pilate passed the sentence on Jesus that they were asking for. He set free the man they wanted, the one who had been put in prison for riot and murder, and he handed Jesus over for them to do as they wished.

THE FINAL TESTING

'The last and fiercest strife is nigh.' Jesus enters the time of trial. In quick and bewildering succession we will see him taken before the Jerusalem council, the Sanhedrin, who will send him to Pilate the Roman Governor, who will send him to Herod Antipas, the ruler of Galilee, who will send him back to Pilate, by whom he will be reluctantly condemned. It is a shameful story of an innocent man being bundled from pillar to post, maltreated and finally killed by the very forces of law and order which should be there for his protection. Religious leaders, officials of two jurisdictions and soldiers are all shown in callous or fearful abuse of their power. Before the public trial of Jesus, he faces his own moment of profound inner testing. The story of Jesus' trials begins as he returns once more to the Mount of Olives, his evening retreat, with his disciples.

He bids them pray that they may be able to withstand the time of testing ahead. And he goes off, some distance from them, to be alone. From now until his resurrection, how powerfully and poignantly the word 'alone' describes Jesus' condition. What he must now do, what he must now allow to happen to him, must suffer, must endure, he must go through alone. The crowds have gone, the disciples waver and fall away; before his accusers and tormentors he is alone. Now, at the Mount of Olives, he wills to be alone, alone with God and alone with his doubts and wrestlings. This is the time of the final testing, the hour of agony, the moment of decision in which the die is cast. Up to this moment he can walk away from what lies before him. Will he? Or will he have the strength to stand fast? What lies before involves not only his own fate, but the fate of others. How much more pressure does that knowledge heap on the head of one whose whole ministry has been so full of compassion for others. 'The horrors he has foreseen need not happen, if he were to slip quietly into obscurity: Judas need not offer the traitor's kiss, nor Peter hear the accusing cock, the conspiracy of priest and Pharisee need not bear its grim fruit, nor need Jerusalem commit her crowning iniquity' (Caird 1963, p. 242).

Falling down on his knees he prays. 'Father, if you will, take this cup of suffering from me.' What poignancy there is in the mention of the cup from the lips of the one who has so recently shared the cup with his friends. His sweat falls like drops of blood on the ground in his struggle of soul. 'Not my will, however, but your will be done' (22:42). In this gospel of prayer, this key moment of prayer has heightened significance. Jesus' prayer has a twofold request; that he might bend his will to God's will and continue to be the instrument of God's peace, and that he might have the strength to carry through what lies ahead. 'Your will be done' continues to take a central place in the pattern of our prayers. We pray this petition, seeking the guidance and resources we need to live faithful lives. As we pray, we are led out into making the prayer real through our own lives in the world. Do we dare to pray this prayer, in sincerity, trusting in the strength God will give us? The prayer is made, the issue is settled, Jesus rises, resolve renewed. He finds the disciples asleep, worn out by the grief and tension of the hours they are living through. The picture is of the contrast between Jesus who is so fully alive and awake to this critical moment, and the disciples dead in the denial of sleep. Again he bids them pray for the strength to endure.

ARREST

He is still speaking when the arresting party, led by Judas, interrupts. We presume that Judas has arranged with the temple guard that he will identify Jesus with a kiss in a shameful betrayal of solidarity, friendship and intimacy. The disciples, seeing the danger, pick up their inappropriate and impotent swords. One of them manages to inflict damage on the ear of the High Priest's slave. Jesus repeats the same word he has said when swords were previously mentioned. 'Enough!' he says, and heals the wound in the slave's ear. 'Enough, this is not the way!'

He turns to the considerable crowd who have come to arrest him, chief priests, temple guards, and elders and upbraids them for this violent and stealthy act. 'Why did you not dare to arrest me when I was teaching daily and openly in the Temple? This affair reeks of the night and its dark powers' (22:53).

DENIAL

Jesus is taken to the house of the High Priest while Peter follows at a distance (22:54). The disciple finds his way to the fire lit at the centre of the courtyard: he is shivering from more than just the cold. Three times in quick succession, by a woman and two separate men, Peter is fingered as having been part of Jesus' company. Thrice, with vehemence, Peter denies that he ever knew Jesus. And a cock crows. And Jesus turns and looks straight at Peter (Luke alone has this telling detail). Peter remembers, turns tail, and weeps, bitterly.

We've all been in that courtyard with Peter, and known these times when we've been less than loyal to our friends, failed to stand up for the truth and, through fear, sold them and ourselves short. We know that haunting sense of self-accusation and failure. We well understand Peter's tears. The cock-crow signals the approaching dawn. For Peter there is now only darkness, in the pain of Jesus and his sense of impotence and failure to be able to do anything to help him. As so often in this story we are confronted by the strangeness of things. If Peter had had the moral courage to admit to his part in Jesus' company, where would that have taken him... to a cell or cross beside his master? And what would the history of the young church have been then? It is out of Peter's failure, redeemed, that a key link in the church's history is forged.

What happens next is not strange. In the hands of the temple guards, Jesus is mocked and beaten. The bullies have their day in a shameful but all too familiar misuse of their power. They blindfold Jesus. 'Guess who hit you!' is the cruel taunt. In this moment Jesus stands in solidarity with all victims of torture and official maltreatment, then and now.

BEFORE THE HIGH PRIEST

At first light Jesus is brought before the hurriedly-convened Council of the Sanhedrin. Luke's version of the trial before the Jewish authorities is significantly different from that of Matthew and Mark. They concentrate on the charge of blasphemy, of Jesus' claim to raze and rebuild the Temple in three days. Perhaps because the charge of blasphemy might seem obscure to his Gentile readers, Luke concentrates on the question, 'Are you the Messiah?' If Jesus says 'Yes' then he can be delivered to the Roman authorities as a political insurrectionary. Jesus says neither 'Yes' nor 'No.' To the leaders of his people he says, 'We don't understand each other. We are not speaking the same language at all. What you understand by "Messiah" and my understanding are completely at cross-purposes.' He then uses his favoured title for himself, 'the Son of Man'. 'But from now on the Son of Man will be seated on the right of Almighty God' (22:69). The Son of Man is ruler, judge and liberator. Who is judging who?... is the question these words of Jesus provoke. 'Are you the Son of God?' ask the accusers. 'You say so,' says Jesus. Such a scant and ambiguous reply is enough for the court. They rise to take him to Pilate, accusing him of fomenting civil disobedience and insurrection. This is the response of the highest court in the land, committed to upholding the Law of Moses and the justice of God. The action of the Jewish leaders in taking Jesus to Pilate forces them to be more loyal to Rome than to one of their own people. Already we have seen Jesus suffer at the hands of faithless and fearful friends, petty bullies, and religious and political leaders committed to administering God's justice. 'Were you there when they crucified my Lord?' asks the spiritual. Most of humanity, including ourselves, would have to say, 'Yes'... not just as innocent bystanders, but somehow complicit in this terrible wrong.

PILATE

Jesus is next dragged and accused before the Roman Governor, Pilate. The charges mentioned above are a blatant misrepresentation of the words and work of Jesus. Pilate finds no reason to condemn Jesus, and says so. The Jewish leaders are insistent: 'He caused trouble in Galilee and now he's causing trouble in Judea' (23:5). As soon as Pilate hears mention of Galilee, he sees a get-out for himself. If the trouble started in Galilee, then Jesus is under the jurisdiction of Herod Antipas. Passing the buck, he sends Jesus to Herod. Compromise is not necessarily a dirty word. Often in life, and in public affairs in particular, it is the only way forward. But there's a time to waver and a time not to waver. If Pilate had had the courage of his convictions, he could have nipped this lynch-mob injustice in the bud. He ducks his opportunity to stand firm, and from now on he's on the slippery slope to his final role in this drama, displaying the powerlessness of the man in power.

HEROD

The accused is now hauled before Herod. Luke alone reports the 'trial' before Herod. It's a curious episode. Luke states that Herod had been keen to see Jesus. It appears the sentiment was not reciprocated by Jesus. Herod hoped that Jesus would perform some miracle. Not only does Jesus not oblige, he says nothing at all to Herod; not a word. He keeps silence in face of both Herod's many questions and the strong charges from the travelling band of his accusers. Herod and his soldiers continue the process of roughing up the prisoner, they add their mockery, putting a fine robe upon him to symbolise the king he isn't. Still without a guilty sentence, Jesus is returned to Pilate. Throughout this appearance the words of Isaiah 53: 7 echo strongly:

> He was oppressed, he was afflicted,
> yet he did not open his mouth;
> like a lamb that is led to the slaughter,
> and like a sheep that before its shearers is silent,
> so he did not open his mouth.
> (Isaiah 53:7, *NRSV*)

PILATE AGAIN

The round of 'pass the prisoner' comes to its final end with Jesus' second appearance before Pilate. Adding pressure on the compromised governor is a local crowd, baying for blood. The scene is played out as a battle of wills between Pilate and Jesus' accusers, aided and abetted by a thoroughly roused crowd. Three times Pilate tells both the religious leaders and the crowd that he (and Herod) can find no fault with Jesus deserving death. Three times they respond with the cry 'Crucify!'

There was a custom that at every Passover Pilate would free one prisoner for the people - some manuscripts add this explanation after Pilate says for the first time, 'I will have him whipped and let him go' (23:16). A contest develops between Pilate's wish to free Jesus, the Galilean outsider, and the crowd's shouts for the release of Barabbas, the local man from Jerusalem. The cry for Barabbas is full of ironies. The name 'Barabbas' means in Hebrew 'son of the father'. Barabbas has been sentenced as a rebel insurrectionist, precisely the charge against Jesus, of which he is innocent. He is a killer; Jesus has done no violence. In the end Pilate succumbs to the shouts of the baying mob. Barabbas, the guilty one, is released and the innocent Jesus is condemned.

Throughout this final confrontation Jesus remains a silent spectator. He waits and watches, mute and powerless, in this battle for his life.

INNOCENCE AND SILENCE

In the scenes of Jesus' trials, two impressions are conveyed powerfully by Luke. The first is of Jesus' innocence. The charges brought against him by the Jewish authorities are obviously ludicrous misrepresentations of him and his words, and Luke lays great stress on Pilate's multiple declarations that he can find no reason to condemn him. The stress on Jesus' innocence of the charge of insurrection can be seen as part of Luke's larger plan in Luke/Acts, where he is at pains to make clear that the church as it spreads through Asia Minor and into Europe represents no threat to Roman authority. While Luke may have had this apologetic purpose in his mind, the reality remains, Jesus is innocent of the charges laid against him. Others are guilty. Jesus is on his way to the cross through the weakness and lack of faith of the disciples, the fear, self-interest and cynicism of the powerful, the fickleness and parochialism of the crowd. 'The Lord has laid on him the iniquities of us all' (Isaiah 53;6b *NRSV*).

The second strong impression coming from Luke's description of the trials of Jesus is of his silence. He either refuses to answer the questions of his accusers directly, or he stands in mute dignity before them. It is a powerful picture of one who suffers, but is not cowed. There is a strange majesty about the bearing of Jesus throughout his trials. Richard Cassidy comments:

> When we recall Jesus' earlier refusal to alter his ministry as a consequence of Herod's threat, and his refusal to accord any privileged position to the Roman empire in responding to the tribute question, the lack of cooperation that Luke attributes to him at his trial becomes considerably more understandable. Indeed, seen against the backdrop of Jesus' earlier sarcastic references to "benefactors" who dominate their subjects and his deprecating reference to Herod as "that fox," Jesus' lack of deference to both Pilate and Herod is surprisingly consistent with his earlier response to them or their counterparts.
>
> We should also recall here the great differences between the patterns Jesus advocated and those in effect around him. Jesus' approach to material possessions and that followed by Herod and the top Roman officials could hardly have been greater. Similarly, Jesus' advocacy of an enhanced status and new roles for women put him at variance with the social patterns that these authorities supported. Again, Jesus' rejection of the use of violence contrasted startlingly with the violence and domination upon which Roman rule was premised. In general, Luke shows Jesus as deeply committed to establishing social relationships based on service and humility; since such qualities were little valued in the society around him, there was a constant tension between his positions and those sanctioned by the existing order... The stance which Luke shows Jesus adopting toward Pilate and Herod at his trial is substantially the same as that which he had previously adopted. It is not a stance of either cooperation or deference.
>
> (Cassidy 1978, p 74-5)

It is the silence of one who is sure of the source of his authority and sure of his own ground. 'Are you the Messiah?' 'If I tell you, you will not believe me: and if I question you, you will not respond' (22:67-68). Jesus is not the Messiah his accusers would make him out to be; his is another kingship, within the royal rule of the imminent Kingdom of God. Throughout the trial scenes, there is a sense of something going on about the ironies of power. Pilate, representative of Roman might, is weak and allows himself to be overruled: Herod is ignored by Jesus' silence; the crowd is swayed by cheap and easy emotion. In a strange way, Jesus is both victim and the most powerful person present. No one can penetrate his silent presence. Both the silence and the presence keep exposing the weaknesses of power. One of the most powerful ways to confront power is to expose its presumptions. By his silence Jesus exposes these presumptions. In effect his silence says, 'There is no reason for you to crucify me except that you've decided to crucify me.' Power always pretends and presumes to be reasonable. Jesus exposes that pretension. The power of weakness is demonstrated.

STUDY

BY YOURSELF
Throughout this passage we see Jesus at war with worldly powers and identified with the pain of the world. Jesus is falsely condemned through the abuse of power by the powerful. Reflect on where you see political or economic power being abused in our world today. Are you complicit in this abuse by your silence? Can you pray in a way which is informed and connected, for organisations which campaign against the abuse of power, like Amnesty International or Trade Justice? And use this Gethsemane prayer.

> Jesus, our brother,
> once you knelt sleepless
> in the darkness of a garden
> alone
> and wept and prayed,
> sweating, bleeding,
> with the pain of powerlessness
> with the strain of waiting.
> An angel offered you strength -
> but it was a bitter cup.
>
> We pray for all
> who wake tonight
> waiting, agonising,
> anxious and afraid,
> while others sleep:
> for those who sweat
> and bleed, and weep alone.
> If it is not possible
> for their cup to be taken away -
> then may they know your presence
> kneeling at their side.
> Amen
> (Jan Sutch Pickard in N Paynter 2002, p. 81)

chapter 36

CrucifixiOn

LUKE 23:26-56

Jesus is Crucified
(Mt 27:32-44, Mk 15:21-32, Jn 19:17-27)

The soldiers led Jesus away, and as they were going, they met a man from Cyrene named Simon who was coming into the city from the country. They seized him, put the cross on him, and made him carry it behind Jesus.

A large crowd of people followed him; among them were some women who were weeping and wailing for him. Jesus turned to them and said, "Women of Jerusalem! Don't cry for me, but for yourselves and your children. For the days are coming when people will say, 'How lucky are the women who never had children, who never bore babies, who never nursed them!' That will be the time when people will say to the mountains, 'Fall on us!' and to the hills, 'Hide us!' For if such things as these are done when the wood is green, what will happen when it is dry?"

Two other men, both of them criminals, were also led out to be put to death with Jesus. When they came to the place called, "The Skull", they crucified Jesus there, and the two criminals, one on his right and the other on his left. Jesus said, "Forgive them, Father! They don't know what they are doing."

They divided his clothes among themselves by throwing dice. The people stood there watching while the Jewish leaders jeered at him: "He saved others; let him save himself if he is the Messiah whom God has chosen!"

The soldiers also mocked him: they came up to him and offered him cheap wine, and said, "Save yourself if you are the king of the Jews!"

Above him were written these words: "This is the King of the Jews."

One of the criminals hanging there hurled insults at him: "Aren't you the

Messiah? Save yourself and us!"

The other one, however, rebuked him, saying, "Don't you fear God? You received the same sentence he did. Ours, however, is only right, because we are getting what we deserve for what we did; but he has done no wrong." And he said to Jesus, "Remember me, Jesus, when you come as King!"

Jesus said to him, "I promise you that today you will be in Paradise with me."

The Death of Jesus
(Mt 27:45-56, Mk 15:33-41, Jn 19:28-30)

It was about twelve o'clock when the sun stopped shining and darkness covered the whole country until three o'clock; and the curtain hanging in the Temple was torn in two. Jesus cried out in a loud voice, "Father! In your hands I place my spirit!" He said this and died.

The army officer saw what had happened, and he praised God, saying, "Certainly he was a good man!"

When the people who had gathered there to watch the spectacle saw what happened, they all went back home, beating their breasts in sorrow. All those who knew Jesus personally, including the women who had followed him from Galilee, stood at a distance to watch.

The Burial of Jesus
(Mt 27:57-61, Mk 15:42-47, Jn 19:38-42)

There was a man named Joseph from Arimathea, a town in Judaea. He was a good and honourable man, who was waiting for the coming of the Kingdom of God. Although he was a member of the Council, he had not agreed with their decision and action. He went into the presence of Pilate and asked for the body of Jesus. Then he took the body down, wrapped it in a linen sheet, and placed it in a tomb which had been dug out of solid rock and which had never been used. It was Friday, and the Sabbath was about to begin.

The women who had followed Jesus from Galilee went with Joseph and saw the tomb and how Jesus' body was placed in it. Then they went back home and prepared the spices and perfumes for the body.

On the Sabbath they rested, as the Law commanded.

'Weep not for me'

The indecent haste of the summary trials continues as Jesus is led away to be crucified. Physically broken by the events of the preceding hours, Jesus is unable to carry the crossbar of his own cross. The soldiers press-gang a man from Cyrene in North Africa to carry it for him. His name is Simon; Simon the disciple is posted absent.

As Jesus staggers along his *via dolorosa*, a crowd follows; by the roadside he meets a group of women weeping for him. There is time for a final word from Jesus about his beloved Jerusalem, which will not learn the things that make for her peace (19:42). He tells the women not to weep for him but rather to save their tears for themselves and their children. Their city's fate will be so terrible that it will be a blessing to be barren and childless, a complete overturning of people's normal hopes and expectations. He continues, 'If such things as these are done when the wood is green, what will happen when it is dry?' (23:31) Jesus is saying that if he, the green wood, can suffer the fate he does as one who comes in peace and offers no violent threat to anyone, how brutally will authority put down those who kindle the dry wood of rebellion. It is a final fruitless warning for Jerusalem to change her ways.

In the introduction to a series of Holy Week addresses, John V Taylor has this comment on the weeping women of Jerusalem:

> Pity is one of the most deceptive of human emotions. It is a half-way stopping place on the way of discipleship. Yet at no time did Jesus ask us to pity him, or pity his brothers and sisters in whom we are meant to find him. We are called to feed and clothe them, visit them in sickness and in prison. We are called to become involved in them at the level of our wills and our action.
>
> We must not be content to form a little cluster of devout people engaged in a religious exercise for the improvement of our souls. If that is all we are doing we shall have no more part in the real event than those wailing daughters of Jerusalem had then. But if we will dare to be honest and to take the whole world into gaze we shall have cause for weeping. "Weep for yourselves and for your children for the days are coming..." so Jesus prophesied the self-destruction of his beloved nation and we who contemplate his Cross again this week are not far from our own self-destruction.
>
> The true perspective of our lives is not the small, moderate bourgeois world that we pretend is ours but a cosmic stage on which the great extremes of the Gospel are stark realities - light and darkness, life and death, luxury and starvation, heaven and perdition. In this struggle of immense opposites the Cross of Jesus Christ towers to its true height. For in the world as it is today, nothing can avail to save us but an act of God making available once more to humanity the divine wisdom and strength and love.
>
> (Taylor 1985, p 3 & 4)

The procession arrives at the place of crucifixion, the place called, 'The Skull' (23:33). Jesus is crucified between two convicted criminals. 'They made his grave with the wicked...' (Isaiah 53:9). The soldiers throw dice to decide who will keep the clothes that were stripped from his back. The Jewish leaders, his main antagonists, mock him. 'He saved others; let him save himself if he is the Messiah whom God has chosen!' (23:35) What irony there is in these words. He has saved others, many others; this is true. And it is precisely *because* he will not save himself that he makes plain that he is the Messiah whom God has chosen and *not* the Messiah who is merely the construct of his people's nationalistic frustrations, hopes and dreams. The irony continues. Over his head is written the charge sheet: 'This is the King of the Jews.' Throughout his ministry, Jesus has thrown out the challenge to see kingship and rule in a completely new light, in terms of the values and reality of God's upside-down, outside-in, inside-out Kingdom. Luke bids us look and see this strangest of kings, and the yet more strange manner of his coming to reign. To help us look in relevant wonder, here are some words from a series of meditations on the Stations of the Cross, *Way of the Cross, Way of Justice*, by the Latin American liberation theologian, Leonardo Boff. In the meditations, Boff invites us both to stand before the original cross, and also to discern the cross in human life today. Here is part of the station where Jesus is nailed to the cross; then and now.

> *Then: Jesus was crucified.*
> Through his life and message, Jesus,
> acting in the name of God,
> strove to inculcate in human beings a spirit
> that would never cause crosses for others;
> and now he himself hangs on a cross.
> His cross is not the result
> of an arbitrary whim on God's part.
> It results from the way in which the world is organized.
> Sinfully closed in upon itself,
> The world rejected the God of Jesus
> and eliminated Jesus himself. ...
>
> God does not will death
> but life in all its fullness.
> That is another name for God's Kingdom.
> Even though human beings rejected that Kingdom
> and crucified Jesus,
> who proclaimed and embodied it,
> God did not cease to will it. ...
>
> It is now through the death of his Son
> that God will realize the Kingdom.
> Jesus freely accepted condemnation to death.

He died for our sins.
In other words,
he died because our rejection of conversion
brought him to his death.
He took our sins upon himself,
establishing solidarity with sinners
in order to free them from their wickedness.
In particular, he established solidarity with all the victims of human
  sinfulness.
Nailed to the cross,
Jesus expresses his freedom to the fullest,
surrendering himself to God and human beings
out of love. ...

Now: Jesus continues to be nailed to the cross.
There is a mysterious presence of God within humanity.
The Incarnation means that the Son
really did assume our sinful condition.
Once he did that, he continues to remain in it forever.
He became incarnate,
not to sacralize the world and humanity,
but to liberate them,
to make the old world new
and the sinful human being just.
His struggle to achieve this liberation
goes on through the centuries,
confronting all the obstacles
that the hardness of the human heart
and the iniquity of socio-historical relationships can create. ...

So Jesus continues to be crucified
In all those who are crucified in history.
There are not enough Stations of the Cross
to depict all the ways in which the Lord continues to be
persecuted,
imprisoned,
condemned to death,
and crucified today in the ongoing Passion of human life. ...

But Jesus does not just suffer.
He continues to offer himself to God
and his brothers and sisters,
to pardon,
and to love all human beings
to the very end.
(Boff 1980, p 88-93)

THE FIRST WORD

We have heard the sound of weeping from the mothers of Jerusalem, and the noise of baying, cynical mockery from Jesus' opponents. There is a third and most significant voice in Luke's account of the crucifixion: Jesus' own. Three times he speaks 'a word from the cross'; with each word we are reminded of one of the key aspects of who he is. In the excruciating moment when he is nailed to the cross, he says, 'Forgive them, Father! They don't know what they are doing'. To the end he remains faithful to his own extraordinary words about love of enemies in the sermon on the plain (6:27ff). At the cross, we see the reality of vicarious suffering and freely offered forgiveness which breaks the charmed and deadly escalating spiral of violence. The liberating power of forgiveness has been central to Jesus' words, and works throughout the gospel. It concentrates and climaxes at the cross.

THE SECOND WORD

Throughout the gospel, Luke has shown Jesus having a special concern for the outsider, whether the outsider be the poor, the sinner, the alien, the enemy, the misfit. Crucifixion itself is a mark of solidarity with outsiders, with the excluded, banished and condemned. In the midst of the horrors of Jesus' last hours, Luke gives us a small cameo picture of one final human encounter. One of the criminals hanging with Jesus picks up the mockery of the Jewish leaders and the Roman soldiers: 'Save yourself and us!' The other rounds on him, saying that their sentence is deserved since they were guilty as charged, while this man has done no wrong - yet another declaration of innocence. The dying criminal says to Jesus, 'Remember me, Jesus, when you come into your Kingdom!' The way he addresses Jesus is striking in its directness: their critical situation cries out for directness. Whatever the dying man means by 'coming into your Kingdom' - and there is plenty of scholarly debate - clearly, he recognises in Jesus the stamp of heaven. Jesus' reply is brief and wonderful: 'I promise you that today you will be in Paradise with me' (23:43). 'Paradise' was a Persian word, meaning a 'park', which was used in the Greek Septuagint version of the Old Testament to refer to the Garden of Eden. It came to refer not only to the original perfection of God's creation but also to the future hope of a world redeemed, and a promise of a state of bliss for God's people. Jesus' promise to the dying man is not for a fulfilment in a future Kingdom at an indeterminate time - probably the thief's hope - but of entry into new life now, this day.

This is Jesus' last word to a human being. It is to an outsider, a sinner, a criminal, one well beyond the pale. Jesus' word, typically, is of welcome, forgiveness and hope. The dying criminal receives the ultimate welcome; he will be at home with Jesus.

THE LAST WORD

During Jesus' last hours, the sky itself darkens. The very atmosphere is thick with menace and gloom. After three hours, Jesus' travail is ended. With a loud voice he cries out. His final word is to God. 'Father, into your hands I commend my spirit!' (23:46) It is a word which speaks of the attitude of complete trust in God which has characterised Jesus from beginning to end and which has endured through these last days and hours, in spite of everything. The words are from Psalm 31:5. 'I place myself in your care. You will save me, Lord; you are a faithful God.'

Many years ago at the service of the Three Hour Meditation on the Seven Words from the Cross in Glasgow Cathedral, I heard the Minister, Bill Morris, contrast the words of Jesus with our modern attitudes. While Jesus casts himself on God the Father in trustful abandon, our modern words often are 'Into your spirit, I give my hands.' There is much to be said for the activism contained in such a prayer, particularly to a church too often guilty of an unbiblical quietism and retreat from the cross at the centre of life. In the abandon of Jesus' final prayer comes first the surrendered will, the confidence in God, the ever-renewed place of prayer. This is the contemplative well which never fails, the trusting committal of ourselves into God's hands. It secures our hold on the things that last; it prevents our activism from becoming brittle, bitter and worn-out.

In trusting faith, Jesus dies. It is another outsider who first makes comment: 'This man was innocent!' (23:47) he says. Luke then tells how the sorrowful procession makes its way home. It includes all Jesus' friends, and draws particular attention to a further group of outsiders according to the conventions of the time: the women who have followed Jesus all the way from Galilee. We shall shortly meet them again; their role in what ensues is critical.

BURIAL

For the moment it remains only for the body of Jesus to be given decent burial. When darkness fell, it would be the Sabbath; there was need for some haste. Joseph of Arimathea was a wealthy and influential man, a member of the Council of the Sanhedrin, although in disagreement with their findings and action on Jesus. This good man went to Pilate and asked for the release of Jesus' body. The body was taken down from the cross and wrapped for burial. Joseph had a new tomb, just cut from the solid rock, and the body of Jesus was placed there. The fact that this was a new tomb will prove important later: there is no possibility of the remains of Jesus being confused with those of anyone else. Once again we meet the women from Galilee: they went with Joseph to see the last resting place of Jesus. They still had the work of anointing the body to do. They went home to prepare the spices; their work would have to wait. The Sabbath rest had come.

After the activity and passion of the preceding hours, there is now dead silence in this day of uneasy rest and restless waiting. Alan Lewis draws us movingly and powerfully into the reality of the day we call Holy Saturday, the time and experience between cross and resurrection, in the book which was his own final testament; *Between Cross and Resurrection*. Let this short quotation hint at the significance of this day between the two days of monstrous significance, Good Friday and Easter Day:

> The very function of Easter Saturday is to prevent the rubbing out of Friday and its grievous memories by the instant and overwhelming exuberance of Sunday. Easter Saturday says that Jesus was gone and finished, subjected to death's power for a season. So Christ himself did not - despite centuries of popular and homiletical deceit - survive the grave! He succumbed to death and was swallowed by the grave - his Sabbath rest in the sepulchre a dramatized insistence that his termination was realistic and complete, a proper subject of grief and valediction. This was departure - painful, ugly, uncurtailed; no docetic illusion, no serene transcendence of the spirit high-floating over purely physical distress, no momentary, insignificant hiccup in Christ's unstoppable surge to glory. God's victory over death, as the Christian gospel tells it, is not a matter of smooth ensured survival but a new existence after nonsurvival - a quite different reality, for us as well as God.
> (Lewis 2001, p. 428)

And so we wait; for the morning we wait.

STUDY

BY YOURSELF
Reflect on these words from this ancient hymn of the Passion:

> Vinegar and gall they offer
> mocking him with thorns and reed.
> Nails and spear, the Saviour piercing
> make his sacred body bleed;
> by that blood the whole creation
> from the stain of sin is freed.
> (Venantius Fortunatus, c. 535-600, tr. J M Neale)

FOR GROUP WORK
Reflect together on Jesus' three words from the cross in Luke's gospel. These words from a hard place will repay time spent wrestling with them together.

1 'Forgive them, Father! They don't know what they are doing' (23:34). Forgiveness is a central theme of Luke's gospel. Here we see its wonder and its cost. Look again at the story of the prodigal in Chapter 23 (p. 155-161). Get each group member to complete a sentence beginning 'Forgiveness is...' Don't be satisfied with your first responses. Explore together. What do you do when you find it hard to forgive? Bring that response below the cross.

2 'I promise that today you will be in Paradise with me' (23:43). What do these words mean to you? What is the significance of these final words of Jesus being spoken to an outsider, a sinner, a criminal?

3 'Father! In your hands I place my spirit!' (23:46); what does the idea of trusting God in this complete way mean for you personally, and for your group?

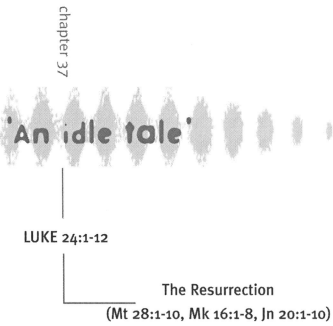

chapter 37

'An idle tale'

LUKE 24:1-12

The Resurrection
(Mt 28:1-10, Mk 16:1-8, Jn 20:1-10)

Very early on Sunday morning the women went to the tomb, carrying the spices they had prepared. They found the stone rolled away from the entrance to the tomb, so they went in; but they did not find the body of the Lord Jesus. They stood there puzzled about this, when suddenly two men in bright shining clothes stood by them. Full of fear, the women bowed down to the ground, as the men said to them, "Why are you looking among the dead for one who is alive? He is not here; he has been raised. Remember what he said to you while he was in Galilee: 'The Son of Man must be handed over to sinners, be crucified, and three days later rise to life.'"

Then the women remembered his words, returned from the tomb, and told all these things to the eleven disciples and all the rest. The women were Mary Magdalene, Joanna, and Mary the mother of James; they and the other women with them told these thing to the apostles. But the apostles thought that what the women said was nonsense, and they did not believe them. But Peter got up and ran to the tomb; he bent down and saw the linen wrappings but nothing else. Then he went back home amazed at what had happened.

HE IS NOT HERE

'Christ is risen!' 'He is risen indeed! Alleluia!' It is with some such loud, joyous, exuberant, affirmation that most services on Easter morning very properly begin. Luke's account of the resurrection morning begins more quietly. Let us start from the place where the story left off, in the silence of Holy Saturday, the in-between day. From that restless silence comes the beginning of the Easter story. Very early, at first light, the women go to the tomb. Dawn is breaking and the birds are beginning to sing; they remain locked in their silent loss. At least now the day of inactivity is over, they have a task of love to do, properly to embalm the body of their loved one, lying in Joseph's tomb. They have no other expectation. What they find does not conform to their expectations at all. The stone which sealed the entrance has been rolled away, and of the body of their Lord they can find no trace. They stand puzzled, astonished.

Two men in dazzling white, whom the women describe as angels (24:23), stand before them. Astonished puzzlement is replaced by fear. The silence is broken by a question, a statement, and a reminder. 'Why do you seek the living one among the dead? He is not here; he has been raised. Remember what he told you while he was in Galilee.' These words repeat what Jesus has told his disciples three times in Galilee and on the way to Jerusalem about his death and rising (9:22, 44, 18:31-33). In the centre is the crucial announcement of the work of God: Jesus has been raised.

The women, now named as the key witnesses to this transforming event, go to tell the eleven disciples and those who are with them. They are greeted with disbelief. Some manuscripts except Peter from this general scepticism, and in verse 12 have him go to the tomb and discover it empty but for the discarded grave clothes. He went home amazed. In the narrative of the discovery of the empty tomb, the key notes struck are of puzzlement, astonishment, fear, amazement, disbelief. The women were met with something confounding their expectations. The disciples heard a story simply beyond their powers of comprehension. This story is not like any other story. It is the shock of the new which confronts the community of the male and female followers of Jesus in the resurrection event. Significantly, neither in the gospels nor elsewhere in the New Testament, is any account given of Jesus' actual rising from death. It is hidden in the mystery of God. For the believing community, the experience of resurrection is like that of emerging from a dark tunnel into sunlight so strong as to be dazzling, blinding. After the experience of the dark night of the cross, there is this new shock in store in this bright light of wonder. Let our Easters begin with that powerful sense of being struck by a wonder, coming from beyond us, which is beyond all expectation. We are surprised by joy.

THE WOMEN

Are we sufficiently struck by the witness of the women? It is to the women, outsiders to the world of power and influence, that the angels entrust their news of hope and liberation. It was too much for the male disciples who simply reacted with sceptical disbelief. It is no accident that the prime witnesses to the wonder of Easter are women. Once more, established expectations and cultural patterns are turned upside-down. In the culture of the times the women's evidence would have been considered 'unreliable', 'an idle tale'. Men simply would not believe the word of truth entrusted to the women by God, at this most vital, critical moment in the whole human story. For too long in the church's history, women's words of truth, bearing their insights and wisdom, have not been allowed to be heard. Let the revolution continue to roll until our churches are genuine communities of women and men together, where all can speak and be heard, and roles of leadership and service are shared without the intrusion of considerations of gender.

'REMEMBER'

It is worth pausing over the angels' instruction to the women to 'remember'. The theme of remembering will be developed in the following story of the Emmaus road (24:13-35). The followers of Jesus are reminded that there are clues to what is now happening, contained in the earlier life and words of Jesus. He had told them of this wonder: in a characteristically human way they had heard only the bad news of the cross, and failed to comprehend the good news of his being raised. So much of our faith is based on remembering. At the heart of Communion is the injunction, 'Do this to remember' (22:19). For us Jesus is risen in our remembering. It is as we call to mind his words and works that his living voice speaks to us, in the power of the Holy Spirit. Memory brings life.

THE EMPTY TOMB

The tomb is empty, of his body there is not a trace, he is alive and gone. The body of the one who was the innocent victim of our malign human violence, masked by the spurious respectability of official religion and the justice of the state, cannot be found. *Violence Unveiled* is an important book by Gil Bailie, in which he makes a powerful case that the violence endemic in human life has religious roots and sanctions, both throughout history and in present-day society. In human history, however, Bailie argues that the Easter event of cross and resurrection is a key moment in our liberation from the cult of violence and the ideology of revenge. In the Easter event the empty tomb is of great significance.

> The empty tomb is essential for understanding the resurrection, not because it announced the resurrection, but because it deprived those who were later to experience the resurrection of a cathartic religious ritual that might have been substituted for it. The discovery of the empty tomb meant that Jesus' corpse and its resting place could not be made into a shrine and become the locus for a new religious cult. Had Jesus' tomb not been empty, the explosive force that scattered the gospel revelation out beyond the culture-world in which it originated and broadcast it to the corners of the earth might have been upset by the gravitational pull of a central shrine. Had the tomb not been empty, what Paul feared might have happened. The Cross might have slowly moved to the margins of Christian awareness and the Christian message.
> (Bailie 1997, p. 231)

The empty tomb by grace deprives Christians of a shrine for a dead hero, a revered martyr whose veneration can so easily spill over into lust for vengeance on those who killed him, or their descendents. In the early chapters of the book of Acts, much of the preaching of Peter and the apostles centres on Jesus' cross and resurrection. The preaching is to the people of Jerusalem, the very ones who have been complicit in his death. Through Jesus' non-violent acceptance of death and the reality of his rising, the vicious circle of revenge is broken and the apostles' message is one of forgiveness, repentance and a new beginning (see Acts 2-8). After the narrow way of the cross and the shut door of death, the gates swing open for us and the widening road stretches on and on ahead.

Sadly, the church has a sorry history of failing to live by the liberating faith entrusted to it. Two legacies haunt us; the poisonous and deadly story of Christian anti-Semitism, particularly in Europe, and the sad and cynical story of the Crusades. When Pope Urban II launched the First Crusade, his specific appeal was for European Christendom to sally forth to reclaim from the infidel the 'holy sepulchre of Christ'. Conveniently or otherwise, he had forgotten it was empty. Bailie comments, 'Christianity's most notorious revival of sacred violence involved a repudiation of the story of the empty tomb and a more or less spontaneous revival of the structures of sacred violence whose perversities the crucifixion had exposed' (Bailie 1997, p. 232). In our world, where today's leaders all too often still invoke and seek to co-opt divine authority for their pursuit of the institutional violence of war - see the pronouncements of George Bush junior on the Iraq war of 2003 - we can and must continue to pray that they be surprised by the wonder and mystery of Easter, and continue, in the name of the crucified and risen one, to protest tirelessly against them in the name of the God they so carelessly invoke.

STUDY

BY YOURSELF
An Easter prayer:

> Almighty God,
> through the rising of your Son from the grave,
> you broke the power of death
> and condemned death itself to die.
> As I rejoice in this great triumph
> may I also make it the model for my living.
>
> Help me to identify in my life
> all that should rightly die -
> redundant relationships,
> tired habits,
> fruitless longings.
> Resurrect in my life faith, hope and love,
> as surely as you raised Jesus Christ
> from the grave. Amen
> (*Common Order* p. 441 - adapted)

chapter 38

The way to Emmaus: the road confirmed

LUKE 24:13-35

The Walk to Emmaus
(Mk 16:12-13)

On that same day two of Jesus' followers were going to a village named Emmaus, about 11 kilometres from Jerusalem, and they were talking to each other about all the things that had happened. As they talked and discussed, Jesus himself drew near and walked with them; they saw him, but somehow did not recognise him. Jesus said to them, "What are you talking about to each other, as you walk along?"

They stood still, with sad faces. One of them, named Cleopas, asked him, "Are you the only visitor in Jerusalem who doesn't know the things that have been happening there these last few days?"

"What things?" he asked.

"The things that happened to Jesus of Nazareth," they answered. "This man was a prophet and was considered by God and by all the people to be powerful in everything he said and did. Our chief priests and rulers handed him over to be sentenced to death, and he was crucified. And we had hoped he would be the one who was going to set Israel free! Besides all that, this is now the third day since it happened. Some of the women in our group surprised us; they went at dawn to the tomb, but could not find his body. They came back saying they had seen a vision of angels who told them that he is alive. Some of our group went to the tomb and found it exactly as the women had said, but they did not see him."

Then Jesus said to them, "How foolish you are, how slow you are to believe everything the prophets said! Was it not necessary for the Messiah to suffer these things and then to enter his glory?" And Jesus explained to them what was said about himself in all the Scriptures, beginning with the books of Moses and the writings of all the prophets.

As they came near the village to which they were going, Jesus acted as if he were going farther; but they held him back, saying, "Stay with us, the day is almost over and it is getting dark." So he went in to stay with them. He sat down to eat with them, took the bread, and said the blessing; then he broke the bread and gave it to them. Then their eyes were opened and they recognised him, but he disappeared from their sight. They said to each other, "Wasn't it like a fire burning in us when he talked to us on the road and explained the Scriptures to us?"

They got up at once and went back to Jerusalem, where they found the eleven disciples gathered together with the others and saying, "The Lord is risen indeed! He has appeared to Simon!"

The two then explained to them what had happened on the road, and how they had recognized the Lord when he broke the bread.

MEETING THE STRANGER ON THE ROAD

Luke's resurrection pictures are unforgettable. The empty tomb event, which Luke shares with the other evangelists, is dramatic, mysterious, full of the shock of surprise. It is followed by the story of the encounter on the road to Emmaus, beautifully and vividly told, mysterious and yet transparently human. 'The good news of the resurrection involves the affirmation that grace does not become abstract with the event of Jesus' physical death' (Rowan Williams 2002, p. 93). Rowan Williams' words find concrete expression in the Emmaus story.

The story begins by introducing us to two of Jesus' followers journeying from Jerusalem to a village called Emmaus. There is great uncertainty about the physical location of this village. Metaphorically speaking, the road to Emmaus is the road to nowhere, rebounding from the blank wall of the cross. The couple's leaving Jerusalem shows that they are in retreating defeat. One of the pair is named, Cleopas; there is a strong suggestion that he can be identified with the Clopas of John 19:25. Perhaps the other was his wife, Mary, whom John's gospel states stood at the foot of the cross. In the agitation of their despair, defeat and confusion, they are talking together when they are joined by a stranger whom they do not recognise. He breaks in on their conversation and asks them what they're talking about. His question brings them to a standstill. They are so taken aback by it that they respond brusquely. 'Are you the only visitor to Jerusalem who doesn't know what's been happening there in recent days?' (24:18) The stranger encourages them to tell their story. It pours out, the narrative of Jesus' death at the hands of authority, the confusion of the story of the women from earlier that morning, and their intense feelings of loss and blighted hope. The stranger replies with a similarly brusque introduction. 'How daft you are!...' (24:25).

MORE ABOUT MEMORY

The stranger then goes on to unlock for them the clues to the meaning of what's been happening in the Scriptures. 'What Luke is here claiming is that, underlying all the Old Testament writings, Jesus detected a common pattern of God's dealings with his people, which was meant to foreshadow his own ministry' (Caird 1963, p. 258). That meaning is to be found in the pattern of the Exodus event with its twin themes of going out and liberation; and also in the intertwined themes of redemption and suffering. The mystery of the cross is revealed as the action of the Messiah who brings redemption, not from suffering but through suffering, through his own vicarious sacrifice.

At the end of the story the stranger is revealed as Jesus, when the three travellers stop for the night and share bread together. Memory plays a vital part in preparing for that moment of revelation. It is the store for our experience, we are lost without memory. The store is not an unmixed treasure trove; there are memories of pain as well of joy, and bitter, guilty memories, as well as the varied multitude of memories which are the daily resources for our living and our hope. Memory holds our experience, made from what is unique to ourselves and what we share with others. Along the Emmaus road the as-yet unknown Jesus invites the travellers to remember, to bring to mind and articulate what they have heard, seen, felt and suffered in recent days. Permission to tell the story of our pain is part of the process of healing. Jesus does more. His words allow the couple to reinterpret their experience and see it in a new, different and hopeful light. It has been well said that faith is what we do with our experience; what gives our experience a different cast. Jesus' invitation is to look again at the cross and the pain of life with the eye of faith. This too is part of the healing process. We can go deeper still. Around the cross broods a deep shadow of common guilt; shared for different reasons by the authorities, the crowd and the disciples. In his book *Resurrection*, Rowan Williams shows that one way to understand the mystery of the Easter event is that Jesus, the victim, becomes transformed into a vibrant sign of hope. The risen one comes offering forgiveness and a new beginning, beyond the unholy cocktail of hate, fear and violence which is the cross. We see this in the experience of Peter, particularly in the final chapter of John's gospel (Chapter 21) - where both his relationship with Jesus is restored, and he is given back his responsibilities of pastoral leadership among the disciples - and we see it also in the preaching of Peter and the disciples to the people of Jerusalem, in the early chapters of Acts. This story encapsulates some of the central features of the resurrection for us; it brings healing, the healing of our memories and experiences of pain; it brings forgiveness, the release from guilt and the possibility of a new beginning beyond condemnation; and it brings reconciliation, as the wounded one, the victim, offers hope, new life and a restored relationship.

HOSPITALITY AND COMMUNION

Back on the Emmaus road, the evening light is failing, but the village is in sight. The two travellers offer the stranger hospitality as the day is almost over. He accepts and sits down to eat with them. As he takes, blesses, breaks and gives the bread, they see who the stranger is. It is Jesus. As soon as they see who he is, he is gone from them. Sharing their experience of the journey, they tell each other how it felt like they were on fire as Jesus talked to them and opened his meaning through the Scriptures. Now the dark of the night is of no account to them, they hurry back to Jerusalem to tell the other disciples. The travellers add their confirmation of an appearance of the risen Jesus to the excited disciples, who tell them, 'The Lord is risen indeed! He has appeared to Simon!' (24:34) Their testimony is 'He had been made known to them in the breaking of the bread' (24:35, *NRSV*).

Although this is a much more human and 'earthy' story than that of the empty tomb, it retains some of its sense of mystery. A common theme of the post-resurrection appearances of Jesus is of an ongoing process, where disciples initially fail to recognise him until some significant moment of truth - in this case, the breaking of the bread. The evangelists clearly wish to convey both that there is a continuity between the risen one and Jesus of the ministries in Galilee and Jerusalem, and also that there is a discontinuity. The risen one is also changed, transformed, no longer bound to the limitations of space and time which circumscribe all mortals. There is a nuanced mystery in all the gospels' narratives of the resurrection; sadly, all too easily broken by dogmatic pronouncements or futile argument about the precise nature of events and appearances. Let the mystery remain a mystery and the truth confront us.

The Emmaus story is clearly about Communion. From earliest times it has been one of the church's central affirmations that Jesus is made known in the breaking of the bread. Jesus here reveals himself after an invitation to hospitality, in the moment when the travellers move out of their own self-preoccupations to think on the needs of their fellow traveller, and invite him to become their guest. It is also at a transparently ordinary meal-table, with no special ritual or liturgical connotations, that Jesus reveals himself. Therefore not just the holy table of Communion, but every table and every meal contains the possibility of the encounter with the holy.

The hospitality which springs from grace is a key theme of Luke's gospel, and it should be no surprise to find its recollection in this post-resurrection narrative. Welcoming the stranger remains one of the key ways in which the church continues the work of Christ. It is encouraging to discover that more and more churches are engaged in a ministry of hospitality of one kind or another - the complexities of modern Health & Safety regulations notwithstanding. The Christian obligation to welcome the stranger has long roots in Scotland, well expressed in this *Rune of Hospitality* after the pattern of the Celtic Church:

> I saw a stranger yestreen.
> I put food in the eating place,
> drink in the drinking place,
> music in the listening place,
> and in the sacred name of the Triune,
> he blessed myself and my house,
> my cattle and my dear ones.

And the lark said in her song
often, often, often,
goes Christ in the stranger's guise.
(Kenneth Macleod 1959, p. 295)

The Rune makes clear our duty to meet the needs of the stranger. In the Emmaus story the stranger is one not only with needs to be served, but someone with an explanation to give, a truth to tell. Remembering the place of the stranger, the outsider, the Other, throughout Luke, the Emmaus encounter serves as a reminder that the Other always has a truth to share, just by being 'other' - whether the Other is our partner of many years, or someone of a different country, colour, language, faith and experience, and we are meeting them for the first time. In the diverse, plural, multi-faith world we inhabit, meeting the needs and being open to the truth of the stranger are vital for us, both as human beings and Christians. Apart from anything else, the truth of the Other keeps us humble, as Rowan Williams pointed out in his Lent book for the year 2001, *Christ on Trial: How the Gospel Unsettles our Judgement*: 'It is not that the outsider is by definition right, nice or superior, but simply that the outsider's very presence puts a question that reminds me that my account of things, my way of making the world all right and manageable, is not only an incomplete enterprise, but may be an enterprise that is keeping out God because it lets in the subtle temptation to treat my perspective as if it were God's' (Williams 2000, p. 65).

STUDY

BY YOURSELF

'The story as a whole is often used, and rightly so, as a focus for meditation, not least when people find themselves in difficulties. Bring your problem, your agony, on the road to Emmaus with Cleopas and his companion; be prepared to share it in prayer with the stranger who approaches; and learn to listen for his voice, explaining, leading forwards, warming your heart by applying scripture to what's going on. Learn to live inside this story, and you will find it inexhaustible' (Wright 2001, p. 293).

FOR GROUP WORK

Read the story slowly. Be present as the journey unfolds. What is Jesus saying to you? Discuss this together, using your reflections from the 'By yourself' section. End by exploring this question: How do we make this story our story?

chapter 39

The road ahead: the widening road

LUKE 24:36-53

Jesus Appears to his Disciples
(Mt 28:16-20, Mk 16:14-18, Jn 20:19-23, Acts 1:6-8)

While the two were telling them this, suddenly the Lord himself stood among them and said to them, "Peace be with you."

They were terrified, thinking that they were seeing a ghost. But he said to them, "Why are you alarmed? Why are these doubts coming up in your minds? Look at my hands and my feet, and see that it is I myself. Feel me, and you will know, for a ghost doesn't have flesh and bones, as you can see I have."

He said this and showed them his hands and his feet. They still could not believe, they were so full of joy and wonder; so he asked them, "Have you anything here to eat?" They gave him a piece of cooked fish, which he took and ate in their presence.

Then he said to them, "These are the very things I told you about while I was still with you: everything written about me in the Law of Moses, the writings of the prophets, and the Psalms had to come true."

Then he opened their minds to understand the Scriptures, and said to them, "This is what is written: the Messiah must suffer and must rise from death three days later, and in his name the message about repentance and the forgiveness of sins must be preached to all nations, beginning in Jerusalem. You are witnesses of these things. And I myself will send upon you what my Father has promised. But you must wait in the city until the power from above comes down upon you."

Jesus is Taken Up to Heaven
(Mk 16:19-20, Acts 1:9-11)

Then he led them out of the city as far as Bethany, where he raised his hands and blessed them. As he was blessing them, he departed from them and was taken up into heaven. They worshipped him and went back into Jerusalem, filled with great joy, and spent all their time in the Temple giving thanks to God.

'PEACE BE WITH YOU'

We come to the end of the gospel's story. While the disciples from Emmaus are telling their story, Jesus suddenly appears in the midst of them with the precious words of blessing, 'Peace be with you'. Far from being a moment of reassurance, the disciples are filled with fear, thinking they have seen a ghost. Jesus' next words are to invite them to see his hands and feet, presumably still carrying the wounds of the cross, and to ask for, and eat, a piece of fish.

This scene raises for our modern minds the puzzle about the nature of Jesus' risen presence. On the one hand, his appearances are shown as transcending the limits of the space-time continuum which defines our humanity - with his ability to be present with startling suddenness, go through locked doors, ascend to heaven - on the other, both Luke here and also John's gospel are at pains to stress the physicality of the risen Christ - no mere ghost. The gospels make clear that Jesus has now moved beyond the limitations of our mortal existence; they also want to stress the continuity of the risen one with Jesus of Nazareth. It is he who has been raised, his ministry, life and death which are affirmed and lifted high. There are other reasons for stressing that the risen Jesus has a physical presence. To the Hebrew mind of Jesus' time, resurrection involved the raising of the physical body. By the time of Luke's writing, the church had to counter strong Gnostic views, which emphasised the reality of the spirit over against the material. The heresy of docetism, which denied the reality of Jesus' humanity, was also showing the first signs of the influence it continues to have on Christian minds up to this present day. If we see the question of the nature of Jesus' appearances as a problem to be solved, we will have an interminable wait for a solution. We can say that the gospel writers, including Luke, confront us with a mystery which is life-affirming. With Rowan Williams we can simply be witnesses of 'the transfiguring expansion of Jesus' humanity which is the heart of the resurrection experience' (Williams 2002 p. 89). We can rejoice in Jesus' liberation from death and his exaltation, which is a vindication of his words and way, and be assured that the one who is raised is the same Jesus of the ministries in Galilee and Jerusalem, the Jesus who welcomes, the Jesus of the wounds.

BEGINNING FROM JERUSALEM

After eating his piece of fish, Jesus offers his disciples some final instructions. As he did with the disciples on the Emmaus road, he opens up to the gathered disciples the confirmations of who he is and what he is about, which are to be found in the Hebrew scriptures. He confirms the message they are to carry as his witnesses, 'repentance and the forgiveness of sins must be preached to all nations, beginning in Jerusalem' (24:47). It is a universal message of liberation for all people, everywhere, but it begins in Jerusalem at the heart of the old faith which has been its cradle. From Jerusalem it will spread outwards to encompass the *oikoumene* - the whole inhabited world. The disciple witnesses will not be on their own, left to their own devices and limited resources. Jesus promises he will send the Holy Spirit promised by the Father. In the meantime the disciples are to wait in Jerusalem till the Spirit's power descends on them. These words are clearly a trailer for, and a link into, the events at the start of the book of Acts. 'The resurrection is now a point of transition from the story of the earthly Jesus to the story of the movement which went by his name, and also the basis of that movement' (Evans 1990, p. 887).

'IN ORDER TO BE EVERYWHERE, HE MUST DEPART'

The movement of transition continues as Jesus leads the disciples out of the city to Bethany, where he blesses them and parts from them. Some manuscripts of the gospel omit here the words 'and was taken up into heaven' (24:5-1), on the basis that 1) it was unlikely that Jesus' ascension took place on the same evening as his resurrection, 2) mention of the ascension here contradicts the story of many appearances of the risen Jesus as told in Acts 1:1-5, and reduplicates the ascension story in Acts 1:6-11. The transition between the end of Luke and the start of Acts is a bit messy.

The omission is probably better on balance, but since we are not now venturing into Acts we should end with the departure of the risen Jesus into heaven and the promise of his return (Acts 1:11). One of the Wild Goose songs by John Bell and Graham Maule captures the meaning of the moment.

> He has to go, as from the grave
> He had to rise:
> In order to be everywhere
> He must depart
> To live, not in one place,
> But in each heart.
> ('The Saviour Leaves'; Bell and Maule 1988, p. 99)

Jesus departs to go upwards and outwards. He is the one who bears our humanity to the right hand of the Father, our intercessor in heaven. And he goes before us, into all the world, in the power and presence of the Holy Spirit.

We leave the disciples, returned to Jerusalem, back in the Temple courts where this gospel began, filled with joy, spending their time giving thanks to God and awaiting the imminent arrival of the Spirit. Through Jesus Christ the way is open both to the Father and out into all the world. We have seen the way as the ever-widening road of life and peace breaking through all the barriers we humans continually create in our personal lives and our lives in society. Will we walk along it?

STUDY

BY YOURSELF

Reflect on your journey through the gospel of Luke. In what ways has it taught you more about Jesus or changed your view of him?

Ask yourself now the question from the introduction: 'What about Jesus excites, scares, perplexes, challenges, reassures me?' (See 'Suggestions on how to use this book', in the Introduction.)

FOR GROUP WORK:

In the story of the Emmaus Road, Jesus is made known to the disciples in the breaking of the bread. Celebrate a resurrection meal together at the end of your journey together through Luke's gospel. Share with each other what you have learned of Jesus on the journey and the ways in which he lives and speaks to you now. Here are two suggestions of tools to help your shared reflection.

1 The leader might provide each member of the group with a sheet of common road signs; asking each group member to pick out three which speak of their journey through Luke. Each member in turn then share their reflections with the group.

2 Ask each member to bring something to the meeting which speaks of their journey: It could be a piece of art-work, a poem, a collage, etc. Each member in turn can then introduce their object to the others.

As the gospel leaves the disciples waiting expectantly for the coming of the Holy Spirit, end by praying together:

> Come Holy Spirit,
> Spirit of understanding and communion,
> Spirit of grace and power,
> renew our faith,
> revive our hope,
> deepen our loving.
> Come Holy Spirit,
> touch us with the living presence of Jesus;
> send us out to meet him on the road before us,
> for his name's sake. Amen.

chapter 40

Epilogue

In her book, *A Story to Live By,* Kathy Galloway tells of how as a child she was fascinated by addresses and maps. Our address speaks of where we are at home; maps point to the strange, fascinating, diverse world out there to be explored. Kathy would write her address thus:

> Kathryn Orr,
> 2 Caiystane Terrace,
> Edinburgh 13
> Scotland,
> UK,
> Europe,
> The World,
> The Universe.
> (Galloway 1999, p. 15)

Kathy's child's address speaks volumes about a confidence of being at home in a very large world. Does part of that confidence which has seeped into the marrow of our modern Western bones come from the gospel of Luke? In the combined works of Luke/Acts we are offered a powerful vision of people everywhere being the children of the one and only God, and of Jesus as the one sent by God to break through all the barriers which have previously divided one human being from another, and nation from nation, race from race.

This confidence is hard-won. The price is a cross, and the continuing way of taking up the cross life. Luke's life of Jesus shows that the clash of grace with the multifarious powers of this world is a strenuous and wounding battle. The gospel doesn't confirm the easy confidence of those who are at home in the world because they are financially, culturally, religiously secure. In telling the story of the one who came to be born outside the house, who spent himself reaching out to the stranger, the outsider and the excluded, and who was crucified 'outside the gate', Luke challenges all who see in Jesus the claim and truth of God to leave the security of the home-place; and find their meaning and peace in a journey outwards, to meet and hear the voices of the stranger, the excluded, the powerless, to see the world through their eyes and to walk with them.

The call is to the discipleship road and the Emmaus road. Both are widening roads. As we seek to take the open ways of grace and hospitality we see in the life of Jesus, the promise is that we shall encounter the grace and hospitality of God, in and through our struggles and our meetings. We meet the grace which comes from below, the divine hidden in the humble, and the Lord who always comes, 'as one who serves' (22:27). Confidence has long been seen as one of the classic aspects of faith. My prayer is that on our journey through Luke, we have met with Jesus in whom we can place our trust, who gives us confidence to take his way in the midst of our world of today, and who confirms our faith.

If faith and confidence belong together, so also do faith and prayer. The Jesus we meet in Luke's gospel is constantly found in the midst of people, immersed in their joys, struggles and humanity. He is also found frequently withdrawing to be alone and at prayer. Let our ending be a prayer that our lives be formed so that we become both listening, waiting people, and active, serving people, as we walk the widening road. The prayer is to Jesus, who left the heights of heaven to creep down beside us, who walks the roads with us and ahead of us, and in the glory of the Father, forever speaks for us.

> Be thou my Vision, O Lord of my heart;
> Naught be all else to me, save that thou art,
> Thou my best thought, by day or by night, -
> Waking or sleeping, thy presence my light.
>
> Riches I heed not, nor man's empty praise,
> Thou mine inheritance, now and always:
> Thou and thou only, first in my heart, -
> High King of Heaven, my treasure thou art.
> (Ancient Irish, tr. Mary Byrne, versified by Eleanor Hull; in *Church Hymnary 3*)

References

Bailie, Gil (1997), *Violence Unveiled*; The Crossroad Publishing Company

Barclay, John (2003), *Annual Report of the British Regional Committee of St George's College*, Jerusalem

Barclay, William (1953), *The Gospel of Luke*; St Andrew Press

Bell, John and Maule, Graham (1988), 'I will give what I have to my Lord', and 'The Saviour Leaves'; *Wild Goose Songs Volume 2*; Wild Goose Publications
- (1989), 'Knocking at the Door' *Wild Goose Prints*; Wild Goose Publications

Berrigan, Daniel (1996), *Isaiah: Spirit of Courage, Gift of Tears*; Augsburg Fortress

Boesak, Alan (1984), *Walking on Thorns* (Risk series no 22); World Council of Churches

Boff, Leonardo (1980), *Way of the Cross, Way of Justice*; Orbis Books

Bonhoeffer, Dietrich (1953), *Letters and Papers from Prison*; SCM Press Ltd
- (1963), *Sanctorum Communio*; Collins

Booth, Nan (2000), *75 Icebreakers for great gatherings: Everything you need to bring people together*; Brighton Books

Brown, Raymond E (1993), *The Birth of the Messiah*; Doubleday Dell Publishing Group

Caird, G B (1963), *Saint Luke*; Pelican Books Ltd

Cassidy, Richard J (1978), *Jesus, Politics and Society*; Orbis Books

Cassidy & Scharper (eds) (1983), *Political Issues in Luke-Acts*; Orbis Books

Church Hymnary, (1973), third edition no 87; OUP

Church Without Walls: The Report of the Special Commission anent Review and Reform (2002), Church of Scotland; Scottish Christian Press

Common Order (1994), Church of Scotland Panel on Worship; St Andrew Press

Common Ground (1998); St Andrew Press

Crawshaw, Richard (1613-1650), 'At Bethlehem' from *A Treasury of Christian Verse*, edited by Hugh Martin; SCM Press Ltd

Derrida, Jacques (2001), *On Cosmopolitanism and Forgiveness*; Routledge

Dillard, Annie (1994), 'The Book of Luke' from *The Reader*; HarperCollins Inc

Drewermann, Eugen (1991), *Open Heavens*; Orbis Books

Esler, Philip (1987), *Community and Gospel in Luke-Acts*; Cambridge University Press

Evans, C F (1990), *St Luke*; SCM Press Ltd

Ferguson, Ron (1979), *Geoff*; Famedram Publishers

Forrester, Duncan (2001), *On Human Worth*; SCM Press

Fortunatus, Venantius / Neale, J M *Jubilate Hymns*; Jubilate Hymns Ltd

Galloway, Kathy (1999), *A Story to Live By*; SPCK

Gutierrez, Gustavo (1997), *Sharing the Word through the Liturgical Year*; Geoffrey Chapman

Herzog II, William R (1994), *Parables as Subversive Speech*; Westminster/John Knox Press

Iona Community Worship Book (1998); Wild Goose Publications

Jenkins, David (2002), *The Calling of a Cuckoo*; Continuum

Lewis, Alan (2001), *Between Cross and Resurrection: A Theology of Holy Saturday*; William B Eerdmans Publishing Company

MacGregor, Neil with Langmuir, Erika (2000), *Seeing Salvation: Images of Christ in Art*; BBC

Maclean, Sorley (1989), *From Wood to Ridge: Collected Poems in Gaelic and English*; Carcanet Press

MacLeod, George (1985), *The Whole Earth Shall Cry Glory*; Wild Goose Publications

Macleod, Kenneth (1959), 'Rune of Hospitality' (from the island of Eigg), translation from the Gaelic; from *A Book of Scotland* ed G F Maine (p 295), Collins

Maddox, Morris (1981), *The Christian Healing Ministry*; SPCK

Mandela, Nelson (1994), *The Long Walk to Freedom*; Little, Brown and Company

Mead, Joy (2001), *The One Loaf – an everyday celebration*; Wild Goose Publications

Morton, Ralph (1956), *The Twelve Together*; The Iona Community (now Wild Goose Publications)

Muir, Edwin (1963), *Collected Poems*; Faber & Faber

Nouwen, Henri J M (1994), *The Return of the Prodigal Son: A Story of Homecoming*; Darton, Longman and Todd Ltd

Paynter, Neil (ed) (2002), *Lent & Easter Readings from Iona*; Wild Goose Publications

Pray Now (annual); St Andrew Press

Quesnell, Quentin (1983), 'The Women at Luke's Supper'; p 59-80 in Cassidy & Scharper (eds), Political Issues in Luke-Acts; Orbis Books

Rowland, Christopher (1988), *Radical Christianity: A Reading of Recovery*; Polity Press; quoted in *Radical Readings*; SCM Press Ltd (2003).

Shehadeh, Raja (2003), *When the Bulbul Stopped Singing: A Diary of Ramallah under Seige*; Profile Books

Taylor, John V (1985), *Weep not for me* (Risk Series No 27); World Council of Churches

Thomas, R S (1993), *Collected Poems*; J M Dent, The Orion Publishing Group

Weber, Hans-Reudi (1984), *Immanuel: The Coming of Jesus in Art and the Bible*; World Council of Churches
- (1989), *Power: Focus for a Biblical Theology*; World Council of Churches

Wengst, Klaus (1987), *Pax Romana and the Peace of Jesus Christ*; SCM Press Ltd

Wink, Walter (1986), *Unmasking the Powers*; Augsburg Fortress

Williams, Rowan (2000), *Christ on Trial: How the Gospel Unsettles our Judgement*; HarperCollins Religious - (2002), *Resurrection*; Darton, Longman and Todd Ltd

Wright, Tom (2001), *Luke for Everyone*; SPCK

Yoder, John Howard (1972), *The Politics of Jesus*, William B Eerdman

ABBREVIATIONS:

AV   Authorised Version
GNB   Good News Bible
NRSV   New Revised Standard Version

Acknowledgements

Except where otherwise attributed, scriptures and additional materials quoted from the Good News Bible published by the Bible Societies/HarperCollins Publishers, Ltd., UK, © American Bible Society, 1966, 1971, 1976, 1992, 1994. Used by permission.

Iona Worship Material © 1991 WGRG, Iona Community, G2 3DH. Excerpts used by permission.

Quoted material from the Annual Report of the British Regional Committee of St George's College, Jerusalem, February 2003 by John Barclay, is reproduced by kind permission of the author.

Material from *Common Ground* © Panel on Worship of the Church of Scotland, 1994. Excerpts are used by permission.

'And now we are come into Lent' by Charles Robertson is reproduced by kind permission of the author.

'The Kingdom', from *Collected Poems* by R S Thomas; © 1993 J M Dent/Orion Publishing. Reprinted by permission.

'The Highland Woman', from *From Wood to Ridge: Collected Poems in Gaelic and English* by Sorley Maclean; © 1989 Carcenet Press. Reprinted by permission.